GARLAND STUDIES IN HIGHER EDUCATION
VOL. 2

REFORM AND CHANGE IN HIGHER EDUCATION

GARLAND REFERENCE LIBRARY
OF SOCIAL SCIENCE
VOL. 961

GARLAND STUDIES IN HIGHER EDUCATION

This series is published in cooperation with the Program in Higher Education, School of Education, Boston College, Chestnut Hill, Massachusetts.

PHILIP G. ALTBACH
Series Editor

THE FUNDING OF HIGHER EDUCATION
International Perspectives
edited by Philip G. Altbach and D. Bruce Johnstone

REFORM AND CHANGE IN HIGHER EDUCATION
International Perspectives
edited by James E. Mauch and Paula L.W. Sabloff

HIGHER EDUCATION IN CRISIS
New York in National Perspective
edited by William C. Barba

REFORM AND CHANGE IN HIGHER EDUCATION

International Perspectives

edited by

James E. Mauch
Paula L.W. Sabloff

GARLAND PUBLISHING, Inc.
New York & London / 1995

Library of Congress Cataloging-in-Publication Data

Reform and change in higher education : international
perspectives / edited by James E. Mauch and Paula
L.W. Sabloff.
    p.   cm. — (Garland reference library of social
science ; vol. 961. Garland studies in higher education ; vol. 2)
    Includes bibliographical references and index.
    ISBN 0-8153-1706-9
    1. Education, Higher—Cross-cultural studies.
2. Higher education and state—Cross-cultural studies.   3. Education, Higher—Administration—Cross-
cultural studies.   4. Educational change—Cross-cultural studies.   I. Mauch, James E., 1930– . II. Sabloff, Paula L.W.   III. Series: Garland reference library
of social science ; v. 961.   IV. Series: Garland reference library of social science. Garland studies in higher
education ; vol. 2.
LB2322.2.R44   1995
378—dc20   94–31729
                                                        CIP

Printed on acid-free, 250-year-life paper
Manufactured in the United States of America

Contents

List of Tables and Figures

Series Editor's Preface

Higher education is a multifaceted phenomenon in modern society, combining a variety of institutions and an increasing diversity of students, a range of purposes and functions, and different orientations. The series combines research-based monographs, analyses, and discussions of broader issues and reference books related to all aspects of higher education. It is concerned with policy as well as practice from a global perspective. The series is dedicated to illuminating the reality of higher and postsecondary education in contemporary society.

Philip G. Altbach
State University of New York at Buffalo

Introduction

Through time and space, the relationship between governments and universities has vacillated between tight control and relative autonomy, symbiosis and laissez-faire, mutual respect and suspicion. The purpose of this volume is to enable the reader to view the issue of higher education reform within a contemporary and international context and to see how this relationship has changed over time both within nations (or parts of nations) and between nations, especially industrialized nations of the free world and the former communist bloc.

Reform Is Controversial and Important

As Altbach (1990) observed, the reform of universities is a matter of importance and controversy throughout the world, occurring in rich and poor nations, totalitarian and democratic governments, industrialized and pre- and post-industrialized economies. Universities, and higher education in general, consume enormous resources, and governments are constantly seeking ways to make them more efficient and relevant, eliminate redundancies, raise fees, orient them to national development goals, and spread the costs.

Clearly, the changes government and the public seek from higher education are filled with controversy. Many a minister of education or higher education has lost the post over proposed "reforms." Governments, in Korea, Czechoslovakia, and France, for example, have even been toppled by students seeking reform of higher education and of the larger society as well. Students who see access to free public higher education as a basic right of citizenship tend to get angry when the government attempts to charge student fees or tighten access. Institutions and faculty tend to object strongly when the government wants them to be publicly accountable and puts financial teeth into its demand for accountability. Taxpayers tend to revolt when they perceive higher education as an elitist enclave for iconoclastic professors, overpaid administrators, and privileged students.

Altbach (1990) defines reform as "planned change," and he notes that the concept of reform applies to substantial changes in structure, organization, or curricula in higher education. In that sense, the chapters in this volume are concerned with reform. These changes, as defined here, occur as a result of purposeful reform, not simply expansion or reaction to changes in the environment. To some extent, reform is in the eye of the beholder, and while some constituent groups perceive reform as a benefit, others see it as a mortal threat. The definition of reform used here does not necessarily connote improvement, only planned change.

Serious reform brings serious controversy because its effects will change power relationships and will enhance or destroy opportunities among a large segment of society. Reform may contribute to or seriously inhibit social change and economic growth. Nations and peoples, particularly in the less developed countries, have such high hopes for higher education that any university reform, or lack of reform, is controversial.

Government-Initiated Reform

The state plays such an important role in higher education around the world that reform is often seen as a government-initiated process. That seems to be the case, at least in large measure, in each of the chapters in this volume. University-initiated reform is rare indeed. Perhaps this should not be a great surprise. Universities are, after all, essentially conservative and bureaucratic, regardless of the nonconservative and nonbureaucratic self-perception many faculty members and students hold. The strong sense of tradition; the fact that in many countries faculty are civil servants employed by the state for life; the deeply entrenched curricula, disciplines, departments, and chairs—all contribute to the perception that universities are much better at describing, researching, and analyzing organizational change than they are at changing themselves in any planned way. After all, university traditions such as academic freedom, tenure and lifelong employment, disinterested and independent scholarly enquiry, institutional autonomy, the academic cultures of the separate disciplines and professions, *Lehrfreiheit* and *Lernfreiheit*, are deeply valued and thus deeply entrenched, and any attempts at reform will be fought, usually by asserting that these academic values are being threatened by destruction. We are reminded by de Rudder's chapter that universities are essentially conservative institutions, and while they may see the need for reform, and even lead the rhetoric about reform, they find it hard to reform themselves.

Given this point of view, it is not hard to see why reform comes from government. One might think that this is related to the level of support government furnishes higher education, but as Park indicates, governments can find ways to control private institutions while providing little financial support.

The Need for Reform

To guide the development of universities in meeting national needs, the state continuously restructures its relationship to higher education. The state, which in many countries has been the main engine of modernization, is placing new demands on higher education to lead the competitive struggle in the new post-industrial society, based as they see it on research capability, knowledge availability, and information technology.

In the 1980s and 1990s, many free world nations have begun massive economic restructuring, based on the belief that the market economy operates on a global scale, and that nations form a single economic system, as Wallerstein (1974) wrote. Realizing that international competition partly depends on a highly skilled work force and the continuous development of high-technology products, governments have pressured universities to increase productivity in teaching as well as applied research. The increase in access to higher education, the ostensible goal of governments and citizens alike, has been described as the shift from elite to mass education (Trow 1974). And emphasis on applied research has sometimes come at the expense of theoretical research. These trends may be seen in chapters by Iram, Sabloff, Scott, and Smyth.

Reform is also needed in the former communist societies where isolation and repression have kept the institutions out of the mainstream of academic thought, research, and scientific advances. Nowhere is this more clear than in the former communist societies (see de Rudder, Darvas, Freeman, and Fogel and Mauch), and nowhere are the effects of this isolation more destructive to the quality of academic life.

For at least 40 years (in some countries longer), communist governments dominated and controlled higher education. Faculty and students were manipulated, spied upon, used as spies, jailed, banished to years of hard labor or no work at all, and sometimes killed. Institutions were so politicized that they became essentially re-education camps to form the "new communist man."

In an Alice-in-Wonderland world, up became down and down up; old scholars and intellectuals were destroyed; politically correct new leaders proclaimed the new orthodoxy of Marx. Academic freedom, critical analysis, divergent thinking, independent and disinterested scholarship were punished. Group re-education, correct thoughts, and political indoctrination classes were not only encouraged, they were mandatory. Higher education was vocationalized in the interests of heavy industry, and research was directed in narrow channels, politicized, and separated from students and the university. Students and faculty, as one would expect, became cynical and uninterested; they saw education in their Marxist paradise for what it was: a massive political re-education project carried on inside a prison. Thus they learned to devalue education and put their faith in the credential at the end (to be obtained by any means), hoping it would lead to a little better life. They saw the failure of central planning to meet the needs of the students, society, and eventually even industry. They increasingly lost respect for any pretense of moral authority the leadership might once have had.

Given this past, the reform process will be long and hard. Perhaps this is put most clearly in the de Rudder chapter. The newly elected democratic governments, often retaining powerful bureaucratic elements of the former communist state, need to reform higher education, but the process of change is slow. Universities still distrust government planning; therefore, there is great resistance to any central planning, even though the need is present more than ever. There are too few resources, too many of the old faculty (higher education was often used for social employment), too many institutions (the communist governments typically created new vocational institutions that were easily controlled and narrowly vocational) and outdated curricula (in law, psychology and the social sciences in particular, academics were cut off from foreign influences and relegated to lowest status, and research was oriented to showing the glories of the communist state).

In addition, higher education reform takes resources, and the new governments have fewer resources now than before. Universities, as in the Czech Republic, are being asked to find new resources outside of government, but there is no structure, experience, or institutional culture to support or guide such activity. Meanwhile, able faculty in critical areas of innovation and reform are leaving for the greater freedom and rewards of international or national entrepreneurial or other private organizations, and governments have so far been unable or unwilling to cope with the problem.

Universities in former communist societies—Hungary, Poland, the Czech and Slovak republics—now more free to set their own goals, are in the process of undergoing political as well as economic change. They simultaneously seek political democratization and entry into the global market economy. Reform in these countries means less control and less central planning by the state. Both state control and state planning were so rigidly shaped by Marxist dogma that they have been thoroughly discredited. Universities now want to be modern (emulating the models they see in the West), autonomous, and self-governing, with no central government interference. Such reforms are laudable of course but, in the long run, not likely to be achieved without structural changes. For example, the experience of universities under communism was one of dependence and lack of responsibility, conditions fostered and encouraged by the system; thus universities—always dependent on the government and party for financing, curricular direction, political manipulation, central planning, and the control of students—naturally responded to state control over the decades by avoiding responsibility, by cynicism, by lack of trust in anything associated with the state, and by doing as little as possible in reaction to a state that valued them little and demonstrated at every opportunity a lack of trust in its own citizens.

Autocratic governments of the right also face reformulation issues. Faced with increasing international communication and competition, they find it more and more difficult to control what people think and do. The walls of the prison-state are being breeched now that students and faculty have access to information and modern tools of communication and persuasion (such as computers, fax and xerox machines, cellular phones, and electronic mail).

Critical Issues of Reform

Worldwide, the concept of high-quality, free public higher education is under threat because governments cannot allocate enough resources to meet quality goals in the face of enrollment pressures. In the case of Korea the recent growth of higher education has been largely in the private sector. Examples could be cited in Latin America also, e.g., Columbia, Brazil, Venezuela. Part of the concept of reformulation is financial. Governments, in the face of growing social demand for higher education, can no longer provide free higher education for the numbers of students now demanding it. Further, in some countries, the public sector has become so politicized that few tears are shed when the budgets for huge public higher education systems are cut or capped in the face of inflation. Public higher education may be seen by the government—and to some extent by the public—as an expensive and inappropriate use of scarce public resources. Hence, nations which previously prohibited private institutions now welcome them.

Governments are under pressure not only to expand higher education but also to make access more open and equitable. As Freeman and Darvas show, even under communism, the classless society which prided itself so much on equality and on guaranteeing the children of peasants and workers access to education, the intelligentsia continued to dominate the examinations for and admissions to higher education. Governments throughout the world will have to resolve issues of equal access if they have not done so already, and in doing so, they will intervene to reform higher education. Even in the U.S., the bastion of independent and autonomous universities, a major area of government regulation may be categorized as achieving equal access, e.g., affirmative action, scholarships for minority students, aid for black colleges, need-based grants, and guaranteed student loan programs. Some of this intervention, that which brings financial aid, is grudgingly accepted by universities; but that intervention which regulates is often resented and resisted.

Even where public higher education is still a serious enterprise, governments are requiring more user fees and, as Sabloff points out, not only increased university fees but also increased regulation. The concept of accountability is in, and higher education—even in privileged nations of North America, Australia, Israel, and Western Europe—will have to pay attention. Already these nations have shifted resources gradually from the university to lower-cost—and perhaps more efficient— institutions such as technical institutes, regional universities or colleges, community colleges, and short-term specialized professional training programs aimed at meeting present occupational needs. As Scott notes, governments have to balance the claims of higher education against those of other parts of the education system and other public services.

Universities have always faced an uncertain future in which their relationship with government (and in some cases, church) power and authority often changed. Scott reminds us in his chapter that popes, kings, and republics have always taken the keenest interest in higher education, and the way of expressing that interest has varied in time and place. The chapters in this volume imply that in the next decades some governments may be moving toward less regulation of higher education while others move toward more, and that all expect institutions to be more accountable and to assume more responsibility for their own growth and financial support. If institutions are unable to assume that responsibility, governments may either abolish them, let them wither away, combine them with others to form new institutions under new leadership and new rules, or step in and reform the institutions by means of state power and authority.

What is interesting is that several of the former communist bloc governments are adopting such Western practices as increasing access, balancing autonomy with accountability, and emphasizing applied research in order to align universities with economic goals. Will the Western-structured relationship between the state and higher education therefore emulate former communist bloc nations' adoption of Western goals? In other words, does form follow function or government goals in this case? Again, comparison of former free world and communist bloc countries will enable the reader to form his or her own conclusions.

This volume grew out of a symposium, "International Perspectives on the Relationship Between Governments and Universities," held at the 35th Annual Meeting of the Comparative and International Education Society held in Pittsburgh, Pennsylvania, on March 14–17, 1991. The purpose of the double session was to explore how government policy (including resource allocation) affects universities—both public and private—and how universities influence government policy. As governments in industrialized nations change their requirements and perception of universities, how will universities respond to new government demands? The participants included Paula L.W. Sabloff (Chairperson; University of Pittsburgh), James E. Mauch (University of Pittsburgh), Peter Scott (London *Times Higher Education Supplement*), Helmut de Rudder (University of Luneburg, Germany), Namgi Park (University of Pittsburgh), John Smyth (Flinders University of South Australia), Gail R. Benjamin (University of Pittsburgh), Ann M. Dykstra (University of Pittsburgh), and Mary Jane Trout Barretta (Salem-Teikyo University).

The conference was immediately followed by a special UNESCO Forum of Experts on Strengthening Capacities for Research in Higher Education (Pittsburgh, Pennsylvania, March 17–19, 1991). Here, the volume editors made contact with other contributors and were able to extend national representation in the book to former communist bloc countries and former colonies of Western nations. Contributors now included Yaacov Iram (Bar-Ilan University, Israel) and Kassie Freeman (Vanderbilt University). Later, Daniel S. Fogel (University of Pittsburgh) and Peter Darvas (New York University) were added.

Each chapter focuses on a different country and presents the author's perspective on how the state relates to reform in higher education. The nature of that relationship is the common thread binding together chapters on Western and formerly communist bloc nations, industrialized and non-industrialized nations, colonial and formerly colonized nations. Upon reviewing the chapters, interesting themes began to emerge, based of course on a very limited sample. These themes had no role in the selection of chapters, but appeared to the editors after the chapters were read.

The first theme is that all of the institutions reported in this volume—public or private—are dependent on the state; that is, the universities are really clients of the state, which acts as their patron. Universities are clients because they rely on the state for revenues and because the state regulates teaching, research, and administrative activities (see the Korean example for little public financing but great state control).

A second theme, a corollary to the patron-client model, is that universities maintain the ideal of university autonomy even in its absence. Members of university communities appear to desire to negate the institutions' dependence on the state. Autonomy is defined in several of the chapters, but a basic definition was offered by Justice Felix Frankfurter who said that universities should be free from government interference when deciding "who may teach, what may be taught, how it should be taught and who may be admitted to study" (Frankfurter in Marcus & Hollander, 1981, p. 23). If autonomy is divided into freedom from government interference in administration, teaching, and research, then one must ask if government regulation of any one of these sectors is necessarily harmful to the institutions, interfering with—or even hampering—the work to be done. According to Park, the effects of government regulation depend somewhat on the motives of the government. Smyth, however, argues that government regulation—by its very nature—subverts the proper role of the universities (that is, disseminating knowledge to all who wish it), to further the government's economic aims. Scott, on the other hand, makes a compelling point when he asserts:

> The democratic state has a vital interest in upholding a free university tradition. Perhaps it must even force universities to maintain their freedom in the face of external demands—many of which, paradoxically, grow out of the state's own detailed requirements as well as those of business, industry, and community. Moreover, a free university tradition provides optimal conditions for scientific progress. . . . It is no accident that the world's best universities are generally to be found in the world's freest societies.

Autonomy is also tempered by the role of the university in government regulation. While Scott alludes to collaboration between the universities (via the University Grants Committee) and government, Iram describes the universities' role in setting and modifying government policy affecting university autonomy.

A third theme, accountability, is tied to the issue of autonomy. While governments often tell universities that accountability will be used to protect the seeming autonomy of institutions (see de Rudder, Iram, and Scott), it is actually a means whereby the state sets limits to autonomy. In order to prove that universities are accountable to the government (i.e., meeting government needs for trained manpower and applied research, treating citizens according to government wishes, etc.), these institutions will have to abide by government regulations and meet government goals. But whether or not accountability works to the detriment of universities' productivity, the sense of community or cooperation with (government) goals is not clear.

The fourth theme that emerges is the adaptation of two basic models of government-university relations to the nations represented here. The first model is the interposition of some semi-autonomous (often quasi-government) agency between the universities and the government to assure a measure of academic independence. This model is exemplified in the British University Grants Committee (see Scott). Many former colonies adapted this model, each modifying it to their nation's particular higher education system and national goals and values. The chapters on Australia and Israel exemplify such adaptation. The second model is direct government control (via government agencies), developed to assure that universities help the government meet its goals (usually economic goals). Many of the former communist bloc case studies are examples of institutions under tight government control now moving to more autonomous (but accountable) relations with their new governments (see de Rudder, Darvas, and Fogel, Mauch).

Growing out of the fourth theme is one final theme: How much of the government-university relationship is determined by historical roots and how much is determined by present national goals? This volume shows that the Western and former communist bloc, colonial and colonized nations may come from different historical and cultural traditions, yet they are moving toward a similar structure (pattern of government-university relationship) as they adopt the same goals (success in the world economy) and organize along similar, democratic principles in the 1990s. There seems to be a movement from the extremes to a mean whereby the most controlling states have moved to allowing institutions somewhat more freedom and autonomy, and those states (such as Germany, the U.S. and the U.K.) with traditions of university autonomy are moving slowly toward more regulation and, thus, a bit less autonomy.

No doubt some of this apparent movement from extremes reflects changes in governments in the last decade, and that of course is the point of the volume. But there may be an additional point operating, succinctly put by that quote from Scott above. If the modern state—authoritarian though it may be—wishes to compete successfully in the 21st century, it will have to release its higher education sector, and especially its great research universities, from tight political control and offer a greater measure of freedom and autonomy than thought necessary before. The modern democratic state, on the other hand, also needing to compete, faces a different dilemma, that of requiring its traditionally autonomous and independent higher education institutions to be more accountable to public demands for greater efficiency, greater and more equitable access, and more relevance to social needs—all this of course requiring more government regulation of the institutions to assure compliance.

Paula L.W. Sabloff
Department of Anthropology, Faculty of Arts
and Sciences, and Administration and Policy
Studies, School of Education, University of Pittsburgh

James E. Mauch
Administration and Policy Studies,
School of Education, University of Pittsburgh

REFERENCES

Altbach, P. G. (1990). Perspectives on comparative higher education: Essays on faculty, students and reform. Special Studies in Comparative Education No. Twenty-two. Buffalo, NY: Comparative Education Center, SUNYAB.

Marcus, L. R. & Hollander, T. E. (1981). The capital and the campus— each in its proper place. *Policy Studies Journal*, pp. 19–31.

Trow, M. A. (1974). Problems in the transition from elite to mass higher education. In *Policies for higher education*, pp. 51–101. General report of the conference on the future of post-secondary education. Paris: OECD.

Wallerstein, I. (1974). *The modern world-system I*. New York: Academic Press.

CHAPTER I

University-State Relations in Britain
Paradigm of Autonomy

Peter Scott

Introduction

One of the proudest claims made by universities is that they are autonomous institutions, insulated from direct political pressures and able to pursue their own agendas in both teaching and research. Such autonomy is generally regarded as a primary characteristic of universities. In fact, during most of their history and in most of the world today, the freedom of universities has been and is severely restricted. The universities of early modern Europe were often agents of state policy. For example, the University of Lund in what is now southern Sweden was founded in 1667 to establish a Swedish presence in provinces which had recently been Danish. Most of the universities established in Europe during the seventeenth and eighteenth centuries were closely bound up in the formation of dynastic and nation states. Nineteenth-century universities were created to meet the urgent needs of an expanding industrial economy. The universities of the twentieth century were designed to satisfy the growing demand for higher education in a complex modern society.

Even at times when universities seemed to enjoy an unchallenged independence, as in Britain between 1919 and 1981, and in places where a commitment to academic freedom is em-

braced within a wider democratic culture (notably North America and Western Europe), their effective autonomy can easily be
exaggerated. As higher education systems have increased in size,
and therefore cost, their freedom to set their own agendas un-
hindered by political and other external intervention has been
progressively reduced. Where universities have retained a high
degree of formal autonomy, the reason has generally been a close
alignment between their interests and those of the state. In effect,
political and academic leaders have agreed about the objectives
universities should pursue.

Nowhere has this claim of institutional autonomy been
made more strongly or seemed to be realized more completely
than in Britain. Until the 1980s it was assumed that a near perfect
balance had been created between the interests of universities
and those of the state. British universities were almost entirely
dependent on public expenditure for their income, like universities in the rest of Europe. Yet they were protected from direct
political interference. One reason was that they were, and are,
independent rather than state corporations and their staff were
not civil servants. But more significant were the special arrangements made to create a buffer between universities and the
state.

The key to these arrangements was the University Grants
Committee (UGC), established in 1919 and only abolished in
1989. The UGC was responsible for offering the government
formal advice on the needs of the universities (in effect, a privileged form of lobbying) but also for distributing to individual
universities the funds made available by the government without any reference to the wishes of politicians. Indeed, so determined was the UGC to keep political influence at arm's length
that civil servants who acted as assessors (observers) at its
meetings were asked to leave when matters involving individual
universities were discussed.

These arrangements appeared to offer an ideal model for
combining state funding of universities with university autonomy. As such, they were widely admired outside Britain (e.g.,
Berdahl 1959). Attempts were also made to emulate these arrangements; some countries such as India and Sri Lanka established university grants committees, or commissions, of their

own, while in Australia a tertiary education commission was created to act as a similar buffer between universities and the government. However, beginning in the mid-1970s and with demoralizing effect through the 1980s, these happy arrangements were violently unraveled. The UGC became a mere agent of the state before being ignominiously abolished.

The Politics of Expansion

This standard account of university-state relations in Britain over the past quarter century—a story of the relentless erosion of university autonomy by an aggressive state interest, the expulsion of the universities from an academic Eden—is largely a myth. It exaggerates both the freedom the UGC—and through the UGC, the universities—enjoyed in the "golden time" of political innocence and also the more recent subordination of the UGC and its successor agencies to the government. British universities had never been as free in the past as people imagined; nor were universities so utterly enslaved by successive post-UGC regimes. To the extent that a real shift in university-state relations had taken place, it was the result of larger structural factors rather than the weakness of university leaders or the aggression of politicians.

The first factor was the growing size, and so cost, of the university system. The number of universities in Britain increased from 24 in 1960 to 45 in 1991. The promotion of the English polytechnics and parallel institutions in Scotland to full university status has increased the total again, to 87. The number of students has risen over the same period from 113,000 to 357,000 (over 600,000 if students in the now-promoted polytechnics are included). The growth in public expenditure on universities has been most dramatic of all, rising from $129 million in 1962 to more than $3 billion in 1989. Such a fundamental transformation of the scale and cost of the university system was bound to affect its relationship with its principal paymaster, the state.

No government, even one ideologically committed to free-market principles like the Conservative government that has been in power in Britain since 1979, can avoid taking a view about the efficiency and effectiveness of a system in which such substantial public resources are invested. In practice it is difficult to establish a clear demarcation between funding and planning or between financial accountability and academic development. It is impossible to measure efficiency without considering effectiveness, which can only be determined in the light of institutional missions. Nor is it possible to determine whether money has been well spent unless the purposes of this expenditure are taken into account. In any case, universities play a key role in fulfilling public purposes, whether meeting the demand for higher education places from those graduating from secondary school or assisting with economic development. Again, no government, even one committed to the primacy of private over public goals, can afford to be entirely agnostic about the goals universities should pursue.

The second factor was the increasing competition between universities and other sectors of education for scarce public resources. Up to 1963, when the UGC negotiated directly with the Treasury on behalf of the universities, such competition was muffled. With the creation of the Department of Education and Science (DES), a single department became responsible for the whole of the educational system, from universities to nursery schools, and for establishing public expenditure priorities within that system. In 1966 the Labor government created the polytechnics by merging colleges of technology, business, art and design, and later education into large multifaculty institutions which rapidly came to rival the universities. However, universities were still insulated to some extent from direct competition. The polytechnics remained the responsibility of local education authorities (city and county councils), although their income came almost entirely from the national government; the universities continued to be shielded by the UGC.

From the late 1970s, the DES placed increasing emphasis on the need to coordinate policies in both halves of higher education, which meant adjudicating between the rival claims of universities on the one hand and polytechnics and other (nonuniversity) colleges on the other. And in 1989 the latter were freed from the control of local authorities and established as independent corporations like the universities. As a result, the polytechnics and colleges formed a rival "national" system, responsible to a Polytechnics and Colleges Funding Council (PCFC) just as the universities after the abolition of the UGC had to answer to the Universities Funding Council (UFC). Both these funding councils were subordinate to the DES, which set their respective budgets.

Finally, in 1992 a single Higher Education Funding Council was established in England (separate councils were created in Scotland and Wales). At the same time, the polytechnics were granted university status. In less than three decades (from 1963 to 1992), therefore, the original universities moved from a position of exceptional privilege in terms of the allocation of public expenditure, insulated from serious competition with other parts of higher education, to a position in which they were treated like all other institutions, having to compete on the same terms for scarce resources.

The third factor was closely linked to the second. Until the late 1960s, little effort had been made in Britain to plan state expenditure as a whole. Instead, detailed sums of money were voted by Parliament for individual departments and the public services they provided. In 1969 the Public Expenditure Survey (PES) system was introduced. Under the PES system, expenditure by departments is coordinated by the Treasury. Any disputes that arise are referred to a special subcommittee of the Cabinet. Not only is each department's share of public expenditure predetermined, but its makeup is shaped by government-wide assumptions on wage levels, inflation, efficiency gains and similar issues. Such planning is now routine in most countries but was still comparatively uncommon a generation ago. Under the PES system university budgets could no longer be privileged. During the 1980s the Conservative government's efforts to roll back the frontiers of the state by cutting public expenditure paradoxically placed even greater emphasis on centralized control because of the need to establish stricter priorities and devise tougher tests of efficiency and accountability.

The fourth factor was the growing complexity of the British university system. When this system was still made up of a comparatively small number of homogeneous institutions with similar and settled missions, the government was content to trust the UGC to distribute state grants among them without interfering. No significant political issues were at stake in this distribution. Similarly, the UGC itself was able to operate a loose-rein planning regime. Although advice had always been given to individual universities, the UGC did not see the need to steer policy for the entire system until 1967, when it issued its first "memorandum of guidance."

But as the number of universities and students grew and as the system became much more heterogeneous, with new disciplines and new patterns of study, the need to plan university development increased. A much larger and more differentiated university could not be left to manage itself in the old voluntarist way. Its priorities could no longer be determined by informal and confidential negotiations among the academic establishment from which political leaders were largely excluded. Many of the policy choices in an expanded system could only be resolved within a political process, in which judgements played an important but subsidiary role.

Universities and the State

Oxford and Cambridge, established in the twelfth and thirteenth centuries respectively, and the two oldest Scottish universities, Glasgow and Aberdeen, which were founded in the fifteenth century, are exceptions to the normal pattern of university development in Britain. During the sixteenth century, two more universities were created in Scotland, Edinburgh and St. Andrews, the former on the initiative of the town council.

But most British universities are more recent foundations. In the nineteenth century nearly all the rapidly expanding industrial cities of the north and midlands acquired universities. They were generally established by civic and business leaders proud of their cities and anxious to train local professional elites, e.g., lawyers, teachers, and engineers. These universities were small and depended heavily on fees paid by students, although some had modest endowments. They were granted Royal Charters and the right to award their own degrees but did not receive significant and systematic state support until late in the century. These early grants dating from the 1880s went to teacher training and technical education.

In the first decade of the twentieth century, an ad hoc University Colleges Committee was set up to channel the increasing flow of public money into universities. In 1919 the committee, renamed the UGC, was established on a permanent basis. The experience of war had convinced politicians that universities were national assets, key producers of the science and technology so urgently needed by a nation facing a formidable enemy. Coincidentally, it was also during the First World War that the state began to subsidize research in universities.

But public expenditure on universities, although sufficiently large by the end of the First World War to require a permanent committee, was not intended to provide universities with the bulk of their income. This was still supposed to come from endowments, industrial and civic subsidies, and student fees. State grants were given to make good any deficit. However on the eve of the next world war in 1938, universities depended on the UGC, and so the state, for a third of their income. In 1951 state subvention had risen to two-thirds. By the 1960s British universities had become—in political fact if not legal form—public institutions. In effect rather than intention, the UGC had been the instrument that produced this radical shift from private independence to public dependence—to which, of course, there was little alternative. The state, it seemed, was the only realistic sponsor of the much larger and more diverse higher education systems that developed after 1945.

In Britain the state also took over responsibility for student support. Originally students, or their families, had to pay tuition fees, although scholarships were available. Gradually the number of scholarships increased so that by the 1950s most students received them. Finally, in 1962 scholarships were transformed into a system of universal entitlement. Students were paid grants to support themselves through college, and their fees were paid. Although recently these grants have begun to be replaced by repayable loans, the principle of universal entitlement has been maintained, and the state, through local education authorities, still pays for tuition. The nationalization of Britain's universities, in terms of their budgets, appears to be irreversible.

Despite its reputation as a buffer between universities and the state, the UGC never had a proper legal status to guarantee its independence from the government. It was created by a Treasury minute, an informal record of the decision to establish it. Its members were first appointed by ministers and then, after 1964, by the Secretary of State for Education and Science. Its officials were civil servants. But this lack of legal definition was a strength rather than a weakness. It enabled the UGC to develop a powerful mystique and surround itself with eloquent conventions of academic freedom which no politician dared to challenge for a long time. Although formally appointed by the DES, UGC members actually resembled a self-perpetuating oligarchy. Various academic interests, such as medical schools, were always represented, and the DES almost invariably accepted the suggestions made by the UGC's chairman about new members. The committee jealously defended its apolitical status almost until its abolition.

The UGC's freedom from political influence had two other main sources. First, the government did not interfere with the UGC because the UGC did not interfere with the universities; the freedom resided in the universities not in the UGC. The latter was simply the gatekeeper. Once the UGC began to interfere with the universities, imposing its own policies rather than simply endorsing their initiatives, it became more difficult for the committee to resist interference by the DES. Second, for the first half of its life the UGC's role was more financial than academic, which is why it was responsible to the Treasury rather than the Ministry of Education. At the start its terms of reference were strictly limited, although they were widened by the postwar Labor government in 1946 to require the UGC's advice to ministers (in effect, its budget bid) to take account of "the needs of the nation."

In retrospect this signaled a significant shift. Before the war British universities had seen themselves as private institutions which were assisted by the state. After the war they increasingly came to see themselves as public institutions, although enjoying a privileged status. But only when university expansion got under way in the 1950s and, in particular, after 1960 was there any need to modify this commitment to an arm's-length relationship between universities and the state. When a large-scale extension of higher education was first contemplated, it was not clear whether the government would allow the UGC to take the lead in steering this expansion. Following the 1945 Percy Committee report on higher technological education, the Labor government had chosen to upgrade further education by establishing regional colleges of technology rather than expanding the universities.

A decade later, in 1956, the government, now Conservative, followed the same approach, creating the colleges of advanced technology outside but alongside the university sector and directly funded by the Ministry of Education. (The colleges of advanced technology [CATs] eventually became universities in 1965 following the Robbins report on higher education.) Ten years later, in 1966, the government, again Labor, established the polytechnics, largely based on the old regional colleges of technology but also embracing colleges of art and design, business, and education. Like the CATs, the polytechnics were designed to be an alternative to the universities, offering more vocational courses, being more locally oriented, and having a limited research mission. In all three cases the government attempted to bypass the universities, largely because, protected by the UGC buffer, they appeared less amenable to political direction.

But in the decade between 1956 and 1966 the UGC was the main organizer of expansion. It implemented the government's decision to expand the existing universities and to found new campus universities on green-fields sites; it decided where they should be based and oversaw their physical and academic development. But in doing this the committee accepted, perhaps unwittingly, two new roles which were eventually to undermine its old independence.

First, the UGC became a large-scale planner, which obliged it to behave in a new, more managerial and intrusive, way in its relations with the universities. No longer mainly an advisory body, it took on important executive functions. Increasingly, as has already been pointed out, the UGC found itself forced to give instructions to universities, at first gently through the medium of euphemistically described "letters of guidance" in the late 1960s and 1970s but, as the 1980s unfolded, more brusquely by means of a stream of detailed circulars. Second, it acted as the state's agent in the development of higher education. As a result the committee could no longer reasonably keep the government at arm's length. The creation of brand-new universities and the large-scale expansion of existing ones, both requiring resources which only the state could provide, were inescapably political decisions. The UGC's job was confined to overseeing their detailed implementation.

The consequences of both changes became apparent, slowly but inexorably, through the 1970s and 1980s. First, when inflation rose rapidly in 1973 following a successful miners' strike and the Arab-Israeli war, the Conservative government decided it would no longer be able to agree automatically to upgrade university budgets. Soon afterwards, it abandoned the system of five-year grants. Both measures struck at the heart of the traditional university funding system. Now the UGC had to constantly negotiate and renegotiate with the DES while universities were no longer insulated from the changing political climate. In 1977 the reelected Labor government tried to restore the old order by offering universities a rolling "triennium," a fixed budget for one year followed by provisional totals for the two subsequent years, to replace the lost "quinquennium."

But two years later Labor fell from power and Margaret Thatcher became Prime Minister at the head of a new Conservative administration committed to rolling back the frontiers of the welfare state. In 1981, as part of a general reduction in public expenditure, university grants were cut by 15% over three years. The UGC, its members having momentarily contemplated mass resignation in protest, decided to implement these cuts, although many critics condemned this as collaboration. The committee told universities to reduce their student admissions by 5% in order to protect the "unit of resource," so that professors and lecturers would still have time for research. This policy was subsequently reversed when it became clear that the displaced students were simply enrolling in the polytechnics instead. The UGC also cut its allocations to universities—but on a highly selective basis. A few universities (Bath, York) suffered no reduction at all, while others (Aston, Salford) saw their UGC allocations cut by more than a third. This selectivity further undermined the old idea that the UGC was the universities' friend.

Having agreed to manage the reduction of public investment in universities on behalf of the government, the UGC in its last decade became involved in a flurry of managerial initiatives. Some were positive. One example was the "restructuring" fund it secured from the government to help universities pay for the redundancy (firing) or transfer of academic staff they could no longer afford to employ (complicated by the fact that until 1989 most university teachers enjoyed tenure). Another example of a more hopeful initiative was the "new blood" scheme designed to allow universities to recruit younger staff despite the cuts.

Other UGC initiatives were more negative—or were seen as such by many in the universities. First, the committee took the lead in urging the universities to operate more productively, sponsoring various efficiency studies in the mid-1960s. Then it embarked on a series of rationalization exercises in particular disciplines, intending to close weak departments and to strengthen others. Predictably, these exercises ran into stiff opposition. Some (for example, in earth sciences) were carried through. Others (as in the case of veterinary science) were effectively abandoned. Others (such as large-scale reviews of physics and chemistry) again were shelved.

Finally, the UGC reformed its method for allocating grants to universities. Previously this had been done according to an informal system stigmatized by its critics as "informed prejudice," incremental funding based on historic costs qualified by private and subjective assessments of quality. No serious attempt had ever been made to disaggregate teaching and research elements in overall university grants. Such a system had been acceptable during a period of expansion but could no longer be justified at a time when significant cuts were being made in university budgets. More robust and public criteria were demanded. So the UGC developed a more complex funding methodology.

In subsequent initiatives, university teaching budgets were determined by student numbers (weighted by discipline), while their research budgets were fixed according to a number of factors. One was the success of universities in attracting grants and contracts from research councils and other external agencies (British universities benefit from a so-called dual-support system for research, receiving some money in their baseline budgets and the rest from research councils). But another—the UGC's most controversial initiative—was its decision to assess the quality of research in every department of each university in Britain. At first, departments were graded on a five-point scale ranging from "outstanding" to "below average." In the most recent research assessment exercise (1992), the number of points on the scale was reduced to four. Universities and the former polytechnics included for the first time were now free to exclude those departments with weak research reputations for which they were not seeking funds.

Despite its managerial activism and willingness to accept political subordination, the UGC was abolished by the 1989 Education Reform Act. However, this was less a comment on its performance in the eyes of ministers than their desire to create a parallel agency to the Polytechnics and Colleges Funding Council (PCFC). The PCFC had been established to manage the polytechnics when they became independent corporations and were no longer responsible to local education authorities. So the UGC had to be replaced by a Universities Funding Council (UFC).

In one respect the UFC had a more secure footing than the UGC. It had proper statutory backing, and its staff was no longer administratively attached to the DES. But in three more significant respects the replacement of the UGC by the UFC further diminished the effective autonomy enjoyed by the universities. First, unlike the UGC, the new council did not have a formal responsibility to advise the government on the needs of the universities. Privileged lobbying was no longer among its terms of reference.

Second, under the 1989 act, the UFC—and through it, the DES—was granted for the first time legal power to tell universities how to use the money they received from the state. Previously, universities had been free to spend UGC allocations as they liked—although they risked getting less next time if they spent their allocations in ways the UGC disliked. Third, the UFC was deliberately designed by the Conservative government to be less representative of the universities. While the chairman of the

UGC had always been a distinguished scholar or scientist, generally a former vice-chancellor (university president), the first chairman of the UFC was a businessman first and an engineer second. A similar shift took place among the remaining members. Whereas those on the UGC had been overwhelmingly drawn from the universities, at least half of UFC members had to come from industry and commerce.

Despite the advantages the UFC possessed in the eyes of politicians, it too was abolished by the Further and Higher Education Act of 1992, along with the PCFC. The main purpose of this act was to end the so-called binary system which divided British higher education into universities on the one hand and polytechnics and colleges on the other. But the creation of a unified system meant that there was no need to maintain two separate funding councils. Both, therefore, were replaced by a single Higher Education Funding Council (HEFC) responsible for all higher education. But while the PCFC was replaced with regret, the UFC was abolished with relish.

During the UFC's brief existence, relations between universities and the state in Britain sharply worsened. The council no longer reflected academic opinion and was seen as ineffective. It continued the UGC's policies on research virtually without change. But the UFC attempted to introduce an "internal market" system for allocating teaching funds, which would have forced universities to bid against each other for student places. Predictably, the universities refused to cooperate, forming what was in effect a cartel by agreeing to bid at the same, or very similar, prices. The system collapsed. Rivalry between the UFC chairman, Henry (Lord) Chilver, and its chief executive, Sir Peter Swinnerton-Dyer, who had served as the UGC's last chairman, exacerbated this failure. Both the UFC and the universities were blamed by politicians, the former for incompetence and irresolution and the latter for sabotaging the move towards an "internal market" in the university system.

Faced with this resistance from the universities, the government attempted to encourage competition by other means. In 1989 it reduced the grant paid directly to universities through the UFC and increased tuition fees paid by students—or rather, paid on their behalf by local education authorities, which were then reimbursed for their expenditure by the national state. The intention was not to get students to make a direct personal contribution to the cost of their higher education. An earlier attempt in the mid-1980s by the then Secretary of State for Education and Science, Sir Keith Joseph, to make students from rich families pay their own fees was defeated by parliamentary opposition, much of which came from within the Conservative Party. Britain's closer links with other European countries that do not charge tuition were a further constraint. Instead, the idea was to channel state funds to those universities which were most successful in the marketplace, as measured by their ability to attract more students. But the incidental effect was to reduce the power of the UFC and PCFC and of their joint successor, the HEFC.

In April 1992 the HEFC formally took over from the two abolished funding councils, but it started work at least a year earlier. Most of its staff came from the UFC. So did its chief executive, Graeme Davies, formerly vice-chancellor of Liverpool University, although its chairman, Sir Ron Dearing, former head of the Post Office, had been chairman of the PCFC. Its initial approach was to continue the UGC's and UFC's policy of research assessment, modified to allow the former polytechnics a better chance of winning research funds. But it has followed the PCFC's lead in allocating funds for teaching, devising a system which guarantees universities and colleges a core allocation of students and distributes the remainder selectively, mainly to those institutions able and willing to expand most rapidly and efficiently. Whether this gradualist approach can be sustained in the long term against a background of rapidly rising student numbers and radically transformed institutions is more doubtful.

Rights and Responsibilities

It is necessary to identify the various aspects of the modern state's stake in higher education. Five different levels of that relationship need to be emphasized, while the relationship is better seen as a web of two-way links rather than a one-way system of control.

The first level is *managerial*. As has already been suggested, the growing size and complexity of modern higher education systems demand that they be managed in more explicit and professional ways than in the past. At times, the ethos and practices required for effective management are difficult to reconcile with long-standing assumptions about academic culture, in particular the autonomy of the individual teacher or researcher and the pattern of collegiality within universities. So the drive towards more efficient management has generated conflict. The state's role has been to ensure that the growing sums of public money invested in universities are being properly used and accounted for and that its investment is securing the best possible return.

In the past, when higher education systems were simpler and smaller and relations between university leaders and politicians were more intimate (and therefore, trusting), these aims could be achieved without an elaborate bureaucracy or open intervention, as the experience of the UGC in Britain clearly demonstrates. The state could accept the universities' assurance they were properly managed. Today that is no longer possible. Categorical assurances are demanded, too often against a background of collapsing trust.

This phenomenon of accountability has not been confined to public institutions; something similar has happened to private universities. They, too, have to account in much more detailed and direct ways to those who provide their resources, whether students through fees, alumni or corporations through donations, or the state through long tax regimes.

The second level is *public policy*. The provision of higher education, both private and public, raises important political issues. In the case of private institutions, these are often oblique—for example, to what extent should gifts to these universities reduce the tax obligations of donors and to what degree should their operation be subsidized by a benign tax regime? In Britain, unlike the United States, the Treasury has always regarded tax forgone, through exemptions and write-offs, as exactly equivalent to public expenditure, which has discouraged private and corporate giving.

In the case of public universities, public policy issues are more explicit. Politics, as the British Labor Party leader Aneurin

Bevan once remarked, is the language of priorities. Therefore, governments must balance the claims of higher education against those from other parts of the educational system and from other public services. There is no way that universities, because of their privileged origins, can be insulated from such competition, as has been clearly demonstrated in Britain.

Also, most governments make further public policy claims on higher education. In the United States the desire to promote equal opportunity through affirmative action is an example of such a claim. In many European countries, where the state is a more active partner in the economy than in the United States, universities are expected to play a powerful role in economic development. Their student intakes are often influenced by manpower-planning policies and their research agenda by policies on technology transfer. In most developed countries, the political demands that states make of higher education systems are complex and often crosscut.

The third level is *contractual*. The state, as a customer for the services that universities provide, has important contractual relations with higher education. In most European countries the state is the employer, direct or indirect, of a high proportion of skilled professionals. Teachers and doctors, effectively if not always legally, are state employees. Similarly, the new professions that have grown out of the postwar welfare state (and which are intimately related to the growth of the social sciences within the university, with the possible exception of business administration) are made up almost entirely of public employees.

Many private corporations that employ large numbers of university-trained workers and the voluntary sector, which is also staffed by highly skilled personnel, most of them graduates, are both often heavily dependent on the state—the former for contracts and the latter for subsidy. And of course, the state is the direct employer of large numbers of graduates, in the civil service and other public agencies, the armed forces, and so on. Although different governments have shown more or less enthusiasm for detailed manpower planning, there can be no doubt about the modern state's commanding interest in higher education's production of graduates.

The state has an equally intense interest in higher education's production of research. It is no accident that the most important advances in public investment in university research have come in wartime. In addition to general support for fundamental research, which has grown along with universities, the state contracts with institutions for specific projects. Here the military and medicine are the two big focuses. Much of the research in the social sciences is commissioned by public or semipublic agencies. And an increasing fraction of high-technology research, even if it is carried out in private corporations, is funded by the state whether through direct subsidy or indirect tax concessions. So there is a myriad of contractual links between the modern state and higher education systems.

The fourth level is *political economy*. Talk of postindustrialism, the knowledge society, and the supersymbolic economy is now commonplace. According to these interpretations, theoretical knowledge will itself become a primary resource for economic development in the future, especially in advanced societies with highly skilled (but expensive) work forces. Within corporations the growing emphasis on human capital can also be traced back to the influence of these theories of post-Fordist society. Although the university will not be the only player (high-technology corporations like IBM, government agencies, the mass media, and other cultural institutions will also make important contributions to the building of postindustrialism), it will be a key one.

But emphasis on the university's role in economic development will bring in its wake new and more insistent demands for accountability. In the competencies-based economies of North America, Western Europe, and the Pacific Rim, higher education has already assumed a new importance and acquired fresh responsibilities. The state, which in many of these nations has been the main engine of modernization, is placing new demands on universities, especially as R and D institutions. In the long run, these links between a postindustrial economy, a modernizing state, and advanced higher education systems may be the most significant of all.

The fifth level is *culture*. Universities have always played a central role in cultural production and reproduction. It has been their role to produce intellectuals as well as scientists; indeed, the production of the former preceded that of the latter by many centuries. Today this function is of continuing importance in free societies where criticism of traditional patterns of thought is essential to their democratic development. In an age of mass culture, globally extended, the responsibility of universities is greater than ever. They must conserve the best and the brightest of traditional culture(s) and foster disciplined discrimination in their students. But at the same time they must strengthen individual intelligence in the inevitable contest with mass tests. The formation of critical minds is more than ever at the heart of the universities' mission.

The democratic state has a vital interest in upholding a free university tradition. Perhaps it must even force universities to maintain their freedom in the face of external demands—many of which, paradoxically, grow out of the state's own detailed requirements as well as those of business, industry, and community. Moreover, a free university tradition provides optimal conditions for scientific progress. The absence of this tradition in Eastern Europe and the former Soviet Union was a crucial element in the social and economic underdevelopment of that region and a primary cause of the disintegration of the communist regimes there. It is no accident that the world's best universities are generally to be found in the world's freest societies. So the state's long-term interests, both in terms of scientific productivity and cultural responsibility, are best served by restricting the short-term demands it places on universities—even if this means creating buffer bodies to make it easier for universities to resist the persuasive pressure of politicians.

The relationship between the state and higher education, therefore, is inevitably highly complex. The political and academic systems touch each other at so many points. The state has not one but many interests to consider in its links with universities. As the supplier of public funds, it must ensure they are well used. As the ultimate source of legitimate authority in a democracy, it must ensure universities respect public policy concerns. As a contractor, it must make sure the terms of the contract are met. As a grand socioeconomic planner for facilitation, it must try to match higher education's key contribution to this wider enterprise. And as the promoter of a progressive science and guardian of a democratic culture, it must defend the responsibilities of universities as free institutions. To reconcile these various roles is not easy. At different times and in different places different balances will be struck, depending on historical circumstances, the weight of present administrative arrangements, and the force of future aspirations.

The relationship between the state and higher education is also ambiguous. It is wrong to regard the state as predator and the university as victim. Sometimes it is political leaders who insist on higher education's moral mission while academic leaders are prepared to sell out—provided the price is right. Both the complexity and ambiguity are inevitable because neither the state nor the university is a monolithic institution. They contain within themselves competing interests (e.g., a division between legislative and executive powers, a division between different layers of government, or a complex stratification of higher education systems), even when these are not structurally defined.

Conclusion

The temptation to categorize university-state relations in terms of key variables such as the legal status of universities, the presence or absence of intermediary agencies, dependence on public funds, or acceptance of market strategies is obvious. Yet the dangers are also obvious. The historical record in Britain suggests that such neat categorization can be misleading. The safest conclusion, therefore, is that in trying to understand the complexity of university-state relations, what matters is not simply the visible structure of funding patterns, organizational controls, and constitutional arrangements but the invisible values which give these patterns, controls, and arrangements a deeper structure. It is much too simple to conclude that British universities were once free and now everywhere in chains. In practice the autonomy balance has shifted remarkably little. There have been losses, painful and visible ones, which have been described earlier in this chapter. But there have also been gains. Most strikingly, the resources available to British universities, and so their capacity to engage in both critical enquiry and creative research, are now far greater. And these resources and that capacity have been provided by the same state that is so often accused of restricting their autonomy.

The changing balance of university-state relations, apparently to the advantage of the latter, has generally been deplored by the former—hence the myth of a "golden time" of university freedom described at the start of this chapter. But a more realistic, and optimistic, account would emphasize two points. First, the impression that the UGC acted as an effective buffer between universities and their political paymasters, allowing them to enjoy the luxury of private autonomy while enjoying state funding, was probably always an illusion. Both the academic and political heights were once commanded by members of the same tight-knit national elite. Oxbridge, Whitehall and Westminster, and the old professions formed a golden triangle of intimate power sharing. But during the 1970s and 1980s, the academic and political worlds in Britain drifted apart. The national elite became less clearly defined, as new groups contended for influence, and also more divided, as open ideological differences became more important than cultural solidarities rooted in class. Inevitably it was a painful process for the universities to have made explicit what was once implicit. But this pain does not prove there was a fundamental shift in underlying power relations.

Second, if there has indeed been a significant shift in university-state relations, it is best seen as a positive rather than a negative phenomenon, for it is evidence of the central position now occupied by universities in the life of modern Britain, as of all modern societies, not only in terms of the reproduction of political, professional, and technical elites but also as the culmination of the mass educational systems created by democratic states and as key agents of social, economic, and cultural transformation.

Perhaps the British experience offers a paradigm for a more mature understanding of university-state relations. Those relations have become so complex, contradictory, ambiguous, and sinuous that they resist easy categorization. They can only be properly understood in a wider social context, against a background of democratic change and in anticipation of a rapid advance towards a postindustrial economy.

REFERENCES

Archer, M. S. (1978). *Social origins of educational systems*. London: Sage Publications.

Becher, T. & Kogan, M. (1992). *Process and structure in higher education* (2d ed.). London: Routledge.

Berdahl, R. O. (1959). *British universities and the state*. Berkeley: University of California Press.

Halsey, A. H. & Trow, M. (1971). *The British academics*. London: Faber and Faber.

Kogan, D. & Kogan, M. (1983). *The attack on higher education*. London: Kogan Page.

Minogue, K. (1973). *The concept of a university*. Berkeley: University of California Press.

Phillipson, N. (Ed.). (1983). *Universities, society and the future: A conference held on the 400th anniversary of the University of Edinburgh*. Edinburgh: Edinburgh University Press.

Scott, P. (1984). *The crisis of the university*. London: Croom Helm.

Shattock, M. (Ed.). (1983). *The structure and governance of higher education*. Leverhulme No. 9. Guildford: Society for Research into Higher Education.

Shinn, C. H. (1986). *Paying the piper: The development of the University Grants Committee 1919–46*. Lewes: Falmer Press.

Stewart, W. A. C. (1989). *Higher education in postwar Britain*. Basingstoke: Macmillan.

CHAPTER II

Changing Conceptions of State-University Relationships
The Israeli Case (1950-1990)

Yaacov Iram

Introduction[1]

The history of government-university relations has always been vexatious, witnessing times of harmonious cooperation and periods of contentious confrontations (Perkin, 1984, 1991). However, developments in recent decades have brought universities to confront problems of unprecedented scope and magnitude that challenge fundamental concepts such as institutional autonomy, academic freedom, politicization, and the role of government in higher education. Many governments and societies have shown increasing concern about the role and relevance of their respective higher education systems. Increased government interest in universities seems to be motivated by factors such as financial stringency, increased demand for higher education, a desire to articulate higher education with other levels of education (i.e., basic and post-baccalaureate education), labor force needs, demographic shifts (e.g., aging, immigration and emigration), changing policies of "welfare states," and demands by minority or underrepresented groups (Van Vught, 1989; Meek et al., 1991; Neave and Van Vught, 1991). The transformation of

23

higher education from "elite" to "mass" systems (Trow, 1974) led to increased community involvement and political intervention. Financial pressures and growing government funding for higher education seem to drive the systems to meet national labor market needs, develop new products, utilize new resources, and train qualified personnel.

In a comparative study of the structure of power in seven national systems of higher education (Germany, Italy, France, Sweden, Great Britain, the United States, and Japan), Van de Graaf, Clark, Furth, Goldschmidt, and Wheeler outlined the following factors or specific forces that "have placed traditional university structures under steadily increasing strain, thereby furthering pressure for reform" (1978, p. 7):

1. Quantitative expansion of students and teaching staff, which generated qualitative problems;

2. Labor market demands and pressure on higher education to train students in a wide range of skills and qualifications;

3. Egalitarianism, which focused attention not only on issues of access but also on problems of adapting programs and structures to previously disadvantaged student populations;

4. The knowledge explosion and the central role assigned by society to the development of science in an increasing differentiation and specialization (both within disciplinary lines and among different forms of inquiry and study), in order to make knowledge more relevant to society's needs;

5. Rising costs from the expansion of student numbers, growth in academic and administrative staff, and institutional and disciplinary diversification, causing public expenditure on higher education to grow faster than total educational expenditure, total public spending, and gross national product. This trend resulted in political pressures to increase productivity; and in turn, strengthened governments in their demands that universities be more accountable, frequently at the expense of institutional autonomy (Sheldrake and Linke, 1979); and

6. Politicization, meaning, in a narrow sense, the legit-
imization of the involvement of political parties, government officials, and groups within and outside of universities in policy-making and, in the wider sense, the
recognition that higher education must be coordinated
by national demands and societal needs. Such recognition implied structural diversification of the higher education system, including the promotion of novel forms of
higher education or the upgrading of existing postsecondary institutions.

These six major forces have affected changes in the division of
authority between universities and government bureaucracies.

The purpose of this chapter is to present an overview of
changes in Israel's government-university relations in the last
four decades, with an emphasis on the last two decades, and to
analyze the effects of these changes. The analysis will be limited
to policy changes at what Becher and Kogan (1980) call the
"central authority level" and the "institutional level" but not in
the "basic unit," in what Clark (1983) terms the "superstructure"
(the regulatory mechanisms of government and other systems to
relate organizations to one another) and the "middle" or "enterprise structure" (individual organizations in their entirety) but
not in the "understructure" (basic academic or disciplinary
units).

Israel's Higher Education System—Background

From the mid-1950s to the mid-1960s the universities in
Israel expanded parallel to the increased demand for higher education. The government spent immense resources to support the
increasing needs of the existing universities and to build new
ones. The universities were designed to provide professional
training for a growing industrialized state. The government developed mechanisms and structures to coordinate the growth of
the universities. These structures and basic relationships continue to form the foundations of higher education in Israel.
However, the same structures and mechanisms which were

originally designed to support and coordinate growth were employed in the 1970s and 1980s—in the wake of recession and government fiscal restraint—to constrain and control growth. Government initiatives as of the latter part of the 1980s have been an attempt to stimulate change but within the confines of the existing relatively stable structure; new structures have been introduced only at the margin.

Higher education in Israel, as defined by law, "includes teaching, science, and research which are conducted in universities and other academic degree granting institutions" (Stanner, 1963, p. 244). Within the higher education system there is a clear distinction between "universities" and "other institutions of higher education." In practice, the system is divided into six distinct subsystems, which in 1991 included the following institutions:

1. Six universities, which are authorized to grant all academic degrees: bachelor's, master's, and doctorate.

2. An Open University, which awards only the bachelor's degree.

3. Seven specialized "institutions of higher education which are not universities nor teacher training colleges" and are authorized to award only professional bachelor's degrees.

4. Nine teacher-training institutions that have received or are in the process of acquiring academic status and are accredited by the Council for Higher Education (CHE) to award the Bachelor of Education degrees either for the entire institution or for certain programs of study. These institutions are financed by the Ministry of Education and Culture. Of the nine teacher-training colleges, seven award the B.Ed. to teachers for primary and junior high schools (K–9), one awards the degree B.Ed. Tech. (technology teaching), and one awards the degree of B.Sc.T.E. (science teaching).

5. Eleven regional colleges, which, in addition to serving as centers of adult education, provide academic courses under the responsibility of one of the existing universities, which appoint their teachers and award their de-

grees. The regional colleges are financed by the Ministry of Education and Culture and by various local and regional authorities, which are supported by the Ministry of the Interior. The CHE has appointed a subcommittee to deal with academic courses at regional colleges "in order to make higher education more accessible to broader segments of the population" (Council for Higher Education, 1988a, p. 78) and, as of 1985, made direct allocations to their academic programs.

6. Three extensions of academic institutions from abroad that were granted a permit from the CHE to offer academic programs in Israel. The degrees, however, will be conferred by the parent institutions abroad (Council for Higher Education, 1991).

The Planning and Budgeting Committee (PBC) of the CHE is responsible for the budgets of all the institutions of the first three subsystems. This chapter focuses on these three subsystems.

Except for the Open University, Israel does not have liberal arts colleges per se. This function is performed by universities that are research universities and are also engaged in training professionals in law, medicine, engineering, business, and other fields. The typical bachelor's program in the humanities and social sciences is designed for three years of study in which the student specializes in two disciplines (departments) chosen by the student, provided he or she meets the admission criteria of the departments. Professional education in law, medicine, engineering, etc., commences in the first year of studies at the undergraduate level and continues for 3.5–5 years. Three additional years are generally required for the completion of the master's degree. The Ph.D. degree has minimal formal requirements; it is a research degree designed individually according to the candidate's research project.

The number of students at the seven university-level institutions (including the Open University) reached some 73,500 in 1992, an increase of more than 24% over the last ten years and an increase of about 10% in the last two years (Council for Higher Education Newsletter, 1992). Some 60% of the students are studying humanities, social sciences, and law; 25% natural sciences, agriculture, and medicine, and 15% engineering. Some

72% are studying for the first degree (bachelor's), 21% for the second degree (master's), 5% for the doctorate, and 2% for academic diplomas (mainly secondary school teaching diplomas). Enrollment at the 13 nonuniversity institutions of higher education is about 5,800. Some 15,000 are enrolled in academic courses of the Open University, this number being equal to some 5,000 students in full-time study programs at a regular university, an increase of 10% over 1991 (Israel, Central Bureau of Statistics, 1988; Council for Higher Education, 1992).

It is difficult to compare the rate of study in Israel with the rate in Western countries because of variations in the division between university and postsecondary education. Also, the principal age-group attending universities in Israel is 20–29, which differs from other countries because of three years of mandatory military service for men and two years for women. It may, however, be said that in Israel this rate (about 20% of the 20–29 age cohort receive university education, and another 33% receive some form of higher education) is higher than in most developed nations, similar to New Zealand, France, and Japan but lower than the United States and Canada (Ministry of Education and Culture, 1991, p. 74). The rate of admission in universities in 1990 was as follows: about 65% of applicants were admitted to departments of humanities, about 50% of applicants to social science departments, and about 20% to law schools, medicine, and engineering.

The principal sources of income for the higher education system are (1) government allocations determined and paid to individual institutions by the PBC; (2) current donations; (3) endowment funds; (4) tuition fees;[2] (5) research grants and contracts from government and private sources, at home and abroad; and (6) sale of services (including teaching services). The share of each is shown in table 1. Government participation in the ordinary budget of higher education is 80%, including tuition fees. This rate remained unchanged in real terms over the past decade in relation to the consumer price index; however, it did not compensate the universities for the growth in student population by almost 25% (see table 2) and for the significant increase in wages and salaries of university staff, which is determined by the government.

TABLE 1. Ordinary Budget of the Higher Education System by Sources of Income and Academic Years

Academic Year[1]	Various[2]	Donations from Abroad	Tuition Fees	PBC Allocations				Ordinary Budget
				Earmarked Allocations and Various[3]	Matching Allocations[4]	Direct Allocations	Total	
NIS THOUSANDS, AT CURRENT PRICES								
1979/80	159	126	64	52	50	867	969	1,318[5]
1980/81	450	260	133	108	225	2,228	2,561	3,404[5]
1981/82	1,132	505	272	150	400	4,138	4,688	6,597[5]
1982/83	3,754	1,205	1,405	569	600	13,326	14,495	20,859[5]
1983/84	25,763	5,944	3,290	3,702	1,363	36,623	41,688	76,685[6]
1984/85	43,387	42,199	29,603	24,079	8,820	153,075	185,974	301,163[7]
1985/86	43,503	57,741	99,256	38,629	38,254	253,037	329,920	530,420[7]
1986/87	89,179	80,087	124,085	49,540	43,904	324,625	418,069	711,420[7]
PERCENTAGES								
1979/80	12.1	9.6	4.8	3.9	3.8	65.8	73.5	100.0
1980/81	13.2	7.6	3.9	3.2	6.6	65.5	75.3	100.0
1981/82	17.2	7.6	4.1	2.3	6.1	62.7	71.1	100.0
1982/83	18.0	5.8	6.7	2.7	2.9	63.9	69.5	100.0
1983/84	33.6	7.7	4.3	4.8	1.8	47.8	54.4	100.0
1984/85	14.4	14.0	9.8	8.0	3.0	50.8	61.8	100.0
1985/86	8.2	10.9	18.7	7.3	7.2	47.7	62.2	100.0
1986/87	12.5	11.3	17.4	7.0	6.2	45.6	58.8	100.0

[1] From October 1 up to September 30; [2] Incl. deficits; [3] Incl. allocations for research and for special subjects (earmarked allocations, inter-university activities, aid to students, budgetary transfers and miscellaneous subjects); [4] To endowment funds at the institutions; [5] According to the balance sheets of the institutions; [6] According to financial reports received from the institutions; and [7] Final budget updated prices.

Source: CHE, *Higher Education in Israel—Statistical Abstracts, 1986/87,* p. 56.

TABLE 2. Students in Universities by Academic Years

Year	1969/70 = 100.0	1964/65 = 100.0	Annual Percentage of Growth	TOTAL*
1948/49	—	—	—	1,635
1949/50	—	—	—	2,450
1959/60	—	—	14.8**	10,202
1964/65	—	100.0	12.4**	18,368
1969/70	100.0	197.3	14.6**	36,239
1974/75	143.7	283.6	8.2	52,088
1979/80	158.7	313.0	3.1	57,500
1984/85	179.5	354.1	0.7	65,050
1987/88	187.4	369.7	1.1	67,900

*Including foreign students and students in special programs.
**On the assumption of linear growth within the years.

Source: Compiled from Council for Higher Education, Planning and Grants Committee, *Higher education in Israel—Statistical abstracts 1983/84; 1986/87.* Statistical Abstracts of Israel, No. 39, 1988.

At present, a three-tier hierarchy administers higher education in Israel. At the apex stands CHE, which is appointed by the president of the state and chaired by the minister of education and culture. The CHE possesses extensive legal power to regulate the higher education system. Below the CHE stands the Planning and Budgeting (Grants) Committee (PBC/PGC),[3] which is the "executive arm of the CHE." The PGC is responsible for planning and budgeting the overall operation of the system. At the bottom stand the individual institutions, which are expected to handle their own affairs through their presidents, rectors, and deans, the latter two being elected by senior faculty members.

Developments in Israel's Higher Education

Higher education underwent four distinctive phases since the establishment of the State in 1948. Each of these stages can be discerned in the changing relationships between the government and the higher education system.

Stage 1 (1948–1958): The Proclamation of the State and Increased Demand for Higher Education

Two small elite institutions of higher education and one research institute were in existence before the proclamation of the state of Israel in 1948. The number of students at that time was about 2,500. The universities were isolated from social, political, and ideological controversies within the small Jewish semi-autonomous community in Palestine. They enjoyed academic self-government, including a decisive role for faculty in administrative matters. All positions of power were held by officials who were temporary appointees from within the ranks of senior faculty. The locus of power rested with the academic community rather than with the appointed administrative hierarchy. The excessive participatory democracy of senior faculty and the veto power held by their assemblies and senates prevented the emergence of effective academic administrative leadership (Ben-David, 1986).

The newly independent state of Israel called on the universities to meet its demands, from the need for skilled manpower to growing student enrollments. The post-independence decade saw the few small and relatively weak Israeli universities grow in size and quality. But the power of the state over them grew concurrently. Indeed, government support of universities, which had initially been welcomed for inducing growth and stabilizing funding uncertainties, proved to have quite different consequences from those originally anticipated by academics. A gradual process of centralization, rationalization, and bureaucratization occurred in the Israeli higher education system, similar to the process that Trow (1984) accounts for in other higher education systems. This political trend accompanied great growth in the system.

During the 1950s and 1960s, trends in Israel's higher education institutions paralleled the massive expansion occurring in many countries. Enrollments grew rapidly, from 2,450 in 1949–50 to 18,368 in 1964–65 and 36,239 in 1969–70. New universities were founded, and new types and sectors of post-secondary institutions were founded or upgraded. In the 1950s two new universities were opened, Bar-Ilan and Tel Aviv; while during the 1960s two more were opened, in Haifa and Beer Sheva. National expenditure on higher education increased to meet growing enrollments. The number of senior academic staff members rose from 118 in 1948–49 to 3,122 in 1969–70. New departments in the social sciences and humanities and professional schools in the fields of law and medicine were established in both the old and new universities (see Council for Higher Education, 1988b).

Stage 2 (1958–1973): Formation of the Council for Higher Education and Massive Expansion of the Universities

As a result of expansion of the higher education system and the increased demand for public and government funds, three interrelated issues surfaced: establishing criteria for the accreditation of new universities, channeling public funds to the individual institutions, and increasing governmental control over the system. In 1958 the Council for Higher Education (CHE) was established to serve as "the state institution for matters of higher education in the State" (Stanner, 1963, p. 244). The CHE has the sole authority to recommend whether the government should grant a permit to open a new institution of higher education. The CHE also recommends whether the state should confer academic recognition or accreditation (i.e., the right to confer academic degrees) to such an institution. In an apparent attempt to safeguard academic freedom, section 4a of the law states that "at least two-thirds of its [CHE] members must be persons of standing in the field of higher education" (namely, full professors), and section 15 is meant to guarantee institutional autonomy:

An accredited institution shall be at liberty to conduct its academic and administrative affairs within the framework of its budget. . . . [This liberty] includes the determination of a program of research and teaching, the appointment of the authorities of the institution, the appointment and promotion of teachers, the determination of a method of teaching and study, and any other scientific, pedagogic or economic activity. (Stanner, pp. 244–49)

Thus, the CHE left the governing body of each university to decide upon its policy of development. The CHE could neither interfere with university decisions nor coordinate programs with other universities or with the government. As a result, almost all of the universities incurred increasing deficits, and after creating *faits accomplis*, the state was asked for additional financial resources.

The continuous growth of the higher education system was accompanied by a massive increase in the proportion of public funding, which rose steadily to 45.5% in 1959–60 and to almost 80% in 1974–75 (Council for Higher Education, 1988b). From 1948 to 1971 the universities enjoyed direct access to the Ministry of Finance. The presidents of the universities submitted their budgetary requests independently to senior officials in the finance ministry, officials who were not always familiar with the issues at hand in higher education.

Following increased government funding, the basic issue became how to reconcile the inherent conflict between academic freedom and accountability to the public. Increasing doubts were raised about the competency of the state bureaucracy to cope with funding the rapidly expanding higher education system. Since 1965, committees charged with drafting a mechanism for making government funding more rational and the universities more accountable to the public have presented a variety of proposals (Kleinberger, 1969).

The first step in this direction was to transfer the function of funding universities from the Ministry of Finance to the Ministry of Education and Culture. And a 1972 amendment to the Council for Higher Education Law of 1958 (the "CHE law") specifically charged the CHE with the responsibility for planning higher education. An equitable system for financing higher education, however, was still lacking. In 1972 the minister of education and culture appointed the Shalon Committee to examine alternative models of university finance. Shalon's committee recommended that Israel adopt the British model of the University Grants Committee (UGC) (Dainton, 1977; Shattock & Berdhal, 1984; see also Scott, this volume).

Stage 3 (1974–90): The Planning and Grants Committee and Increased Public Expenditure (1974–79), Fiscal Restraint and Political Indifference (1979–85), and Extended Regulation (1985–90)

In 1974 the CHE adopted the Shalon report and appointed the first Planning and Grants Committee (PGC) as a buffer between the Ministry of Education and Culture, the Ministry of Finance, and the universities. The "Terms of Reference of the Planning and Grants Committee," as set forth in Government Decision No. 666 of June 5, 1977, are as follows:

1. To be an independent body coming between the Government and the national institutions, on the one hand, and the institutions of higher education, on the other, in all matters relating to allocations for higher education, taking into account the needs of society and the state while safeguarding academic freedom;

2. To submit the ordinary and development budget proposals for higher education;

3. To have the exclusive authority to allocate to the institutions of higher education the global approved ordinary and development budgets;

4. To submit to the Government and to the Council for Higher Education plans for the development of higher education, including their financing;

5. To encourage efficiency in the institutions of higher education and coordination between them . . . preventing superfluous duplication;

6. To ensure that budgets are balanced;

7. To express its opinion to the Council for Higher Education before the Council reaches a decision on the opening of a new institution or a new unit in an existing institution having financial implications. (Council for Higher Education, 1987a, pp. 12–13)

These terms of reference were adopted from the British UGC in operation after World War II, which was "directly copied in Australia, Bangladesh, India, Israel, New Zealand, and Nigeria and . . . was partly adapted in many other countries" (Williams, 1984, p. 92; cf. Moodie, 1983). Thus Israel's PGC is essentially a collegial organization. Its members, appointed on the basis of individual merit and not as representatives of their own institutions, view as their prime interest the defense of the essential characteristics of the traditional institutional fabric of the universities as a whole and the autonomy of the individual institutions.

The PGC has six members, including its chairman. At least four of the members, including the chairman, must be full professors appointed *ad personam*; the other two members come from business and industry. "The four professors represent 'the two cultures'; two from the natural sciences, engineering, medicine or agriculture" and two from the humanities and social sciences (Council for Higher Education, 1985a, p. 95). To safeguard against state intervention, all PGC members are appointed by the minister of education and culture only after approval by the CHE by secret ballot. The chairman of the PGC is employed full time and is, ex officio, a member of the CHE. He is assisted by an administrative and professional staff of 18–19 persons.

As in Britain, the PGC's composition, terms of reference, and modes of operation were meant to prevent the erosion of academic freedom and to guarantee the autonomy of the higher education system as a whole. At the same time, the PGC was to provide for greater accountability by requiring that the universities negotiate their budget requests with the PGC before it submitted them to the government. However, the autonomy of these institutions became limited, for ironically the formation of the PGC marked a gradual concession of power by the universities to the authority of the PGC in fiscal and planning matters. Concomitantly, the government conceded power to the PGC, withdrawing from direct involvement in financing higher education. This made the PGC the single most powerful central organization in Israel's higher education system.

The main function of the PGC is to submit the budget request for higher education to the government and, after the Knesset (parliament) approves it, to allocate the global budget to individual institutions. The CHE law states that higher education institutions are at liberty to conduct their academic and administrative affairs autonomously within the limitation of their approved budgets. The institutions' budgets are determined by their administration after their heads "have discussed and finalized it with the PGC" (Council for Higher Education, 1985a). However, from its first term of office (1974–1979), the PGC was not content with the function of channeling governmental funds to universities but determined specific needs and allocated earmarked grants to universities by diverting funds from the ordinary budget.

The planning, funding, and supervisory authority of the PGC increased further during its second term of office (1979–1985) and especially during the third term (1985–1990). No longer merely a mediating participant in the budgeting of universities, it had now become an active initiator of development in higher education as a whole. This development was partly because governmental allocations were at this time being cut or not adjusted to the high inflation rates, while research funds, national and international, had become scarce. While the student population at universities between 1973 and 1983 had grown by 30%, academic staff was decreased by 3% and administrative staff was reduced by 11%. The share of higher education in the national budget (excluding defence expenditure and debt payment) fell during that period by some 44% (see table 3). Thus, in a period when higher education in Israel had been experiencing substantial financial disinvestment "the PGC's authority in the allocation of the higher education budget to the higher education system is, essentially, unlimited" (Council for Higher Education, 1985a, p. 96; 1991, p. 139).

TABLE 3. Ordinary Budget for Higher Education as a Function of the Government's Ordinary Budget (1973–1983)[1]

Budget Year	Share of Allocation for Higher Education in State Budget (as percentage)
1973	7.9
1974	7.0
1975	5.3
1976	4.6
1977	5.6
1978	4.8
1979	5.9
1980	5.5
1981	4.4
1982	4.9
1983	4.4

[1] Not including defence expenditure and interest payments on debts.

Source: The Higher Education System in Israel, 1984.

The PGC's increased regulatory power is reflected in its policy regarding the largest budgetary item: direct allocations to the ordinary budgets of the institutions of higher education. This item, which made up about 85% of the total PGC budget in 1979–80, decreased to only about 75% in 1985–86 and remained at this level in 1988–89 (Council for Higher Education, 1990a, p. 51) because "the PGC preferred to preserve, and even increase, the real value of its special allocations" (ibid., p. 101). However, this item increased in 1989–90 to 79.2% (Council for Higher Education, 1991, p. 64). The PGC's policy is even more evident in its relative share in the ordinary budget of the universities, which decreased from 65.8% in 1979–80 to 45.6% in 1986–87 (see table 1) and increased slightly to 49.6% in 1988–89 (Council for Higher Education, 1990a, p. 54) and 50.8% in 1989–90 (Council for Higher Education, 1991, p. 67). Thus, budgetary restrictions were used primarily to affect the direct allocations by the PGC while increasing the share of earmarked funding which the PGC could use to support special needs in accordance with its own determined priorities, such as basic research, which increased from 2.3% in 1981–82 to 8.0% in the years 1984–85 (see table 1).

The PGC's regulatory power over higher education relates also to its criteria and method for apportioning the direct allocation among higher education institutions. As of 1981–82 the PGC introduced "productivity" criteria to examine the budgetary proposals of each institution, in addition to using the fixed indices to determine direct budgetary allocation. These criteria include the number of undergraduates and graduates by degree and field of study, the value of research grants, and other data reflecting upon the scope and quality of research in the institution. There is no single formula upon which calculations of an institution's "productivity" are based, since "a single, pre-determined formula gives the omnipotent computer the power of decision rather than the collective balanced judgement of the committee members" (Council for Higher Education, 1985a, p. 102). Thus the range of allocation (not a single amount) is determined by two teams: the "regular" team and the "productivity" team. The PGC takes both proposals into consideration. In this way the annual allocation to each institution is based upon its work program, proposed development, research "output," and its training of academic manpower, namely, the number of graduates according to their degrees.

The allocation methods and criteria employed by the PGC were opposed by the universities, which questioned their validity. They argued that the lack of an established definite formula for the "productivity" of an institution gives the PGC the authority to "assess" the "quality" of the universities' performance. This policy, they claimed, weakened the academic freedom of the universities and limited their institutional autonomy.

Another area where the PGC exerts a decisive influence on assessing the quality of particular institutions regards their discretion concerning "competitive funds." The PGC has set up a number of funds which award grants to individual researchers and research teams in the universities, based upon personal or team excellence as recommended by special selection committees. Allocations from the Fund for Scientific Equipment are also awarded by selection committees, which weigh the quality of research programs submitted by teams of researchers. These funds

TABLE 4. Apportionment of PGC Allocations (in NIS and as a Percentage of Total Allocations)

	1985/86		1986/87	
Total (NIS Thousands)	331,121.4	100%	439,381.4	100%
Direct allocations to the institutions of higher education	242,912.0	76.4	311,905.0	73.9
Allocations for electronics and computers	10,125.0	—	12,855.0	—
Matching allocations to endowment funds	38,253.7	11.5	43,904.0	10.0
Earmarked allocations for research and special subjects*	20,398.5	6.2	28,172.1	6.4
Other allocations**	18,230.7	5.5	41,114.9	9.4
PGC's administrative budget	1,201.5	0.4	1,430.0	0.3

*Includes allocations for research, earmarked allocations, and inter-university activities.
**Includes aid to students, miscellaneous subjects and budgetary transfers.

Source: CHE, PGC Annual Report No. 13, 1985/86, No. 14, 1986/87.

amounted to 6.2% of the total budget allocated by the government to higher education in 1985–86 and 6.4% in 1986–87 (see table 4).

Additional PGC means for evaluating the quality of teaching and research include its request for periodic inspection of departments and research units in individual universities by "review committees" from outside the institution. Although "the PGC's policy is not to take part in these checks but to recommend that the university administration from time to time appoint external review committees which would present their reports to the administration" (Council for Higher Education, 1985a, p. 67), it encourages individual institutions to act along these lines. The PGC also reviews periodically different fields of study within the higher education system as a whole by appointing international "survey committees."

All of these practices were questioned by the Committee of Heads of Universities, a voluntary organization that represents the "higher education interest." The committee expressed concern over the power the law gives the PGC to rank the "output" of universities and to evaluate the quality of proposed new programs. The PGC's measures (e.g., the "productivity" criteria, the process of evaluating the quality of proposed new programs, "review committees" of existing departments within institutions, and interinstitutional "survey committees") further eroded the autonomy of the universities. Indeed, similar trends of limiting institutional autonomy were observed in many national systems during the 1960s and 1970s (Perkins & Baird Israel, 1972; Clark, 1983); this autonomy was further limited in the 1980s and had become a common source of concern for universities in many countries (Tight, 1985; Altbach, 1980, 1989).

Worsening economic conditions in Israel in the mid-1970s affected disinvestment trends in higher education; and government allocations to universities were reduced by 20% between 1982–83 and 1983–84. This in turn affected the delicate balance between institutional autonomy and central regulation by the PGC, as well as between direct governmental intervention and the statutory roles of the CHE and the PGC on one hand and the universities on the other hand. In its annual report for 1985–86, the PGC's chairman concluded, "If higher education does not very soon advance in the national order of priorities, it will no longer be possible to repair the damage that higher education has suffered in recent years" (Council for Higher Education, 1987a, p. 5). In the following year, 1986–87, the chairman voiced his concern forcefully: "Is the higher education system in danger of losing its independence?" He worried that budgetary deficits and divesting trends might bring pressure from boards of governors on academic matters in order to impose a balanced budget (Council for Higher Education, 1988a, p. 5).

To halt the risk of further deterioration both in academic standards and manpower training, the PGC submitted a plan to increase government allocations for higher education by 25% for the years 1988–90 (ibid., p. 6). The government adopted the PGC's recommendations in part and increased its allocations to higher education by 2.5% in 1987–88 and by 4% in 1988–89 and added another 9% to cover the universities' debts (Council for Higher Education, 1989, p. 65; 1990, p. 63). This improved the financial status of the institutions, but only slightly. It brought the total budget, in real terms, back to the level of a decade ago despite a growth of about 30% in student enrollment and the increased costs of research (Council for Higher Education, 1990b).

Stage 4 (1990s and Beyond): Academic Freedom, Accountability, Diversification, and Politicization

Higher education in Israel has retained its traditional Central European elitist character (Iram, 1992) despite more than 40 years of rapid growth, which has brought it beyond Trow's "15% enrollment threshold" into the range of "mass" higher education. However, at the beginning of the 1990s, there are growing signs that Israel's higher education system is undergoing major changes. Basic concepts such as institutional autonomy and long cherished tenets such as academic freedom and elitism, which were the foundations of the system, are being reassessed, and awareness of inadequacies such as equity, quality of instruction, and effectiveness of training is growing because of internal self-evaluation and external critiques, as well as increased governmental intervention and politicization. These developments are discussed below.

During the 1980s institutional autonomy was limited by legal enactments and administrative actions in all five constituents of academic freedom defined by the Robbins Committee of Great Britain (Robbins, 1963; Farrant, 1987):

1. Freedom of appointment of academic staff has remained, but the right of an institution to attract the best candidates is limited by national salary scales imposed on universities by the government (though a university is free to determine the position and the rank of the appointee).

2. Freedom to determine curricula and standards is generally maintained by departments and faculties, but the introduction of new programs and any structural or curricular changes in existing programs is subject to the approval of the PGC even though no funds are required.

3. Universities have full discretion in setting criteria and methods for selecting applicants for admission; however, these criteria and methods have been subjected to continuous public pressure to relax admissions requirements.

4. The freedom of an individual institution to determine the balance between teaching and research was infringed upon in recent years by the PGC's "productivity" formula. Thus, the PGC evaluated the scope and quality of the research "output" of an institution and used this evaluation to determine budgetary allocation.

5. The freedom of universities to determine the direction and scope of their own development is limited to what it can negotiate with the PGC. Thus, the autonomy of each university is considerably less than it was until the 1970s and less than was intended in 1974 when the PGC was founded.

The growing participation in higher education of the 1950s and the concomitant growth in higher education's share of public finance, which was followed by economic recession and fiscal restraints by the government since the mid-1970s, raised concerns over accountability in Israel as in many other countries (Hufner, 1991). In Israel these demands were introduced in what Shils (1991) has defined as the "system level" and the "institutional level," and from both intra- and inter-institutional perspectives. Thus demands for "accountability" were expressed in Israel by proposals that the existing need for higher education could be met only through greater efficiency and a more vocationally oriented system. Furthermore, it was proposed that any expansion be measured by the same criteria. These demands were followed by growing pressure for higher "productivity" and "effective" or "joint utilization" of facilities and equipment. The "productivity" criteria applied by the PGC to determine the range of budgetary allocation to individual institutions have added an inter-institutional dimension to accountability, while the periodic inspection of units within universities by external "review committees," as well as the appointment of "survey committees" of entire field of studies such as the schools of education in 1987 and life science in 1988 (Council for Higher Education, 1990a), might have far-reaching restructuring effects on both the intra- and inter-institutional levels. Indeed, university faculty and administrators tended to see some of these demands as a disguise for more direct state control at the expense of institutional autonomy and academic freedom.

Another development which might affect institutional autonomy stems from the PGC-initiated comprehensive study of undergraduate education (Silberberg, 1987). In its guidelines for long-term planning, the PGC foresaw that the student population would reach 85,000 by 1995. It suggested that "the feasibility of establishing undergraduate colleges that will [be empowered] to award the bachelor's degree and for which universities will be academically responsible should be examined" (Council for Higher Education, 1987b, p. 35). But in 1988 the PGC's chairman stated that "the PGC does not see a need for opening new institutions for higher education specializing in teaching toward a general Bachelor's Degree . . . [as] most of the expected demands can be met by the existing system" (Council for Higher Education, 1988a, p. 53). However, in 1990, following increased immigration from the Soviet Union to Israel, the issue of access became more pressing and the PGC changed its policy, stating that "the PBC is of the opinion that preparations should be made for the establishment of an undergraduate college" (Council for Higher Education, 1991, p. 6).

Any future decision to establish undergraduate colleges will necessarily influence the policies of the higher education system in the direction of further diversification and differentiation. In fact, new proposals to establish independent undergraduate colleges were submitted to the Knesset in 1990, and the number of regional colleges expanded between 1990 and 1992. The PGC's chairman has announced that some of these colleges might be upgraded soon to independent undergraduate institutions (Ben-Nahum 1992a).

As of the late 1980s there has been a growing public discontent over restricted access to higher education in general and to highly desired professional studies in particular. As an example of restricted access, we note that while about 65% of the applicants to humanities departments and 50% of those applying to social science departments were admitted during the 1987–88 and 1988–89 academic years, only 20–30% of those who applied to law, medicine, paramedical, and engineering faculties were granted admission. These admission restrictions resulted in public pressure, which led in turn to political intervention and legislative initiatives by the Knesset. In 1990 the Knesset approved a resolution to open new law colleges. Although these colleges will be associated with existing law schools, they will not become an integral part of the universities and will be providing legal training but not granting academic degrees.

Another legislative proposal, pending approval of the Knesset, would permit opening private "extrabudgetary" independent undergraduate institutions outside the aegis of the CHE and the PGC despite these organizations' opposition to this proposal. These developments confirm Cerych and Sabatier's (1986) argument that it may often be easier to set up entirely new institutions than to set out or modify—let alone reform—existing ones. Such was the case with the creation of the Open University in the United Kingdom and in many other countries including Israel, the network of regional colleges in Norway and Israel, and the IUTs in France.

Concluding Remarks

At this point, it is too early to determine how the PGC's use of the "productivity" criteria, "competitive funds," "survey committees," and plans to open undergraduate colleges and private professional schools such as law and business administration will affect university-government relations and the autonomy of the universities over the long term. Some of these policies will encourage diversity at the departmental (faculty) levels within and between universities, namely, the "understructures" (Clark, 1983), while others will probably accentuate the differences among individual institutions of higher learning at the all-university level, namely, the "middle structures" and "superstructures" (Clark, 1983). A more detailed analysis of these policies is required to predict the future course of the higher education system in Israel on the basis of the government's role in recent developments.

Supporters of the PGC argue that it has rendered Israel's higher education accountable while preserving academic freedom. Indeed, the PGC takes credit for having coordinated the development and growth of institutions and standardized governmental and public funding of higher education, encouraged basic research, and expanded and raised the quality of nonuniversity institutions. However, many in the academic community consider the PGC to be a controlling bureaucracy that has brought an excessive degree of standardization to higher education; they regard the changes that have taken place since the 1980s as inimical to academic freedom.

It seems reasonable to speculate that Israel's higher education system is on the threshold of two major and interrelated developments. The first will be a changing relationship between government and universities, i.e., more direct governmental involvement in higher education and reduced authority for the CHE and for the PGC. It is even possible that these institutions will be abolished, as was the fate of the University Grants Committee in Britain (Watson, 1989).

The major issue which the higher education system may have to face in the 1990s is public concern over restrictions on access to higher education. Mounting public pressures have been noted by the media and have enlisted political and parliamentary involvement. At present, various proposals aimed at democratizing access to existing institutions and at introducing new professional and regional colleges are being debated by the parliament. The effect of these proposals on the future course of higher education in Israel remains to be seen.

The second possible development is in the direction (identified by Trow) of moving from "elite" to "mass" to "universal" access, that is, providing postsecondary education to every person wishing it (Trow, 1970, 1976; Fulton, 1981). Israel (like most industrialized nations, except the United States, Canada, and to some extent Japan) has paused at the threshold of a "mass" system, and might start to move towards the "universal" stage in higher education (Altbach, 1989, pp. 68–69). It is too soon to predict with confidence what the outcome of the present tensions between governmental intervention and institutional autonomy will be. It is likely that in the decade of the 1990s, significant changes in all these areas will continue to modify Israel's higher education system, and its structure will be significantly diversified as the 21st century approaches.

NOTES

1. This chapter describes the higher education institutions of the State of Israel; it does not include the Arab universities in the occupied territories.

2. Tuition fees are set by the government and ranged from about 10% of the ordinary budget of universities in the mid-1970s to 4% in 1982; they increased to 16.9% in 1990 (Council for Higher Education, 1991, p. 68).

3. As of 1991 the Planning and Grants Committee was renamed the "Planning and Budgeting Committee" (PBC), which is a more literal translation of its Hebrew name. The acronym PGC will be used for the remainder of this chapter because all the publications until 1991 are under this name.

REFERENCES

Altbach, P. G. (1980). *University reform: An international perspective.* Washington, DC: American Association for Higher Education.

———. (1989). *Perspectives on comparative higher education: Essays on faculty, students, and reform.* Special Studies in Comparative Education No. 22. Buffalo: State University of New York Press.

Becher, T. & Kogan, M. (1980). *Process and structure in higher education.* London: Heinemann.

Ben-David, J. (1986). Universities in Israel: Dilemmas of growth, diversification and administration (pp. 105–30). *Studies in Higher Education* No. 11. pp. 105–30.

Ben-Nahum, Arnon (1992a). Colleges are upgraded. *Ha'aretz* (June 9).

———. (1992b). 10 new undergraduate colleges will be needed until the year 2010. *Ha'aretz* (June 16).

Cerych, L. & Sabatier, P. (1986). *Great expectations and mixed performance: The implementation of higher education reforms in Europe.* Trentham: European Institute of Education and Social Policy.

Clark, B. R. (1983). *The higher education system: Academic organization in cross-national perspectives.* Berkeley and Los Angeles: University of California Press.

Council for Higher Education. (1984). *The higher education system in Israel: Guidelines on the development of the system and its planning for 1988 with a first glance at 1995.* Report of the Planning and Grants Committee (executive body of CHE). Jerusalem: The Planning and Grants Committee.

———. (1985a). *The Planning and Grants Committee annual report* (No. 12, academic year 1984–85). Jerusalem: The Planning and Grants Committee.

———. (1985b). *Higher education in Israel—Statistical abstract 1983/84.* Jerusalem: The Planning and Grants Committee.

———. (1987a). *The Planning and Grants Committee annual report* (No. 13, academic year 1985/86). Jerusalem: The Planning and Grants Committee.

———. (1987b). *The Sixth Council 1981–1986 report* (No. 2). Jerusalem: The Council for Higher Education.

———. (1988a). *The Planning and Grants Committee annual report* (No. 14, academic year 1986/87). Jerusalem: The Planning and Grants Committee.

———. (1988b). *Higher education in Israel—Statistical abstract 1986/87.* Jerusalem: The Planning and Grants Committee.

———. (1989). *The Planning and Grants Committee annual report* (No. 15, academic year 1987/88). Jerusalem: The Planning and Grants Committee.

———. (1990a). *The Planning and Grants Committee annual report* (No. 16, academic year 1988/89). Jerusalem: The Planning and Grants Committee.

———. (1990b). *The first degree in Israel—Guidelines, facts and data.* Jerusalem: The Planning and Grants Committee (Hebrew).

———. (1991). *The Planning and Budgeting Committee annual report* (No. 17, academic year 1989/90). Jerusalem: The Planning and Budgeting Committee.

———. (1992). *Newsletter of the Planning and Budgeting Committee* (Hebrew).

Dainton, F. (1977). University grants committees. In A. S. Knowles (Ed.), *International encyclopedia of higher education* (pp. 1724–29). San Francisco: Jossey Bass.

Farrant, J. H. (1987). Central control of the university sector. In T. Beecher (Ed.), *British higher education* (pp. 29–52). London: Allen and Unwin.

Fulton, O. (Ed.) (1981). *Access to higher education.* Leverhulme No. 2. Guildford: Society for Research into Higher Education.

Hufner, K. (1991). Accountability. In P. G. Altbach (Ed.), *International higher education—An encyclopedia* (pp. 47–58). New York and London: Garland Publishing, Inc.

Iram, Y. (1992). Curricular and structural developments at the Hebrew University, 1928–1948. *History of Universities, 11,* pp. 205–41.

Israel, Central Bureau of Statistics. (1978). *Statistical abstract of Israel,* No. 29. Jerusalem: Government Printer.

———. (1987). *Statistical abstract of Israel,* No. 38. Jerusalem: Government Printer.

———. (1988). *Statistical abstract of Israel* No. 39. Jerusalem: Government Printer.

Kleinberger, A. F. (1969). *Society, schools and progress in Israel.* Oxford: Pergamon Press.

Meek, V. L.; Gedegebuure, L. C. J.; Kivinen, O. & Risto, R. (1991). Policy change in higher education: Intended and unintended outcomes. *Higher Education, 21,* pp. 451–59.

Ministry of Education and Culture. (1991). *Facts and figures on the education and culture system in Israel.* Jerusalem: Ministry of Education and Culture.

Moodie, G. C. (1983). Buffer, coupling and broker: Reflections on 60 years of the UGC. *Higher Education, 12,* pp. 331–347.

Neave, G. & Van Vught, F. A. (Eds.) (1991). *Prometheus bound: The changing relationship between government and higher education in Western Europe.* Oxford: Pergamon Press.

Perkin, H. (1984). The historical perspective. In B. R. Clark (Ed.), *Perspectives in higher education* (pp. 17–55). Berkeley and Los Angeles: University of California Press.

———. (1991). History of universities. In P. G. Altbach (Ed.), *International higher education—An encyclopedia* (pp. 169–204). New York and London: Garland Publishing, Inc.

Perkins, J. A. & Baird Israel, B. (Eds.) (1972). *Higher education: From autonomy to systems.* New York: International Council for Educational Development.

Robbins. (1963). *Higher education: Report of the committee appointed by the prime minister under the chairmanship of Lord Robbins* (Cmnd 2154). London: HMSO.

Shattock, M. & Berdhal, R. D. (1984). The British University Grants Committee, 1919–1983: Changing relationships with government and the universities. *Higher Education, 13,* pp. 471–500.

Sheldrake, P. & Linke, R. (Eds.) (1979). *Accountability in higher education.* Sydney: Allen and Unwin.

Shils, E. (1991). Academic freedom. In P. G. Altbach (Ed.), *International higher education—An encyclopedia* (pp. 1–22). New York and London: Garland Publishing, Inc.

Silberberg, R. (1987). *The studies for the first degree in the higher education system.* Jerusalem: CHE, PGC (Hebrew).

Stanner, R. (1963). *The legal basis of education in Israel.* Jerusalem: Ministry of Education and Culture.

Tight, M. (1985). Academic freedom re-examined. *Higher education review, 18,* pp. 7–23.

Trow, M. A. (1970). Reflections on the transition from mass to universal higher education. *Daedalus, 9,* pp. 1–42.

————. (1974). Problems in the transition from elite to mass higher education. In *Policies for higher education* (pp. 51–101). General report of the conference on the future of postsecondary education. Paris: OECD.

————. (1976). Elite higher education: An endangered species? *Minerva, 14,* pp. 355–76.

————. (1984). The analysis of status. In B. R. Clark (Ed.), *Perspectives on higher education* (pp. 132–64). Berkeley and Los Angeles: University of California Press.

Van de Graaf, J. H.; Clark, B. R.; Furth, D.; Goldschmidt, D. & Wheeler, D. F. (1978). *Academic power: Patterns of authority in seven national systems of higher education.* New York: Praeger Publishers.

Van Vught, F. A. (Ed.) (1989). *Governmental strategies and innovations in higher education.* London: Jessica Kingsley Publishers.

Watson, K. (1989). The changing pattern of higher education in England and Wales—The end of an era? *International Review of Education, 35,* pp. 283–304.

Williams, G. (1984). The economic approach. In B. R. Clark (Ed.), *Perspectives on higher education* (pp. 79–105). Berkeley and Los Angeles: University of California Press.

CHAPTER III

Higher Education Policy Reform in Australia
An Expansive Analysis

John Smyth

Background to Australian Higher Education

In 1987 Australia embarked on a process of restructuring its higher education system, the likes of which had never been seen or even thought possible in that country. The reasons behind this were complex, but they had much to do with the wider restructuring of world capitalism and the so-called economic rationalist view (Pusey, 1991) embraced by Australian politicians as the preferred vehicle for producing a turnaround in the economic fortunes of a small country of less than 20 million people who had been historically dependent on the export of wool, wheat, and minerals for a livelihood. That Australia in the 1980s had arrived at the point where it was largely dependent on its export of unprocessed produce primarily because of earlier political decisions to keep Australia locked into a subservient set of relationships to powerful, predator nations (initially Britain, then the U.S., and more recently Japan) seems to have escaped the attention of the historical politicians.

The decision to break decisively with its neocolonialist history required Australia to totally rethink how it might operate differently. This was when higher education became firmly fixed in the sights of the economic rationalist (Labor) government. The view put was that "Australia [was] not producing the right skills" (ACTU/TDC, 1987, p. 118) in order to enable the country to improve its international competitive position. What we had, then, was a vision of a "high tech" economic recovery in which politicians, employers, and unions arrived at a consensus that higher education was an essential ingredient for at least a particular instrumental form of higher education. The scenario was one in which higher education would be forced to do its "economic work" of national reconstruction and, in the process, "academics [were] to be managed, their institutions amalgamated, [and] their intellectual work measured in market output terms" (Sharp, 1988a, p. 79). In other words, although education, and higher education in particular, was not the cause of Australia's economic problem, it was used as part of the solution.

Australia's restructuring occurred against the larger backdrop of global restructuring. Western economies in the 1980s were generally experiencing a legitimation crisis that hinged on the extent to which governments should continue to operate in directly interventionist ways (as had been the neo-Keynesian approach following World War II) or whether market forces should be allowed to operate in a much more unfettered way. Technology was regarded by many as the preferred response to this global crisis and as holding the possibility of generating a new international division of labor. What was needed, it was argued, was a more "flexible" labor market in which there was a dual labor force: a "core" of skilled (usually male) workers, with a largely "peripheral" or temporary work force (generally female) that could easily be recruited (and just as easily dispensed with) and quickly trained in the new atomistic ways required by the new technology. The universities were viewed as responsible for training this new work force.

The Changed Shape of Higher Education in Australia

It was against this kind of background that the federal minister for employment, education, and training, John

Dawkins, introduced a range of measures to "reform" higher education in Australia in 1987. These appeared as a "Green" discussion paper (Dawkins, 1987) and as a "White" policy paper (Dawkins, 1988), and in the main were characterized by the following features:

1. A persistent rhetoric arguing that because of the declining international competitiveness of Australian primary and extractive industries and as a consequence of an outmoded manufacturing base, we must become more competitive by restructuring existing industries and moving into high technology industries. The implication is that higher education has not been doing its economic work of boosting national productivity.

2. In a related vein, universities must become more *internally self-sufficient* and less reliant upon federal handouts of funding by entering into collaborative funding arrangements with industry. Students shall also be required to play their part through the introduction of a (partial to full) user-pays principle in the form of a tertiary tax (Higher Education Contribution Scheme—HECS) as well as through the payment of full fees.

3. To ensure that universities respond to centrally devised economic initiatives, they will be assessed by means of *performance indicators* that will give "objective," comparative, and compelling evidence on how institutions are doing in terms of meeting centrally prescribed government objectives for higher education. At the institutional level this will mean "performance appraisal" of staff.

4. Efficiencies and economies of scale nationally will be achieved through the amalgamation of significant numbers of existing institutions, "which will merge to create a *unified national system* of institutions with minimum thresholds of viable student numbers. Karmel (1989) has described this as a "cult of the big," which will homogenize higher education.

5. Central control through the Canberra-based bureaucracy of the federal Department of Employment, Education, and Training will be ensured through a process of *"profiling"* in which universities will be required to indicate how academic programs meet national objectives; failure to do this satisfactorily will mean the withdrawal of funding.

6. In the area of research, funding which had formerly been part of universities' recurrent grants distributed according to internal processes will be "clawed back" by the Department of Employment, Education, and Training (DEET), to be redistributed by the Canberra-based Australian Research Council to projects they regard as *meeting national priorities* determined by the government.

7. Activities such as *Asian languages*, which are seen as enhancing our national capacity to engage in business and commerce with our neighbors, will receive favorable funding, as will *engineering, computer technology, management studies*, and *science programs*. (Smyth, 1991, pp. 52–53)

There are a number of broad ideological themes about the nature of the relationship between government and higher education that flow from these reforms and that demand careful analysis.

The Agenda of the New Right and the Slide from a "Public" to a "Private" Good

Brady (1988) summed up the major problem with the Dawkins reforms when she pinpointed their main thrust as being "sheer commonsense" placed in a context that pays due regard to social responsibility by ensuring "a fair chance for all." Who could possibly be against economic rejuvenation, increased international competitiveness, and the process of ensuring that higher education makes its contribution to the better educated work force Australia needs to achieve (Dawkins, 1987, p. 21)? According to Brady (1988, p. 29), "commonsense has little awareness of its own [history] and thus little self-knowledge, taking for granted ideas, practices and values which may be open to question. . . . In other words, it lacks a critical factor." The result, she sees, is that the ideology of the reforms appears to express the view that the only "purpose of higher education is to contribute to 'economic strength and vitality' and that these in turn are the base of our 'future prospects'" (p. 29), a position that needs much more interrogation through a process of "sifting and sorting, selecting some and rejecting other aspects of consciousness" (p. 30). Indeed, the New Right has presented an agenda that promotes "an apparently 'commonsense' discourse and set of assumptions concerning the nature and purpose of education" (Robertson & Woock, 1989, p. 22) and a public philosophy which says that the only value that counts is "economic value" (p. 21).

So far as the Dawkins reforms are concerned, this new economic logic argues that we need a unified national system of higher education (Dawkins, 1988, p. 27) in order to forge closer links with industry (p. 66). To direct research towards national goals and priorities (p. 90) and satisfy what the government regards as efficient organizational effectiveness, we need to amalgamate institutions (p. 41). Robertson and Woock (1989) note: "The rationale for this view assumes that a higher proportion of the population with secondary and tertiary education will cause strong economic performance, and therefore greater national productivity" (p. 20).

Smith, Burke, Smith and Wheelwright, (1988, p. 4) claim that this "new educational orthodoxy" in Australia needs to be challenged because it is seriously unbalanced and distorted in several ways, particularly in the linkages between education, the labor market, and economic growth, which they regard as being based on "dubious economics." Specifically, they regard the Dawkins reforms as being unbalanced in six respects:

1. Undue stress is placed on the economic analysis of education and on the economic goals and benefits of education.

2. Efficiency is exalted: equity is an afterthought. This is particularly evident in discussions of the funding of higher education, and the associated pressures to reintroduce fees.

3. Efficiency does not imply effectiveness: for example, many of the changes proposed may reduce staff morale, the key to effective research and teaching.

4. The Green paper on Higher Education, in particular, demonstrates what could be called a narrow "business management approach to education."

5. The balance has been tipped on the side of technology and business, while the humanities and the social sciences are devalued.

6. Undue emphasis is placed on the needs of young people, while the needs of adult learners have been rather neglected. Like-

wise, informal, nonformal, and adult and community education have largely been ignored, despite the large size, low cost,
and the social and economic contribution of this sector, and its
claim based on equity. (p. 2)

They pull few punches in challenging the so-called economic
imperatives implicit in the new orthodoxy by admitting that education and training are certainly linked to economic growth and
recovery. "But this does not mean that economic imperatives as
seen from Canberra should drive the education system, nor that
we should adopt a narrowly instrumental view of the purpose of
education" (p. 3).

There is also a critical history to the current reforms that
must be exposed and explored if we are to understand what is
occurring in the government's accommodation with the New
Right. Robertson and Woock (1989) describe recent educational
developments in Australia as being a "combination of New
Right barbarism, centralization, and privatization" in a context
where Australia has become the "laboratory of New Right exper-
imentation even more advanced than in Great Britain" (p. 4). The
progenitor of the current new-wave economic rationalist view of
education lies in the conservative years of the 1970s, which
blazed the trail for a human capital approach (Sharp, 1988b,
p. 119) in higher education during a period of postwar expansion. It was the Williams report, however, that launched the
concerted ideological attack on the earlier Karmel report (1973),
which was the centerpiece of an era (1972–75) in Australian
education in which the touchstones were social justice,
democracy, diversity, devolution, and equity (Robertson &
Woock, 1989, pp. 8–10).

What the Dawkins reforms represent, therefore, is the
gradual whittling away of the notion that education (and higher
education in particular) is a "public good" (notwithstanding a
history in this country of its having been restricted until fairly
recent times to a relatively elite group) (see Burchell, 1986, p. 22).

There can be little doubt that the new settlement emerging
from the Dawkins reforms has had the effect of shifting higher
education towards being a "private good" and therefore better
left to the operation of market forces. Two aspects, in particular,
illustrate this point: first, the introduction of the "user pays prin-

ciple" through the Higher Education Contribution Scheme (a form of deferred government-provided student loan) which substantially shifts responsibility for the cost of university education onto the shoulders of individual beneficiaries and opens the way for full-fee programs; and second, the argument in the Green and White papers that the level of federal funding must fall substantially as a proportion of GDP (Gross Domestic Product) (despite the fact that it has already fallen 27.2% from a peak of 1.36% of GDP in 1975, to .99% of GDP in 1988, and is mooted to fall even further).

Both of these represent significant retreats from earlier positions, which reflected a broad conception that higher education is in the public interest (although, there were always significant elements of private advantage to individual beneficiaries). Targeting the cost of education further exacerbates the psychological slide towards a privatization mentality. This tendency rests rather uneasily with the insistence by Dawkins that higher education must be directed towards the national interest, which is clearly a collective or public interest.

Further evidence of this fundamental transformation taking place in the way higher education is regarded by the state can be found in the way universities are being required to operate with respect to one another and in relation to the government. Bartos (1990a) writes:

> The transformation is from a system supported as a public good and funded on an assessment of its needs to a system of autonomous universities [notwithstanding the language of describing it as a "unified national system"] which behave as private corporations in competition with each other. . . . The end point is for public funding for universities to be provided on a contract basis, with universities bidding against each other to offer teaching services at the lowest price. (p. 12)

Both the Green and White papers make it clear that institutions will only be funded on the basis of their performance after negotiating their "profiles" with the government every three years according to their student loads, areas of course offerings, and planned directions for growth. Most commentators regard it as only a small step from here to "contracting," in which the government will determine the price of student places and universities will compete against each other by tendering for them (Bartos, 1990a).

Competition is to be further "encouraged" by reducing recurrent funding to institutions by 1% annually and rising to 2.5% by 1992, and using the funds thus released as a way of "reward[ing institutions] for toeing the line, i.e., for following the Federal Government and the market's directions" (Kenway & Blackmore, 1988, p. 50)—or as Dawkins (1988) put it, the funds are "to be redistributed each year on the basis of institutions' responses to specific Commonwealth initiatives or to identified areas of national priority" (p. 81).

Deregulation and Pedagogy for Profit

One of the ways in which the state in crisis situations seeks to reestablish its own legitimacy is through closer alliances or settlements with private-sector interests. An illustration of this can be seen in Dawkins' vision of the increasing privatization of higher education by having universities become progressively beholden to industry for funding (in research as well as in teaching) and, presumably, having industry shape higher education to its specific needs (by becoming involved in such aspects as curriculum development). While it would be tempting to argue that through this means the autonomy of universities will gradually be diminished as they become increasingly indistinguishable from industrial interests, with aspects considered to be irrelevant (such as the study of the humanities and the social sciences) being allowed to wither and die as a consequence of market forces, this would be altogether too simplistic (see Donald, 1979, p. 15). Slaughter (1985, pp. 220–21) argues that the primacy of private enterprise leads the state to operate in ways in which the "universities are expected to develop a curriculum for multinational executives, one that would teach foreign management practices, foreign language and culture, as well as offer an international studies program," all of course within an embracing rhetoric about the imperative to provide the necessary infrastructure within which the "talents of the private sector can be focused to meet the competitive challenge." The trouble with the "user pays" argument that industry should "support education *because* it serves their interests is that we are stuck with the corollary: employers will support education *to the extent that* it supports their interests" (Junor, 1988, p. 140).

Another blatant instance of the Dawkins fetish for enmeshing universities in the private sector is the "directive" in the Green paper that the government shall look favorably upon higher education institutions that provide programs in Asian language studies. But on other occasions, such patently thin strategies of "pedagogy for profit" (Slaughter, 1985) have gone seriously wrong as the education export drive bears testimony. It was Dawkins who, as minister for trade in 1985, advocated "education as an export industry" capable of earning hundreds of millions of dollars from overseas students, the epitome of the final commodification of education. By July 1990 Dawkins was forced to publicly admit that the whole deregulationist exercise in the education export drive had been "an unfortunate saga" and that he had "learned a bitter lesson" from Australia's efforts to attract large numbers of foreign students—an exercise which had failed as a result of "inadequate regulation of individuals and institutions" (Bartos 1990b). The irony, as Bartos (1990b) described it, is that

> there is real doubt about whether education export is really worth anything, in balance of trade terms. If students borrow in their home country to come to Australia, and if their main motive is the higher wages available in Australia, and if they work while they study to repatriate the amount they borrowed and more, where is the net gain to Australia? (p. 19)

Instrumentalization of Knowledge

Junor (1988) argues that the "new orthodoxy," at least as pronounced by Dawkins, has its more proximate roots in the OECD (1987) philosophy that "social well-being derives from the interplay of micro-economic forces, chiefly 'capabilities' and 'incentives'" (Junor, 1988, p. 133). What is required, the OECD argues, is "structural adjustment" that incorporates and enhances "skills formation." Needless to say, this new orthodoxy offers little to workers who must await the miracle of an export-led recovery. The other problem with this is that "when economies are in crisis and fundamental shifts are occurring in the balance of global economic power . . . then the search for scapegoats and quick fix solutions becomes imperative." The argument is that a peripheral economy like Australia cannot isolate itself from the redistribution of global economic power, but neither can we expect micro-economic reforms (of which education might be regarded as a part) to produce the answers because they are based upon a "comparative competitive imperative" (p. 32) that has its origins as part of a constructed consensus in the West as to what was required for the restoration of international economic competitiveness. In promoting education as one of the mechanisms of reform, what remains hidden from view are ideological judgements about "the nature of work and employment, and the process of productivity generation" (Burgess, 1989, p. 23).

In educational policy-making terms, the Dawkins reforms therefore amount to an expression of the view that problems of accumulation and legitimation can be handled (at least in "structural adjustment" terms) through what Wise (1979) described as a process of "hyper-rationalization," that is to say, through the use of "a range of economic, bureaucratic, and scientific rationales" (Robertson & Woock, 1989, p. 17) that are supposedly capable of harnessing education to the economy and the restoration of a state of relative equilibrium within capitalism. One of the mechanisms for achieving this "structural adjustment," Dawkins argues, is to see higher education as having been a major "cause" of Australia's low international productivity, and as a consequence, what is required are improvements in work practices. As I have argued elsewhere:

> Because of the way in which capitalist systems in general
> have been able to ascribe the cause of our economic ills to
> the personal inadequacies of individuals (illiteracy, lack of
> incentive, and poor work habits among students), it has
> not been difficult to link this with the systematic failure of

> schools [and higher education] to meet the needs of indus-
> try. The argument is such a compellingly simplistic one
> that it is proving almost impossible to dislodge—get stu-
> dents in schools [and universities] to conform through
> more compliant forms of education, and all our economic
> woes will disappear. (Smyth, 1989, p. 408)

For instance, one of the arguments rehearsed ad nauseam in the Dawkins plans is that by deregulating higher education and making it more responsive to industry's needs, the Australian work force will be made more "flexible" (see Pollert, 1988, for a detailed rebuttal of this argument) and that Australia will be able to benefit from increased international competitiveness brought about by a work force able to change quickly and respond to unpredictable situations. Davis (1988) points out that assertions that higher education is not already responsive are grossly inaccurate: "It has long been responsive and its examples of responsiveness to new technological demands could fill several pages" (p. 10) (also see Bourke 1988, p. 3).

Ashenden (1988) further presents evidence that the real problem is not a shortage of graduates or skills but rather the inability of industry to properly use them (p. 26). Both Marginson (1989) and Marceau (1989) present convincing evidence on this argument.

The problem with the deficit skills argument underpinning the Dawkins plan is that it not only deflects the argument away from the broader restructuring of the nature of work and the international division of labor accompanying it but it shifts blame to individuals in a simplistic way that totally misconstrues the nature of skills formation. According to Junor (1988) the terms "skill" and "skill formation" are "central to the new education settlement" (p. 135) in which there has been a fusion of the educational and industrial relations meanings of these terms. Where in educational terms skill has become a human capital concept signifying to employers some kind of "depersonalized 'indicators' of the 'outcomes' of learning" (p. 135), in industrial relations terms skills signify "masculine," "Anglophone" hierarchies of work culture in which the work of women, people of color, and other minorities is largely excluded or marginalized. Jackson (1990) is one of the most eloquent in portraying skills as not purely "technical," but "social," and above all, "gendered" relationships. She argues that the very definition of skills and what constitutes their presence or absence is largely a political process in which the term itself has been "emptied of . . . tangible content and imposed on certain types of work by virtue of the sex and power of the workers who perform it" (p. 6). Discussions about what constitutes skills or skilled work are, therefore, highly charged political debates about how some groups of workers can benefit from the constructed hierarchies of work while others are subjugated.

Dawkins' discussion of the need for national skills enhancement, which is the cornerstone of much of the rhetoric of the Green and White papers, is really a recipe for the segmentation of educated labor in much the same way as has happened with blue-collar labor in the past. According to Jackson (1987, p. 352), what we are experiencing educationally is a "training fever" in which the relationship between education and work is seen to be at the heart of the problem:

> As economic prosperity has faltered across the industrialized world, disrupting the fit between demand and supply of labor, aspects of educational provision have been widely identified as both a cause and a solution to the problem. Public schools have been charged with inefficiency and ineffectiveness in delivering basic skills necessary to both social and employment situations. The postsecondary sector has been criticized for giving priority to the concept of individual opportunity rather than responding to the demands of the view that the education system should be understood in terms of its contribution to economic development and national prosperity. (p. 352)

The resolution of this problem is argued to lie in engineering a better "fit" between the needs of industry and the provision of education and then "restructuring the education system to match these specifications" (p. 352).

Those who take a more expansive view of the problem (Beverley, 1982) regard technocratic and instrumental forms of training as nothing more than a reassertion of the "work ethic" and as a means of social control in a situation of declining job prospects. Jackson (1987) argues that in capitalist countries "skills formation" has become the linchpin in a strategy to orchestrate a broad public consensus on educational goals, with "competency" being used as the yardstick of achievement. "Skills formation" and "competency" are much more palatable, neutral, and apolitical terms, which give all the outward appearances of having been purged of the highly problematic notion of "educational" imperatives. In other words, the problem becomes one of devising means to reach predetermined ends, rather than one of debating the desirability or otherwise of the ends themselves. The problem gives all the appearances of being a "technical" one (Moodie & Acopian, 1988), when in reality it is a complex moral and philosophical one, involving diverse and contradictory possibilities. What the notion of skills hides, of course, is the historical and gendered struggles between labor and capital in which various accommodations have been reached and resistances enacted in determining who has the right to control work. These are crucial framing issues which have to be considered in any discussion of educational policy. Sadly, they are not ones that emerge in the Dawkins agenda!

The crucial companion piece to skills enhancement within the Dawkins strategy is treating knowledge in instrumental terms—for example, singling out science, engineering, computer science, business studies (the so-called strategic disciplines), and Asian languages for preferential funding, on the grounds that widespread possession of these skills will somehow magically generate jobs that will make Australia internationally competitive—all of which is almost unbelievably naive. But if we look even cursorily at recent history, it is not hard to see how this commonsense view has come about. Blaming universities (or at least sections within them) for our economic problems is not that dissimilar from the scapegoating that schools received in the 1970s and early 1980s for high levels of youth unemployment. It is a variant of the same argument mentioned earlier. Freeland (1985) writes that, with respect to schools, both government and employers were keen to find "scapegoats" for unemployment and that "employers [were] hardly likely to blame the capitalist system for unemployment" (p. 227).

It is not hard either to see how Australia's wider international economic woes can be blamed on a higher education system that is not producing either enough graduates or graduates of the right kind. Yet this argument is amply evident in the Dawkins papers in terms of the need to expand higher education enrollments (not on equity and access grounds), and to "speed up" the rate of graduation—clear reference to Fordist notions of speeding up the rate of the production line.

Hinkson (1989) argues that this process is largely supported by the preparation of the myth that the "third industrial revolution" (Mandel, 1976) requires vast increases in "intellectually trained labor-power" (p. 259). The reality, as shown by Levin (1987) in the U.S. and by the detailed labor market predictions of Sweet (1987) in Australia, is that job expansion is likely to be in service areas with low-skill requirements (see Gordon & Kimball, 1985, p. 315). The Dawkins argument, which is linked to "Australia Reconstructed" (ACTU/TDC, 1987) and which regards value-added production as "increasingly com[ing] to mean production in which value is added as a consequence of intellectually reconstituted work practices" (Hinkson, 1989, p. 164), appears to be founded on a totally false set of assumptions.

Redefining the role of higher education according to the scenario described above is certainly possible (although apparently flawed), but what it also does is

> deny education as an exercise of the human capacity for learning: . . . deny[ing] the importance of reflection, of inquiry, of social interaction and of environmental responsibility: . . . negat[ing] relationships, including international relationships, based on understanding and co-operation rather than competition: . . . ignor[ing] meaning and values. The pursuit of such activities is defined as the appropriation of a commodity for which the user must pay. (Junor, 1988, p. 139)

But it is also important to note that instrumentalization of knowledge in this way is not totally orchestrated from outside of higher education; "betrayal from within" (During, 1987, p. 116) has been a feature of Australian universities for some time as the administratively minded grasp at a discourse that gives them a clearer vision of the university as a place to "manage." The crucial issue is not only that knowledge is being construed in terms of a trade school pedagogy, but that what is being transformed in the process is what should be the "relation of university to government . . . [and] the relation of intellectuals, and the traditions of knowledge and interpretation within which they work, to society at large" (Sharp, 1988b, p. 123). He notes how the history of the early postwar years of higher education in Australia was marked by major contestation as universities reacted to protect their autonomy, and "until well into the seventies, the core ideal of university remained strong" (p. 120).

There were, however, processes at work within which "figures of the upper echelon of academic life were writing 'higher education' policies for the government without recognition that these might be discontinuous with the tradition of the modern university" (p. 120). Even now, Hinkson (1987) says, it is inaccurate to portray the picture of "the embattled university overwhelmed by political forces . . . [Rather], dominant influences within universities have seized on the [reforms] with vigor" (p. 123), and as Sharp (1988b) put it, "it has been left to Mr. Dawkins to publicly render unmistakable the process which has been at work for forty years: the rise of the higher education system within the husk of the modern university" (p. 121). None of this is unique to Australia; what Dawkins does is capitalize on a trend towards the deprofessionalization of higher education, which has long been underway internationally. Citing Mills (1951), Wheelwright (1978) summarized the argument in these terms:

> The specialization that is required for successful operation as a college professor is often deadening to the mind that would grasp for higher culture in the modern world. There now is . . . a celibacy of the intellect. . . . The professionalization of knowledge has . . . narrowed the grasp of the individual professor; the means of his [sic] success further this trend; and in the social studies and the humanities, the attempt to imitate exact science narrows the mind to microscopic fields of inquiry, rather than expanding it to embrace man and society as a whole. (p. 90)

Yet, even given all this, along with the contradictory way in which universities over the past 800 years appear to have resisted some external incursions, as McKinnon pointed out recently (West, 1990, p. 9), it is by no means certain that the Dawkins vision of a "hoped-for value-added or 'brain-based' export-led recovery" (Hinkson, 1987, p. 120) will actually come to pass, notwithstanding that life may be made difficult by funding mechanisms and other moves to further proletarianize (Beverley, 1982) labor within higher education. Take, for example, the package of ideas from the Hudson report, "Efficiency and Effectiveness in Higher Education" (1986), most of which have been implemented in one form or another by Dawkins.

1. A salary bar at the mid-point of lecturer and senior lecturer to facilitate "review of performance and recognition of achievement";

2. The use of up to 20% salary loadings' subject to review after three years to allow better competition with industry;

3. While purportedly supporting tenure, a minimum of 10–20% of staff on fixed-term contracts;

4. The establishment of staff assessment schemes which "can assist staff to monitor their performance";

5. The introduction of early retirement schemes;

6. The introduction of rules for the termination of staff on grounds other than misconduct, namely incapacity, inefficiency, or redundancy. (Hinkson, 1987, p. 120)

Without getting too deeply into the complex debate about "professionalism" (see Gouldner, 1979; Larson, 1980; Mills, 1951, for a few examples of this debate), what the above measures signify is the continuation of a much larger and longer process of proletarianization that has been occurring in higher education. Meisenhelder (1983, p. 298) encapsulates the argument in terms of the modern university having become a dependent multi-function institution in most capitalist societies. At the same time he argues that in return for the functions they discharge, faculty in higher education have paid dearly "for the rewards which come with the acceptance of the self-deceptive set of beliefs and norms inherent in the counter-factual definition of themselves as professionals" (p. 298). Meisenhelder (1983) gives examples of the way in which the university as a workplace falls very short of the ideals of professionalism:

> Faculty are relatively poorly paid and their income is de-
> creasing, relative to that of many other workers. . . . [T]hey
> are more or less powerless employees of bureaucratic in-
> stitutions . . . evaluated, ranked, and rewarded according
> to an increasingly rationalized set of pseudo-scientific pro-
> cedures and artificially precise, even mathematical crite-
> ria. . . . Faculty decision-making power seems to primarily
> involve making recommendations to administrators who
> often agree with faculty but who are free to disagree
> and/or ignore them. Faculty are delegated tasks rather
> than power or authority in crucial areas of institutional
> life. . . . Management defines the institution's priorities
> and ensures that employees are judged according to stan-
> dards derived from those goals. (p. 299)

Basically Meisenhelder (1983) is saying that faculty have
become increasingly blinded to the fact that their role is really
that of "subordinated employees," a role they share with many
other workers (p. 300). Given this trend, it is not altogether surprising, when the specter of economic crisis is raised, that the response of management within universities is to act in ways that
standardize the work of faculty, thus intensifying management's
control over the shape and form of university work and knowledge. Processes become Taylorised in the attempt to match
offerings and perceived demand in the pursuit of organizational
efficiency, with "the traditional notion of holistic education . . . [being] replaced by an academic assembly line composed
of a series of esoterically specialized courses . . . preventing very
many faculty from developing a broad general knowledge of the
processes of the institution as a whole" (p. 302).

It is not hard, therefore, to see the new technology of control, of which Dawkins is but one manifestation, as the means by
which institutional managers *within* the formal bureaucracy of
higher education obtain legitimation for intensifying the work of
universities (on efficiency grounds) while regulating the amount
and pace of work according to predetermined and narrowly defined and codified technical tasks. Meisenhelder (1983) summarized this "enemy from within" thesis (my terminology), when
he said:

> While the objective situation of fiscal shortfall created by
> the economic problems of late capitalism may force ad-

ministrators to reduce costs and increase the efficiency of work, it *allows* them to do so in a manner that increases their own power at the expense of faculty. (p. 303)

What we have then is a "condensation of [educated] labor" (Larson, 1980, p. 137) in which the functions of management and planning are effectively removed from the shop floor and the functions "differentiated, hierarchically connected, and bureaucratically integrated." Analogous with what happened when trained craftsmen were replaced by machinery and unskilled workers, what we have through the proletarianization process is

the deepening of a special dimension of *political* alienation; the alienation from decision-making in and about the productive process . . . from the level of decisions about what, for what and how much to produce, to the apparently non-political level of decisions about *how* to produce, about methods, times, and rhythms. (Larson, 1980, pp. 139–40)

Meisenhelder (1983) has argued that while faculty may still seem to have a degree of temporal and spatial freedom within which to exercise their work, "this discretion is diminishing and may soon be limited to questions surrounding how to exercise assigned tasks . . . [i.e.] choos[ing] the means, not the end, of education" (p. 304).

Full accomplishment of what Encel (cited in Stretton, 1989, p. 9) called this "service station role for universities" is dependent upon "no conflict . . . on the role of knowledge [and the hope] that the now prostrate form of the modern university shall not get up and walk around to the embarrassment of the higher education system" (Sharp, 1988b, p. 122). Clearly, an impositional analysis of what is happening in higher education policy reform in Australia is too simplistic, even though most critics in Australia have railed at Dawkins. Hinkson (1987, p. 124) points out in his discussion of the "embattled university" that while it is certainly true that new criteria are being forced upon universities by government and are shaped by conceptions of appropriate management emanating from the corporate sector, there is much more truth in the argument that the major changes of thinking in fact had their origins within universities and it is government that is turning that thinking back upon them. In other words, higher education itself has been at the forefront of creating "instrumental rationality as the dominant form of knowledge" (Sharp, 1988b, p. 125) and propagating it in ways that have seriously undermined the traditional role of universities of interpreting the world and that have lent "support to the means of changing it: means within a capitalist form but expanding beyond its classical limit in a new found conjunction of class power with instrumentalized intellect" (Sharp, 1988b, p. 125).

Gender and Labor Market Segmentation in Higher Education

Building upon the points just made, it is not hard to make a compelling case that another of the accommodations and settlements evident in the Green and White papers hinges on gender (and indeed, equity issues more broadly defined). As alluded to at several points already in this chapter, the Dawkins reforms represent a simultaneous and overlapping manifestation of "proletarianization" (the reduction of work from being an understanding of a whole process to fragmentation, where it becomes impossible for those performing the work to comprehensively see interconnections—see Lawn & Ozga, 1988) and "segmentation" (the gradual insertion of incentives and rewards that change the boundaries of different segments of labor—see Gordon & Reich, 1982).

There is a compelling argument that the "selectively economistic" line taken by the Dawkins reforms is designed to privilege an already dominant group—namely, men (Yeatman, 1988, p. 39)—at the expense of other groups, especially (but not only) women. Yeatman claims that the educational reformist agenda of Dawkins is not only gender-blind but "thoroughly subjugated to its economic rationalist agenda," and that it is not even a genuinely economic agenda because of its decidedly "selective [and] masculinist" pose (p. 41). She backs up her assertions with evidence in four ways: First, reducing the public funding base of higher education and allowing market forces to operate will, she says, selectively reduce the participation, access, and equity for already disadvantaged groups—especially women from low socioeconomic backgrounds. Groups that have been given only limited access to higher education in the past will be excluded even further under the Dawkins plan (regardless of "cross-credentialling," "bridging course," "credit transfers," and "encouragement to women to enter non-traditional areas"—all parts of the Green and White papers) just because these are groups that have neither the credentials nor the personal dispositions to enter the fast tracks nominated by Dawkins (a point I shall return to in a moment).

Second, the "virtually unregulated entrepreneurial buccaneering" (Yeatman, 1988, p. 40), which is the hallmark of the "John Wayne version of economics" (p. 40) implicit in Dawkins, regards the appropriate educational response to the macroeconomic picture as forms of consultancy that are highly dependent on geographic mobility and "patterns of availability and time use which depend on freedom from domestic and parenting responsibilities" (p. 40)—all features that militate strongly against women in academic positions and that will undoubtedly "intensify the already existing gender stratification of academic staffing" (p. 40).

Third, Yeatman fears that the Dawkins "economy of specialization" that will direct research funding to areas of already existing strength and concentration will further push women into the "intensive and mass teaching areas of the social sciences and humanities" (p. 40) which are not to be accorded national priority status. (Shades here of an "industrial reserve army" of relatively cheap labor). This will be further exacerbated as collegiate models of decision making are increasingly replaced by generic forms of hierarchical corporate management. Again, "it is all too likely that women will be situated again on the wrong side of the new binarism" (p. 41).

Fourth, Yeatman has considerable difficulty with the "gender-based mythology about what counts as productive work" (p. 41) that lies behind the Dawkins plan and its neglect of women's skills which, she argues, ought to be the basis of a more humane, communicative, inclusive, and problem-solving "productive culture."

It is Kenway and Blackmore's (1988) contention, like that of Yeatman, that the Dawkins agenda defines some forms of knowledge as being "empowering" and others as being "power neutral or disempowering." The effect is that of diminishing women's "skills, experience, interests, and aptitudes" (p. 52) based upon a "masculinist definition of power" (p. 52) that embodies a "very restricted, often masculinist reading of labor market trends and future directions" (p. 52). Furthermore, what constitutes skill in the restructuring of the economy is distorted and discounted away from the complex interpersonal and communicative skills stereotypically possessed by women, in the rush to ensure the dominance of patriarchal virtues of technology, science, engineering, and management. Yet both Yeatman (1988) and Jackson (1990) make the point that in the normal course of business it is men who make the decisions but women who possess the "invisible skills" (Jackson, 1990, p. 24) and "do the 'shit-jobs' that 'anybody' can do" (Offe, 1985, p. 40). The argument, therefore, really hinges on what constitutes the notion of a productive culture, and who has the right to define what kind of knowledge shall be accorded supremacy and what shall be denigrated. It does not resolve anything, Kenway and Blackmore (1988) argue, to suggest, as Dawkins does, that women be encouraged to enter science, mathematics, and technology areas because taking such steps involves women not simply inhabiting a male domain "but a masculinist culture where success may well depend upon taking on board values antithetical to a feminist cause" (p. 53). The proposal to make research more entrepreneurial not only excludes women because it favors already well-established (male) researchers, but it is women who will increasingly be relegated to teaching responsibilities as a consequence (p. 54).

Barlow (1989) presents some compelling quantitative evidence that the process of academic restructuring and de-skilling is already well advanced, with a *primary* group (of tenured academics) in favored targeted areas of economically and technologically relevant knowledge who will increasingly be permitted and supported to do research, and a *secondary* "teaching only" group (untenured) whose function will be the unquestioning reproduction of knowledge to students, mainly in the areas of humanities and social sciences. Barlow argues that this "vertical" and "horizontal" restructuring will be achieved through a very clear division of labor along gender lines, and through the targeting of the curriculum so that "economically relevant knowledge is [increasingly] redefined as that which consolidates in human capital form those skills, attitudes and knowledge content which more directly serve the needs of economic growth" (p. 35). More short-term contract positions can be expected in the teaching-only areas as the process of de-skilling occurs within the widening and structurally enforced separation between teaching and research. This separation goes right to the very heart of what Marxists describe as "praxis": the interdependence of theory and practice, and the way in which each is continually informed and shaped by the other through experience.

The Dawkins instrumentalist reforms will serve to do nothing more than reinforce the already demonstrable underrepresentation of women in the professions (see Moodie & Acopian, 1988, for evidence of the difficulties involved). Even when government had a clear policy goal (in the Williams report, 1979) over a decade ago for doing something about this, it has largely failed to use education as the vehicle for achieving this (Moodie & Acopian, 1988); the gap between males and females is still huge by any standards. Moodie and Acopian make the sobering point that if the reasonably straightforward goal of redressing gender imbalances has become too complex, uncertain, and "beyond" the reach of governments to alter, then what can we expect from the endeavors to use education to "close the gap on our international competitors" (Moodie & Acopian, 1988, p. 64)?

By way of drawing together some of the threads, it should be said that as a response to the global crisis, the Dawkins reforms are all derivative of strongly masculinist "solutions" or, as Beilharz (1986) put it, "jobs-for-the-boys" (p. 12). We should not, therefore, be too surprised at the gender-oppressive nature of their effects. Neither can we excuse this as being a contemporary phenomenon, for as Beilharz and Watts (1983, p. 102) argue, Labor governments have a notorious legacy of being sexist.

The interrelationships between Labor's current economic reconstruction program was well put by Rosewarne (1988) when he said that despite its public proclamations about equity and concern for women's economic well-being (despite average weekly wages for women having increased from 80% to 83% of average male earnings since 1983, and 60% of new jobs having been taken up by women mostly in casual and part-time work), it is still fundamentally a patriarchical policy of economic management. The argument is that the shift in policies from *public* to *private* investment (Blackman, 1984) as the supposed and preferred engine for economic revitalization transfers the burden of economic restraint to the private (i.e., household) sphere through real wage reductions, by 8% since Labor came to office in 1983 (Rosewarne, 1988). While the "Accord" (ACTU/TDC, 1987) has served to bring together government, trade unions, and employer organizations to work on economic recovery, it has done so with a strong emphasis on manufacturing industry, in which most employees are male, while writing off industries of significant female employment like clothing and footwear (Rosewarne, 1988). Paradoxically, what we are experiencing through the Accord is a "feminization" (Wajcman & Rosewarne, 1986) of work in which there is an increased utilization of female labor precisely because of its greater "flexibility" in terms of hourly rates of pay, piecework, and lack of job security. Even in processes like multiskilling, it has been men who have been the primary beneficiaries because of their strategic location in industries likely to benefit most (Rosewarne, 1988, p. 82). Therefore, what we are witnessing in higher education in terms of the proletarianization of labor and the gender bias reinforced by Dawkins in the higher education labor market is precisely that reflected in the processes at work in the economy at large through the Accord and "Australia Reconstructed," as the real burden of economic recovery is shifted from the public to the private sphere. So, the relationship between the global crisis, the Labor response in its various forms, and the further gender oppression of women is a direct rather than an indirect one.

Postscript

In the intervening five years since the Dawkins higher education reforms, Australia has witnessed the transformation of its higher education system from an elite to a mass system of higher education. Most of the predictions alluded to in the body of this chapter have come to pass, and at a substantial cost to all involved—students as well as staff. For example, there has been a "16% decline in funding per equivalent full-time student since 1983"; research opportunities in universities for small-scale projects have virtually dried up; there has been a "rapid exploitation of education as an export industry and the use of research as a lever of economic recovery . . . [with] institutions now receiving only 73% of their income direct from [government] sources" (Zetlin, 1992, p. 36). Yet, at the same time there are real questions being asked as to whether universities can deliver "the agenda" (in reference to our former prime minister's vision of an education-led high-tech recovery) on "banana republic funding" (in reference to our current prime minister's view as to where we might be headed unless we adopt his vision) (Zetlin, 1992, p. 36).

Five years down the track, we are now in a position to make a sober assessment of the effects of higher education reforms in Australia, and several things have become clear. Bourke (1992) summarized the changing redefinition of the relationship between higher education and society in Australia in terms of:

>•*Dismantling* without public debate of the expert advisory and program funding statutory authority [which had previously insulated universities from the direct interference of politicians] and the subjection of universities to the direct operation of the ministry.

>•*Abolishing* the binary line [between universities and applied colleges of advanced education] and the creation of 15 or so new universities.

>•*The redesigning* of the universities through enforced mergers with former colleges on arbitrary criteria of enrollment size.

>•*The widespread demoralization* of university teachers and researchers . . . [through] intrusion into their activities.

• *A deterioration* of quality control, especially in the post-graduate area [through the removal of scrutiny of college programs].

• *Overwork in the classroom* as effective reduction and redistribution of real resources have worsened the staff–student ratios in high demand areas. (p. 36)

Above all, there has been a fundamental and marked shift in the nature of government control of Australian higher education. As Marginson (1992) writes, there has been a "giving up control over the *process* of higher education, but taking more control of the *product*" (p. 19). The claim, and it is well substantiated by research evidence Marginson has collected through the Center for Study of Higher Education at Melbourne University, is that the federal government has loosened up on administrative control by giving universities more control over their financial resources, while it has tightened up steering control through accountability requirements and by requiring universities to competitively bid against one another for funds:

> Monies for enrollment growth, innovatory programs, quality improvement, better teaching and research are distributed this way. Through control of the criteria used to distribute this funding, the government is able to establish a "culture of compliance" around certain styles of work, and determine program outcomes. (Marginson, 1992, p. 19)

As he says, "the beauty of competitive bidding arrangements is that they are entered on a voluntary basis" (p. 19). So, the widely held view is that the apparent retreat of government from administrative control is more than matched by its replacement with what appears on the surface to be a market mechanism but what really amounts to the government channeling activities in directions it deems desirable. It is not a true market mechanism because invisible (and largely unaccountable) government bureaucrats determine the national priorities, goals, and objectives to which academics shall work. The overall result is a system in which academics have considerably diminished control over their work, with a substantial surrender of academic freedom.

Arguments in this chapter have sought to show something of the complexity of the determination of educational policy in higher education in Australia by particular reference to the recent reforms engineered by Dawkins. By locating discussion of those reforms in the wider gambit of the international restructuring of capitalism generally, an attempt was made to portray educational policy as another form of temporary historical compromise in the endeavor to resolve Australia's economic vulnerability (Castles, 1988, called it a "domestic defense").

The basic thesis of the chapter has been that the Dawkins reforms in higher education in Australia are part of a much broader response by government to economic events of international origin. First, because Australia has become increasingly dependent on foreign capital inflow, and as a consequence of the ensuing high levels of foreign ownership of strategic Australian resources, increasing levels of cooperation from labor have been necessary for capital accumulation to continue. Second, government reaction to these events, partly for historical reasons, was to follow already established corporatist tendencies in Australia by opting for a high-tech solution based around a manufactured political consensus. These were seen as crucial framing mechanisms necessary to engender the kind of widespread change in attitudes, thinking, and support necessary for the Dawkins reforms to seem nonproblematic and natural. Finally, it was argued that the Dawkins proposals did not represent the blind application of an externally determined agenda for higher education but rather the "licensing" of events, processes, and settlements that had been underway for some time. In particular, higher education as a public versus a private good, deregulation and pedagogy for profit, the instrumentalization of knowledge and the proletarianization of educated labor, and gender and labor market segmentation in higher education represented the attempt to establish credible forms of discourse about the "rightful" role of higher education in a situation of economic crisis. Each of these was portrayed as having a gloss of credibility about them, while at the same time representing a significant shift of higher education away from a social agenda towards individualistic, market-regulated modes of responding to broad international economic forces.

REFERENCES

ACTU/TDC. (1987). Mission to Western Europe. *Australia reconstructed: A report by the Mission members to the ACTU and TDC.* Canberra: Australian Government Publishing Service.

Ashenden, D. (1988). Using our graduates is the real problem. *Australian Universities' Review, 31(1),* pp. 24–26.

Barlow, K. (1989). The white paper and restructuring the academic labor market. *Australian Universities' Review, 32(1),* pp. 30–37.

Bartos, M. (1990a, March). Further steps to a new educational order. *Australian Society,* pp. 12–13.

———. (1990b, September). The education exports fiasco. *Australian Society,* pp. 12– 13.

Beilharz, P. (1986). The left, the "accord" and the future of socialism. *Thesis Eleven, 13,* pp. 5–21.

Beilharz, P. & Watts, R. (1983, November). The discovery of corporatism. *Australian Society,* pp. 27–30.

Beverley, J. (1982). Higher education and capitalist crisis. In D. Derber (Ed.), *Professionals and workers: Mental labor in advanced capitalism* (pp. 100–20). Boston: G. K. Hall.

Blackman, D. (1984, Spring). Women and the accord. *Australian Left Review, (89),* pp. 17–23.

Bourke, P. (1988). The green paper: Towards an evaluation. *Australian Universities' Review, 31(1),* pp. 2–5.

———. (1992, September). A new timetable, a new rhetoric. *The Weekend Australian, (13-13),* p. 36.

Brady, V. (1988, February). The long perspective. *Australian Society, (29-30),* pp. 54–55.

Burchell, D. (1986, December). Tertiary education for sale. *Australian Society,* pp. 22–24.

Burgess, J. (1989). Productivity: A worker problem? *Journal of Australian Political Economy, 24,* pp. 223–38.

Castles, F. (1988). *Australian public policy and economic vulnerability.* Sydney: Allen and Unwin.

Davis, D. (1988). Flexibility and future labor needs in the light of the green paper: A consideration of the EHW factor. *Australian Universities' Review, 31(1),* pp. 6–11.

Dawkins, J. (1987). *Higher education: A policy discussion paper.* Canberra: Australian Government Publishing Service.

———. (1988). *Higher education: A policy statement.* Canberra: Australian Government Publishing Service.

Donald, J. (1979). Green paper: Noise of crisis. *Screen Education, 30,* pp. 13–49.

During, S. (1987). Woodchipping in the groves of academe. *Arena, 81,* pp. 111–18.

Freeland, J. (1985). Australia: the search for a new educational settlement. In R. Sharp (Ed.), *Capitalist crisis and schooling: Comparative studies in the politics of education.* Melbourne: Macmillan.

Gordon, D., Edwards, R. & Reich, M. (1982). *Segmented work, divided workers: The historical transformation of labor in the United States.* Cambridge: Cambridge University Press.

Gordon, R. & Kimball, L. (1985). High technology, employment and the challenges of education. *Prometheus, 3(2),* pp. 315–30.

Gouldner, A. (1979). *The future of intellectuals and the rise of a new class.* New York: Oxford University Press.

Hinkson, J. (1987). The embattled university? *Arena, 81(1)* pp. 19–27.

———. (1989). A one-dimensional critic. *Arena, 88,* pp. 163–66.

Hinkson, J. et al. (1986). *Review of efficiency and effectiveness in higher education.* Canberra: Commonwealth Tertiary Education Commission.

Jackson, N. (1987). Skill training in transition: Implications for women. In J. Gaskell & A. McLaren (Eds.), *Women and education: A Canadian perspective.* Calgary: Detselig.

———. (1990). *Skills formation and gender relations: The politics of who knows what.* Geelong: Deakin University Press.

Junor, A. (1988). Australian education reconstructed. *Arena, 84,* pp. 133–40.

Karmel, P. (Chairman) (1972). *Schools in Australia.* Report by the Interim Committee for the Australian School Commission. Canberra: Australian Government Publishing Service.

———. (1989). *Reflections on a revolution: Australian higher education in 1989.* Canberra: Australian Vice-Chancellors' Committee.

Kenway, J. & Blackmore, J. (1988). Gender and the green paper: Privatization and equity. *Australian Universities' Review, 31(1)*, pp. 49–57.

Larson, M. (1980). Proletarianization and educated labor. *Theory and Society, 9(2)*, pp. 131–75.

Lawn, M. & Ozga J. (1988). The educational worker? A re-assessment of teachers. In J. Ozga (Ed.), *Schoolwork: Approaches to the labor process of teaching*. Milton Keynes: Open University Press.

Levin, H. (1987). Improving productivity through education and technology. In G. Burke & R. Rumberger (Eds.), *The future impact of technology on work and education* (pp. 194–214). Lewes: Falmer Press.

Mandel, E. (1976). *Late capitalism*. London: Verso.

Marceau, J. (1989). Australian business sector: Skills, tasks, and technologies. In D. Pope & L. Alston (Eds.), *Australia's greatest asset: Human resources in the nineteenth and twentieth centuries* (pp. 220–38). Sydney: Federation Press.

Marginson, S. (1989). *Labor's economic objectives in higher education: Will they be achieved?* Paper presented to a lecture series, Center for the Study of Higher Education, University of Melbourne, November 1989.

———. (1992, September). Winners and losers in post-Dawkins era. *Higher Education: The Australian, (19)*.

Meisenhelder, T. (1983). The ideology of professionalism in higher education. *Journal of Education, 165(3)*, pp. 295–307.

Mills, C. (1951). *White collar*. New York: Oxford University Press.

Moodie, G. & Acopian, J. (1988). New instrumentation in higher education: another axe being ground. *Australian Universities' Review, 31(1)*, pp. 60–65.

Offe, C. (1985). *Disorganized capitalism: Contemporary transformations of work and politics*. Cambridge: Polity Press.

Organization for Economic Co-operation and Development (OECD). (1987). *Structural adjustment and economic performance*. Paris: OECD.

Pollert, A. (1988). The "flexible" firm: fixation or fact? *Work, Employment, and Society, 2(3)*, pp. 281–316.

Pusey, M. (1991). *Economic rationalism in Canberra: A national building state changes its mind*. Melbourne: Cambridge University Press.

Robertson, S. & Woock, R. (1989). Reform and reaction in Australian education. *Urban Education, 24(1),* pp. 3–24.

Rosewarne, S. (1988). Economic management, the "accord" and gender inequality. *Journal of Australian Political Economy, 23,* pp. 61–86.

Sharp, G. (1988a). Reconstructing Australia. *Arena, 82,* pp. 70–97.

————. (1988b). The university and after? *Arena, 82,* pp. 117–33.

Slaughter, S. (1985). The pedagogy of profit. *Higher Education, 14,* pp. 217–22.

Smith, B., Burke, G., Smith, S. & Wheelwright, T. (1988). Proposals for change in Australian education: A radical critique. *Discourse: The Australian Journal of Educational Studies, 9(10),* pp. 1–38.

Smyth, J. (1989). A critical pedagogy of classroom practice. *Journal of Curriculum Studies, 21(6),* pp. 483–502.

————. (1991). Theories of the state and recent policy reforms in higher education in Australia. *Discourse: The Australian Journal of Educational Studies, 11(2),* pp. 48–69.

Stretton, H. (1989). Life after Dawkins: teaching and research with diminishing resources. *Australian Universities' Review, 32(2),* pp. 9–14.

Sweet, R. (1987). Australian trends in job skill requirements: a critique of the current orthodoxy. In G. Burke & R. Rumberger (Eds.), *The future impact of technology on work and education* (pp. 96–117). Lewes: Falmer Press.

Wajcman, J. & Rosewarne, S. (1986, September). The "feminization" of work. *Australian Society,* pp. 15–17.

West, F. (1990, September 12). AVCC head refreshed with worldly view. *Higher Education, The Australian,* p. 9.

Wheelwright, E. (1978). The higher learning in Australia. In E. Wheelwright (Ed.), *Capitalism, socialism or barbarism: Essays in contemporary political economy.* Sydney: Australia New Zealand Book Company, pp. 87–93.

Williams, B. (Chairman) (1979). *Education, training, and employment.* Canberra: Australian Government Printing Service.

Wise, A. (1979). *Legislated learning: The bureaucratization of the American classroom.* Berkeley: University of California Press.

Yeatman, A. (1988). The green paper on higher education: remarks concerning its implications for participation, access, and equity for women as staff and students. *Australian Universities' Review, 31(1),* pp. 34–41.

Zetlin, D. (1992, September 12–13). Turmoil masks underlying pressures. *The Weekend Australian*, p. 36.

CHAPTER IV

The Reformulation in Korean Private Higher Education
Changing Relationship between the Government and Private Schools

Namgi Park

Introduction

As is the case with many developing countries, Korea has achieved a remarkable quantitative expansion of higher education during the last forty years. But in Korea, higher education has expanded most rapidly in the private sector. The number of enrollments in higher education grew from 7,819 in 1945 to 1,678,750 in 1992; the ratio of private sector enrollments has increased from 55% in 1955 to 78% in 1992. Korea ranks sixth in terms of total enrollment in the world, and third in terms of enrolled students per 100,000 of the population (UNESCO, 1990). This remarkable development was achieved through strong government direction and popular demand. Table 1 demonstrates this rapid growth.

For many years the government controlled not only public universities and colleges, but private institutions as well. Dressel and Faricy (1972) wrote that, "complete autonomy would require complete financial independence, an unattainable state" (p. 13). But in the case of Korea, although private universities and

TABLE 1. Number of Enrolled Students, Private School Ratio, and Cohort Entrants Ratio in Higher Education by Control (1945–1992)*

Year	Total(A)	National and Public	Private (B)	Private Ratio(%) (B/A) x 100	Cohort Entrants Ratio (%)[1]
1945	7,819	4,090	3,729	47.7	—
1946	10,315	—	—	—	—
1947	25,813	—	—	—	—
1948	42,000	—	—	—	—
1949	28,000	—	—	—	—
1950	11,358	—	—	—	—
1951	20,000	—	—	—	—
1952	31,342	—	—	—	—
1953	38,411	—	—	—	—
1954	62,663	—	—	—	—
1955	78,649	35,207	43,442	55.2	—
1956	84,996	34,369	50,627	59.6	—
1957	80,142	30,244	49,898	62.3	—
1958	79,449	—	—	—	—
1959	81,641	30,980	50,733	62.1	—
1960	95,200	35,380	59,820	62.8	6.0
1961	134,779	36,622	98,157	72.8	—
1962	134,480	37,785	96,695	71.9	—
1963	131,777	38,603	93,174	70.7	—
1964	136,158	37,580	98,578	72.4	—
1965	141,636	39,259	102,377	72.3	8.5
1966	175,349	43,079	132,270	75.4	8.0
1967	170,941	46,566	124,375	72.8	8.2
1968	172,410	51,122	121,288	70.3	9.5
1969	165,934	47,732	118,202	71.2	8.3
1970	177,996	53,493	124,503	70.0	7.6
1971	186,789	58,002	128,787	68.9	7.8
1972	195,963	62,015	133,948	68.4	7.6
1973	209,643	65,533	144,110	68.7	7.1
1974	223,151	68,042	155,109	69.5	7.2
1975	238,719	69,832	168,887	70.7	7.1
1976	257,139	73,432	183,707	71.4	7.4
1977	278,987	79,914	199,073	71.4	7.2

TABLE 1. (*continued*)

Year	Total(A)	National and Public	Private (B)	Private Ratio(%) (B/A) x 100	Cohort Entrants Ratio (%)[1]
1978	308,730	90,920	217,810	70.6	8.2
1979	444,578	122,954	321,624	72.3	19.2
1980	601,994	157,806	444,183	73.8	21.9
1981	786,354	198,046	588,308	74.8	32.6
1982	947,334	236,449	710,885	75.0	34.3
1983	1,073,974	264,460	809,514	75.4	36.3
1984	1,192,936	288,823	904,113	75.8	37.4
1985	1,277,825	303,870	973,955	76.2	37.3
1986	1,332,455	311,202	1,021,253	76.6	36.3
1987	1,361,949	309,639	1,052,310	77.3	34.9
1988	1,387,170	309,243	1,077,927	77.7	32.9
1989	1,481,557	335,268	1,146,289	77.4	—
1990	1,542,779	348,162	1,194,617	77.4	—
1991	1,598,342	354,210	1,244,132	77.8	39.2
1992	1,678,750	369,629	1,309,121	78.0	43.5

[1]Cohort Entrants Ratio = (Entrants/Population of 18-Year-Olds) x 100.

*Data include colleges and universities, graduate schools, junior colleges, and miscellaneous schools (exclude air and correspondence universities).

Source: See Notes.

colleges were financially independent from the government, they lacked autonomy and remained under the government's firm control. The government controlled the structure of expenditure, admissions policy, number of students, and tuition rate. Furthermore, the chairmen of boards of trustees and the presidents of universities and colleges were required to receive government approval before being appointed, and the government was able to remove them from their positions if it deemed it necessary. How this was possible in Korea will be answered in the course of this chapter.

University autonomy is defined as "essentially the freedom to use resources and to define and execute programs consonant with institutional (university) purposes" (Dressel &

Faricy, 1972, p. 14). The university seeks autonomy to gain freedom and flexibility in resource allocation, curriculum planning, faculty promotion, and selection of faculty and administrators; to determine instructional practices and admissions policies; and to make decisions about research and educational programs.

Why is university autonomy an important value? According to Polin (1983, p. 39), "autonomy of the university is intrinsic to our understanding of education. It is necessary for fertile teaching, effective research and creative intention." John Gardner remarks that "the issue of university autonomy will never be finally solved. It can only be lived with" (Berdahl, 1971, p. v). Dressel and Faricy assert that without autonomy the university could not exist as we understand the term today and could not perform the essential functions that led to its creation (1972, p. 14). Colleges and universities need freedom, not merely as an administrative convenience to enhance their efficient operation, but as an indispensable means to all other achievements. Without freedom, productive teaching and research in the Western tradition are impossible (Moos & Rourke, 1959, p. 39).

Nevertheless, the Korean government has continuously tried to control its universities. What is the rationale for governmental intervention? Accountability and national development are given by the government as the rationale. In view of the political weight and financial burden of universities, most governments show an increasing tendency to make them accountable to the public and to strengthen central control of finances, teaching and research, personnel appointments, and curricula (Goldschmidt, 1984, p. 66).

Universities that receive financial aid from the government seldom have complete autonomy. However, government funds are not a precondition for government intervention. In the developing countries, the perceived nexus between the role of the university and national development has legitimized government intervention in the university in order to harmonize university activities with national educational and socioeconomic goals. For example, in Tanzania the government intervened to introduce national service for its university students (Paterson, 1986, p. 251). Human capital is a crucial ingredient for economic development in the developing countries, so government plans for universities emphasize national development needs and try to ensure that universities meet these needs. Universities often see these measures as attempts at controlling them.

However, the governments of some developing countries and communist countries have controlled higher education institutions in order to control their own society. In the Third World, students and intellectuals are often the leading groups that criticize the government. To maintain power, the government tries to control students and intellectuals.

This chapter describes the changing government policies with respect to Korean private universities and colleges since World War II, and explains the changing relationship between the government and the private schools. This explanation will help the reader to understand the relationship between the Korean government and private universities and colleges. The chapter also attempts to analyze the effects of policy changes on Korean private higher education from both positive and negative points of view.

The data for this study consist of historical documents and research papers related to Korean government control of private universities and colleges and of their development, as well as interviews with public officers of the Ministry of Education (MOE), private school owners,[*] presidents, professors, and students. These interviews took place in Korea between January 1992 and March 1992.

Expansion and Change of Korean Private Higher Education

The characteristics of the Korean higher education system can be summarized as follows (Park, 1989, p. 4):

---

[*] *Private school owners* is used here to denote individuals or groups of individuals who actually own and control private institutions of higher education. Usually these institutions were established as for-profit organizations (proprietary institutions). In any case, the owners attempted to retain control, even appointing themselves, family members, and friends as presidents, university trustees, and other officers of the institutions.

1. The private sector has three-quarters of the total enroll-ment of students.
2. There is little public financial support for this private sector.
3. All higher education institutions are under the control of the MOE.
4. The ratio of higher education students to the general population is high, but the teaching and learning conditions in higher education institutions are poor by comparison to the United States.
5. Students pay most of their educational expenses. In private universities and colleges, they pay 78% of their total educational expenses, whereas in national institutions they pay 48%.

The first higher educational institution in Korea, Tae Hak (the Great School), dates back to 372 A.D. Tae Hak of Korguryo is the second oldest higher education institution in the world. It was established by the government to educate public officers. There were also private higher education institutions, such as Kyoung Dang, which were established somewhat later than Tae Hak. Private schools were established to meet the provinces' educational demands, which could not be covered by Tae Hak in the capital city. This higher education system, which had a mass-oriented private sector and an elite-oriented public school, was continued to the end of 19th century. The governing classes relied on schools as an important instrument for keeping their status. Throughout Korean history, nearly anyone who wanted to be a public officer had to pass an examination, and the universities were preparatorial institutions for the examination. Access to higher education was gradually widened from a few royal classes to the governing classes.

Higher learning institutions equivalent to the universities and four-year colleges of Western countries have been in existence less than 100 years. There were three different streams to the establishment of Western-style higher education in Korea. The first one was started by Western missionaries. They established private higher education institutions, such as Ewha Kak Dang (1886) and Sungsil Hak Dang (1897). The second stream was started by the Korean government, which established professional schools to teach Western knowledge such as medicine, telegraphy, industry, mining and agriculture, and languages. The third stream was led by the nationalistic pioneers to teach Western knowledge and to rescue the country from invasion by Japan and Western countries. This third stream continued until Korea gained independence from Japanese occupation (1945).

When the Japanese colonized Korea (1910), they forced the closing of private schools, except for those founded by the Western missionaries, to which only a few Koreans had access. The nation-wide independence movement in 1919 forced the Japanese to change their severe style of control to a milder one. Seven private junior colleges were established during the 1920s because of this change. During this period, the movement to found a university in Korea through public donations emerged. The Committee for University Establishment was organized in 1922 to offer more and better higher education to Koreans. The Japanese government considered this movement an independence movement, and in response, established a university, Kyungsung Jaguk Dahak. They did this rather than permitting Koreans to open their own university. The Japanese offered majors that would not contribute to the raising of Korean political consciousness (Kim et al., 1989, p. 135). Only one-third of the students in this university were Korean.[1] Jongchul Kim and colleagues (1989, p. 197) have concluded that the characteristics of Korean higher education under Japanese occupation were strong control of higher education, prohibition of political activity, extremely restricted access, and segregation of Korean students from Japanese students.

Korea gained independence from Japanese colonial occupation in 1945. The system of higher education was restructured and reorganized under the United States Military Government (1945–1948). There were then 19 institutions of higher education in South Korea with a total enrollment of 7,819 students and 1,490 faculty members. The U.S. military government had a receptive attitude toward the establishment of private schools. In 1948, towards the end of the U.S. military government intervention, higher education institutions increased and enrollment rose to 24,000 students (KCUE, 1990, p. 35). There are various explanations of this rapid expansion of private higher education.

One of the major causes of the expansion was the enactment of the Agriculture Land Reform Law in 1949. The Act was intended to build a new economic system by modernizing the Korean rural community. It enabled the government to buy all private agricultural land inexpensively and redistribute it to farmers who had little or no land. There were some situations in which the government could not force large landowners to sell their land. Some of these involved land that government, public organizations, and educational institutions wanted to use; land that was owned by schools, religious bodies, and public welfare organizations; and land that was used for special purposes such as scientific research (Agriculture Land Reform Law, Art. 6).

The Land Reform Law, in effect, encouraged landowners to create universities and colleges in order to keep their land. Many large landowners founded private schools or donated the land to schools to avoid the force of the Act. Twenty-three universities and colleges were founded in a period of three years (C. Lee, 1990, p. 42; H. Lee, 1990, p. 25). Many large landowners regarded the founding of new education institutions not as a charitable donation of property but as a safe investment for profit (H. Lee, 1990, p. 25). Though universities and colleges were supposed to be nonprofit institutions, many founders managed to find profit in the institutions. The chairmen of the boards of trustees were often the founders of the institutions, and the members of the boards of trustees were often friends and relatives of the proprietor. In addition, the founder often became president of the institution. The government did not prohibit that. Private universities in Korea have mixed characteristics of both private institutions and proprietary institutions in the United States.

In 1950, when the Korean War broke out, the government delayed the conscription of university students. The demand for higher education was thus increased, as happened in the United States. From 1952 to 1954, the number of students doubled (Kim, 1979, p. 66).

After the war, a university diploma became an important credential for a good job. The starting salary of college graduates was more than three times higher than that of high school graduates. At the same time, the government permitted citizens to form private institutions easily. The qualifications needed to form this type of institution were so easily attainable that many institutions were formed in a short period of time. As a result of this, the quality of private higher education was often low.

Kim (1979) found that with the exception of some private universities that had a long history, most private universities were of miserable quality, often moved their campuses from one place to another, and frequently changed leadership.

In 1960, the dictatorial government was overthrown by students and a new democratic government was installed. However, this new government was overthrown by a military coup in 1961. The regime took drastic measures, including the Temporary Exceptional Law on Education (1961) and the Ordinance on School Consolidation Criteria (1961). The purpose of the Temporary Exceptional Law on Education was to control the quantitative growth of education and increase the quality of education. The minister of education could abolish departments or schools, and could control the number of students admitted into each university and college through discussions with the Consultation and Reconstruction Committee of the Ministry of Education (Temporary Exceptional Law on Education, Art. 3). Twenty-one universities and colleges were abolished among 71 higher education institutions (Song, 1990, p. 20). The Ordinance on School Consolidation Criteria stated that the minister of education could decide the number of students in every public and private university and college according to the manpower demand of the country, financial ability of the founder, and affordability of education (Ordinance on School Consolidation Criteria, Art. 16). There was a decrease in the number of students from universities and colleges during this period (H. Lee, 1990, p. 26). These drastic policies were unpopular and created many tensions. The government withdrew this radical policy in 1964, and most departments, universities, and colleges that had been abolished by these measures were reestablished. However, the measures became a precedent for governmental control over universities and colleges. The government enacted laws, such as the Private School Law (1963), and promulgated policies (the University

Student Quota Policy of 1965, the Private Institution Financial Affairs Policy of 1969, and the Policy of Tuition and Entrance Fees of 1969) to control not only public universities and colleges but private ones as well. During this period all universities and colleges were under strong governmental control.

The University Student Quota Policy of 1965 centralized the government's power to regulate student quotas in all universities and colleges, including the private sector. Under this policy, individual school admission quotas were established by the Ministry of Education, an arm of the military government. The MOE also determined each institution's departmental-level admission quota. These quotas led to an enrollment decrease starting in 1967 (refer to table 1).

Two policies led to the later expansion of higher education: the policy of free middle school entrance examinations (the lottery system for middle school entrance) and the high school equalization policy.[2] The free middle school entrance examination policy addressed the need to liberate elementary school students from overwork, equalize middle schools, and decrease the educational cost of private tutoring (Hanguk, 1980, p. 119).

TABLE 2.   Middle and High School Student Numbers
and Enrollment Ratio

Year	Middle School Students	Enrollment Ratio (%)[1]	High School Students	Enrollment Ratio(%)[1]
1965	751,341	42.1[2]	426,531	26.8[2]
1970	1,318,808	51.2	590,382	28.1
1975	2,026,823	72.0	1,123,017	41.0
1980	2,471,997	95.1	1,696,792	63.5
1985	2,782,173	97.5	2,152,802	79.2
1990	2,275,751	96.9	2,283,806	87.6

[1](Students/cohort age group) x 100.
[2]This is datum of 1966.

Source: This table is reconstructed from Korean Educational Development Institute, 1990, pp. 27, 67.

As a consequence of this policy, middle school enrollment increased tremendously.[3] Neither government officials nor scholars expected this enormous expansion in the number of students. Table 2 shows the expansion of middle school students and enrollment ratios. The government had to build many new public middle schools and had to permit the founding of private schools to meet demand (see table 3). The increasing number of middle school students brought pressure on the high school system. The free middle shool entrance examination policy made the high school entrance examination highly competitive. Thus all the problems of elementary schools and students moved into the middle schools. Middle school students overworked themselves in order to enter high-ranking high schools so that they subsequently could enter high-ranking universities, and entering high school became extremely competitive for middle school students.

TABLE 3. **Middle and High School Numbers by Control**

	Number of Middle Schools			Number of High Schools		
Year	Public(A)	Private(B)	A:B	Public(A)	Private(B)	A:B
1955	578	371	61:39	334	223	60:40
1965	695	513	58:42	385	316	55:45
1970	910	698	57:43	471	418	53:47
1975	1,248	719	63:37	585	567	51:49
1979	1,313	743	64:36	645	653	50:50

Source: Hanguk Gyoyuk Samsibnyeon Pyeonchanwywonhwae, 1980, p. 115.

In 1973 the government began a high school equalization policy to solve these problems. The government, using a school group system, assigned each student who passed the entrance examination to the school group that was closest to the student's residence. This had the effect of lessening selectivity. Table 2 shows that the total number of high school students and the registration ratios increased very rapidly after this policy was begun. This expansion of secondary school enrollment, of course, transferred the pressure to colleges and universities.

From 1973 to 1978, enrollment in higher education increased by an average of 11.8% per year. The major strategy the government used to manage the increase of enrollments was manpower planning. The government focused on training middle-level technicians, and as a consequence two-year junior colleges increased more rapidly than four-year colleges and universities. For example, enrollment in two-year colleges as a percentage of total enrollment increased from 8.1% in 1962 to 29.0% in 1978.

From the mid-1970s on, there was a growing number of educational problems facing Korean society. For example, repeating and private tutoring for university and college entrance students was common. These problems came from the fact that the high schools were not as selective as they were formerly. To relieve the social pressure, the MOE announced the Comprehensive Measures of Dealing with Repeaters on July 23, 1978. The new policy was to (1) increase admission quotas annually until 1980; (2) redesign two-year colleges as four-year colleges; (3) establish new institutions of higher education for women, increase admission to the Korean Air and Correspondence College, and establish evening undergraduate programs in colleges for young workers; (4) narrow the wage gap between high school graduates and college graduates and exclude requirements for school diplomas in job interviews and tests; and (5) give greater weight to high school records in the university entrance examination and give less weight to the examination results of third-year repeaters on university examinations (Joo, 1990, p. 27). As a consequence of this policy, the number of students increased rapidly from 1978 on. Cohort enrollment ratios suddenly increased from 8.2% in 1978 to 19.2% in 1979 (see table 1). However, these policies did not solve the problems of Korean higher education.

In 1979 President Junghi Park was assassinated, and a new military government was established. This new government (the Fifth Republic: 1981–1987) attempted reforms with the hopes of solving political problems and controlling social unrest. One of these reforms was aimed at higher education. The new government policy on higher education began with the enactment of the 1980 Educational Reform Act. The key policy measures included:

1. Expanding higher education by 30% additional admissions; this additional enrollment to be balanced by an equal number graduating (Graduation Quota System);

2. Changing the system of higher education by the following:

   a. upgrading teachers colleges from two years to four years;

   b. upgrading the air and correspondence universities from two years to four years;

   c. upgrading junior technical schools to technical colleges;

3. Reforming the entrance examination system by abolishing the entrance exams given by each college and university and replacing them with a national exam, the High School Achievement Test;

4. Retaining the government's tight political control on university education. (KCUE, 1990, pp. 40–41)

One of the educational "reforms" indicated above was the Graduation Quota System. Even though the explicit purpose of this policy was to reduce the number of repeaters, to upgrade educational quality, and to help private institutions' financial difficulties (Chulan Joo, 1990), the hidden and major intention was to control student antigovernment movements. The new military government was afraid of student groups because they were perceived as antigovernment and they had overthrown corrupt dictatorships before. Policymakers focused upon controlling student protest movements rather than improving educational conditions. In 1981 the government forced all universities and colleges to double the number of newly admitted students, and forced them to dismiss students before they graduated. Almost 30% of continuing students dropped out as a result. However, the increasing numbers of newly admitted students resulted in an enrollment increase from 601,994 in 1980 to 1,277,825 in 1985, and the cohort enrollment ratio increased from 21.9 in 1980 to 37.3 in 1985 (see table 1).

The Graduation Quota System faced considerable opposition, including student resistance to the enforced dismissals.

Finally, in 1988 the policy was changed back to the original policy, the Admission Quota System. Private universities and colleges, however, continued to be under strong governmental control until this period.

In 1985 the government formed the Presidential Commission for Education Reform with the task of recommending educational policy directions and tasks for Korean Education Reform through the 21st century. This commission made its final report in 1987. The commission recommended that the private universities and colleges be given more autonomy and be encouraged to specialize, to make public their funding sources and expenditures, and open to the public their administrative and financial affairs (The Public Corporation of Teachers' Pension Management, 1991). On the basis of this report, the government of the Seventh Republic (1988–1992) made a Short- and Long-Term Plan for Education Reformulation in 1988. The plan's basic directions for higher education were excellence, autonomy, diversity, and efficiency (Ministry of Education, 1988, p. 2).

In 1987 the government acceded to the demand for democratization, and developed a scheme to carry to it out: the Six-Two-Nine Declaration. This declaration was a result, in part, of student antigovernment movements. The concept of autonomous higher education institutions was included in that declaration. In September 1987 the MOE announced the University Autonomy Plan on the basis of a proposal by the Korean Council of University Education. The key points of this plan were:

1. To grant autonomy to and require accountability from institutions;

2. To enlarge faculty participation in governance;

3. To achieve excellence in higher education by respecting the rights of faculty;

4. To provide a degree of autonomy to each institution, depending on each institution's situation; and

5. To give more autonomy and individuality to private universities and colleges.

The goals of the plan were:

- *Short term:*
  a. To reorganize the boards of trustees in the public higher education institutions.
  b. To give more self-direction to faculty.
  c. To allow the presidents of the private universities and colleges to travel without prior government approval.
  d. To simplify the degree registration system.
  e. To allow each institution to guide student activities.
  f. To allow the institutions to govern scholarly affairs.
  g. To expand financial support for students.
- *Medium term:*
  a. To provide for presidential search committees in public higher education institutions.
  b. To eliminate the right of the MOE to approve or void the appointment of presidents of private institutions.
  c. To expand the right of public universities and colleges to manage faculty.
  d. To reduce the separation between universities and colleges.
- *Long term:*
  a. To allow private universities and colleges to set tuition.
  b. To allow institutions to set student enrollments.
  c. To allow institutions to set entrance examinations. (Kim, et al., 1989, pp. 362–63)

The plan provides an insight into the level of governmental control before 1987. The new plan not only grants much more autonomy to institutions of higher education, it also puts private institutions under the same policies as are under public institutions.[4] Thus the plan to give institutions more autonomy opened a new era to private universities and colleges, although many problems still remain. Some of these problems come from the universities' lack of autonomy experience and from the absence of policies and procedures of self-governance, as well as from the knowledge that the government can take back what it gave.

Korean higher education is now in the eve of a new era. If the new Korean president (1994–98) keeps his election promises, he will open the doors of higher education to larger numbers, and the enrollment rates of Korean higher education may become among the highest in the world.

The next section analyzes the changing relationship between the Korean government and private universities and colleges. It focuses on the factors that have enabled the government to control private institutions without financial aid, the effects of government control on private universities and colleges, and the effects of recent policies encouraging more autonomy and democratization.

The Changing Relationship between the Government and the Private Universities and Colleges

Financially independent private institutions are often assumed to have a degree of autonomy, and it is generally believed that universities develop better when they are substantially free from government control. However, the Korean government has exercised strong control over private universities and colleges even without providing financial support. These private institutions developed in quantity rather than quality over the years and, under strong government control, contributed to the economic development of Korea. Historically, many factors made this possible in Korea. These factors can be summarized as follows:

1. Corruption within the government and the private institutions;
2. The military government's fear of student antigovernment movements;
3. The tremendous demand for higher education;
4. Faculty who were employed as technical intelligentsia rather than as independent intellectuals.

How these four factors collectively contributed to the relationship between the Korean government and the private institutions will be examined in the following section.

First, in 1961 General Junghi Park led a military coup which overthrew the democratic government. The new revolutionary government tried to solve several educational problems. One of the most important was the low quality and corruption of private institutions. This deterioration of private education provided the excuse for government control. Neither parents, students, nor professors opposed government intervention in private institutions; they hoped that it might have an effect on the prevalent corruption among the university founders.

Thus the regime passed a number of laws to control private institutions. In 1963 the government enacted the Private School Law, which proposed the "sound development of private institutions through guarantee of autonomy and increase of publicity" (Private School Law, Art. 1). This law regulated the establishment of private institutions and their faculties; it also gave legal authority to the founder of a private institution. The founder could be the chairman of the board of trustees, a legal governing body. One-third of the board members could be composed of relatives of the founder.

Later, the government enacted the Rule of the Number of University Students, which controlled the new student enrollment in private institutions. In 1969 the government enacted the Rule of Private Institution Financial Affairs and the Rule of Tuition and Entrance Fees. The government controlled the income and expenditures of private institutions through these rules. Gradually, government power grew until the government controlled every aspect of private institutional governance. The founders of the private institutions could not resist this growing power for several reasons. The government was too strong, and it cleverly attacked the private institutions' weak points. Many of the founders were corrupt and in no position to raise objections. Also, the government held out a crucial carrot: it guaranteed the founder's legal position.

The military government regulated private institutions in order to deal with educational problems, but in fact it was also to control the students. The government feared the university students and faculty who had dethroned the previous autocratic government in 1960. The government directly suppressed student movements, and on this position the government and the founders were in agreement. The government and the founders felt that if they did not suppress student movements, they would be threatened by students who wanted to participate in national as well as university governance. Students believed they had the right to participate in university governance because private institutions were dependent on student tuition. According to Dressel and Faricy (1972, p. 28), external probing and pressure are sometimes welcomed by top administration figures as a means of internal control. The founders of private institutions could control the university at their will within the safe house of autocratic government control. After all, the first concern of the military government was controlling student antigovernment movements. Thus student control was of paramount concern to both the private institutions and the government. It served their interests to such an extent that each could overlook the very real faults of the other.

Another reason that the government could control private universities and colleges was the ties of corruption between the government and the private institutions. In the late 1940s, many agricultural landowners founded private universities and colleges to avoid the forced sale of their land to the government for redistribution. The founders regarded these institutions of higher education as their own property and as an investment for the future. They refused to accept any outside influences because they were worried about losing their power. The corruption of the private institutions became a social issue, and the founders were criticized as immoral. This gave the government the excuse to control private institutions.

When the government started to control governance issues (such as resource allocation, appointment of university presidents, the number of new admissions, and tuition), the founders tried to negotiate with the government. The founders submitted to government orders and helped the military government directly and indirectly. In turn, the government gave legal authority to the founders and prohibited faculty and students from membership on the board of trustees (Private School Law). This allowed the founders to control their institutions without strong resistance internally or from the government. Although the private universities and colleges were strictly regulated by the government, the founders could exert substantial power internally. It was well known in Korea that the government did not punish the founders who helped the government, even though institutional budgets were used illegally. If a founder did not help the government and resisted, the government imposed special supervision, including revealing the university's budget management to the public.

Some university founders became congressmen on the basis of their university position and resources. They also were the congressmen who were influential in changing the Private School Law to favor the interests of founders; this was done under the name of private school autonomy in March 1990 (Shin, 1990, p. 75). They increased the limitation on putting relatives of the founders on the board of trustees from one-third to two-fifths. They took away the university president's power to appoint and to dismiss the faculty and administrators, and gave it to the founders (Private School Law). The Ministry of Education rationalized this amendment by saying that the strict control over private institution founders decreased their investment in the school (Shin, 1990, p. 77). Though the government promised more autonomy to private institutions, it gave up no regulating authority. On the contrary, the government continued its control over universities and colleges by strengthening the founders' power.

The third factor that made government control over private institutions possible was the tremendous demand for higher education in Korea. For forty-five years after independence from Japan, private universities and colleges had no worry about losing enrollment. The founders managed their institutions cheaply and provided cheap education. They hired cheap part-time instructors instead of expensive full-time professors. Even without government funds, private universities and colleges grew and prospered.

Korean professors worked not as intellectuals but as technocrats. According to Henry Giroux (1985, pp. 29–30), while technocrats are manipulable and adjustable, intellectuals are critical, are creative, and have the courage to fight for their beliefs. In Korean private universities, faculty could not protest the lack of academic freedom. Before 1976, every faculty member had tenure. Once they were appointed as full-time faculty members, they retained their jobs until they reached retirement age. This "all-faculty tenure system" developed from conditions unique to Korea.[5]

In the 1970s, the autocratic government was strongly threatened by students and the faculty. So, the government formulated the "faculty reappointment system" to control every faculty member in 1975. In July 23, 1975, the Korean government changed the Education Law, the Educational Public Officer Law, and the Private School Law to incorporate the faculty reappointment system. A policy establishing a "faculty reappointment evaluation committee" was adopted on September 15, 1975. According to the Educational Public Officer Law, full-time lecturers and assistant professors would be reappointed every two or three years, and associate professors and professors every six to ten years. Suddenly all faculty lost their tenure. The same rule applied to the private institutions.[6] In the reappointment of 1976, 212 persons among 4,260 faculty of national institutions and 104 persons among 5,511 faculty of private institutions were not reappointed (The Korean Federation of Education Association, 1977–78, p. 117).

In order to survive, faculty had to compromise with the government. If they did not criticize the autocratic government, they could have their job until retirement. Their academic laissez-faire was the product of compromise with the autocratic government. Thus, faculty also became an instrument for government control of private institutions.

Only the student groups protested continuously for democratization of government and higher education. However, the main issue of student demonstrations was not so much democratizing university governance as it was throwing out the autocratic military government. But antigovernment demonstrations brought about stronger governmental intervention in the university. Though students paid almost all of the university costs, they were alienated from university governance by three groups which negotiated for power: the government, the founders, and the faculty. After 1988 the focus of student movement changed from political issues to university governance issues. They wanted to participate in university governance and in university presidential elections. However, the government suspected that the change of issues was a tactic to strengthen the student antigovernment movement. Therefore, the government prohibited student participation in presidential elections and other governance matters and allowed only the faculty to elect the president.[7] Because the government and the private founders were afraid of student power, they gave some privileges to the faculty, who appeared to be more easily regulated than students.

Effects of Educational Policy on Private Universities and Colleges

Government policy toward private institutions affected their development as well as the development of the nation. Many small institutions grew quantitatively, but without student participation in governance. The government encouraged citizens to build institutions of higher education, and as a result, more than 75% of Korean students are educated in private universities and colleges. Thus Korea has a higher enrollment level in higher education than have other developing countries. The founders of the private institutions managed their institutions very economically. Without the devotion of the founders, private universities and colleges could not have prospered and grown as they have today and Korea would not have had the human capital needed for economic development.

Government control also affected the development of Korean private universities in a negative fashion. First, the founders of the private institutions regarded universities and colleges as their own private property and managed them like private companies under government control. The founders appointed presidents of the universities and colleges, or they themselves became presidents. The founders packed their boards with relatives and friends. The boards had nominal power and the founders had real power. The founders negotiated with the government to continue their power. Though the boards of trustees were legally responsible for the governance of the private institutions, they became a hindrance to university autonomy. The struggles between the founders (who controlled the boards of trustees) and university members (the faculty and students) continue to this day, and these struggles deprive the institutions of the authority, leadership, and support for substantial qualitative development. The founders concentrated on producing numbers instead of quality. In most Korean private universities, the student-to-faculty ratio is more than 40 to 1.

Since the autonomy law of 1987, changes have been coming, and may come faster when the new president takes office. The changes will concern, among other things, the relationship between the government and private institutions in terms of governance, finance, presidential elections, and faculty employment conditions.

First, the private institutions have begun to exert their independence of the government. One public officer's complaint is that even simple data to make a statistical yearbook are difficult to obtain from private schools. This is a sign of the changing relationship; before 1987, no school dared to refuse to submit what the MOE demanded. Also, private universities and colleges have joined the Korean Council of University Education (KCUE) to lobby for more autonomy and financial support from the government.

Second, university governance is becoming more democratic than before. The founders and boards of trustees are now sharing some power with faculty representatives, although owners and faculty members still exclude students from power, with the help of the Korean government. The government strongly prohibits the participation of students in the governance of higher education except in some areas of student affairs. This is becoming one of the issues of the student movement.

Third, the revenue gap between the elite and low quality private universities and colleges has grown since 1987. The elite private universities have been receiving more resources from private industry and the government than have the low quality private institutions. The market mechanism, which Trow (1989, p. 619) calls one of the most important characteristics of

American private higher education, may start to work in Korean higher education. Before 1987, private universities and colleges were regulated and protected as a whole by a single policy of the government. There is now a possibility that the tuition charges can differ among institutions; even though tuition differences among schools are not large, they are becoming larger than before (Lee et al., 1989).

Fourth, elections have become widespread for the selection of presidents of universities and colleges (Joo et al., 1988). Only faculty members have the right to vote for the candidate, who usually comes from among their colleagues. Many attempts by students to participate in the presidential elections of their institutions have been undercut by the Korean government, founders, and faculty members. Through voting, faculty can elect a president who will work for them, not for the founders or the government.

Fifth, there is a struggle for power in hiring new faculty members. In the national universities and colleges, the department-level faculty committee has actual power, but in the case of private schools, the founders (or boards of trustees) fight for the actual power to hire new faculty members.

Government control hindered the development of independent, high-quality private universities and, thus, the diversity of the higher education system. Although there are some private universities (like Younsei and Seogang) that do not have proprietors, government control caused almost every institution to maintain the same mediocre level of quality. Though almost 80% of the universities and colleges in Korea are private institutions, most of them do not contribute to the system's diversity.[8] If the government had not maintained the same strict control on all private institutions, some could have developed into excellent private universities as in the United States. Though the Korean economy developed and some Korean private enterprises are among the largest in the world, Korea does not have a university that is included among the 100 finest universities of the world. Korean universities still depend on foreign countries to educate their faculty members and researchers.

Present policies on autonomy and democracy in higher education open a new era to private universities and colleges. It is too early to tell what the positive and negative effects will be. Universities and colleges keep changing their own policies, and their constituencies are competing for power. It seems that Korean higher education needs more time to develop a stable system. The shape of this system is dependent on political and economic conditions. The result of the new presidential policies will be an important factor affecting the shape of Korean higher education.

NOTES

Table 1: Nineteen forty-five data are from *Hanguk Gyoyuk Jungchek Yungu* (Korean educational policy study, p. 185) by J. Kim, 1987, Seoul: Gyoyuk Gwahack Sa; 1947–1959, 1961–1963 data are from *Hanguk Godunggyoyuck Youngu* (Study of Korean higher education, pp. 70, 77) by J. Kim, 1979, Seoul: Baeyoung Sa; 1960, 1964 numbers of students and private ratio data are from *Hanguk Gyoyuck Baljungwa Sahak* (Korean education development and private schools, pp. 380, 400) by Salibhakgyo Gyowon Yungum Gwanli Gongdan (ed.), 1992, Seoul: Salibhakgyo Gyowon Yungum Gwanli Gongdan; 1960 cohort ratio datum is from *An analytic study on the social dynamics determining higher education enrollment quota* (p. 83) by Hyeyoung Lee, 1992, unpublished doctoral dissertation, Seoul: Seoul National University; 1965–1992 numbers of students and private school ratio data are from Mungyo Tonggye Yunbo (*Statistical yearbook of education*) by Ministry of Education, 1965–1992, Seoul: MOE; 1965–1988 cohort data are from *Statistical indicators of Korean higher education* (p. 30) by Korean Council for University Education, 1989, Seoul: KCUE; 1991, 1992 cohort data are calculated from cohort data (Ministry of National Statistics) and admission quota data (Ministry of Education).

1. The Ratio of Korean Students of the Kyungsung Jaguk Dahak

Year	Total Students(A)	Korean Students(B)	B/A (%)
1925	324	91	28.1
1927	623	193	31.0
1932	903	300	33.2
1937	876	291	33.2

Source: Reconstructed from Kim et al., 1989, p. 147.

2. This radical reformation of the secondary school system was possible under a strong autocratic government. Students and parents couldn't protest even when students were assigned by the lottery system to mission schools established by religions different from their own.

3. The middle school students registration ratio of cohorts—1966: 42%, 1970: 56%, 1976: 76%, 1981:94%.

4. And usually the public school system became the model for the private school system in Korea.

5. The first condition was the rapid expansion of higher education and the shortage of faculty. In 1945 Korea was emancipated from Japan. The demand for higher education increased dramatically, and many institutions were founded within a short period of time. However, because very few Koreans received higher education under Japanese control, faculty was now in short supply. Because of this situation, Korean universities and colleges could not use the probationary employment system, and this became a tradition. Second, the probationary employment system is rare in Korea. Elementary and secondary teachers have tenure when they are appointed as new teachers, and there is no probationary period. Though the groundwork of the Korean higher education system was built under the American military administration, Korea could not adopt America's faculty tenure system (Park, 1991).

6. The Rule for Faculty Reappointment Evaluation Committee states that each university and college may include no more than 14 associate professors and full professors on this committee. The committee members are appointed by the minister of education. The president of the institution becomes the chairman of the committee. The evaluation criteria are: (1) research and a special field study activity in ten years, (2) teaching and student guidance, and (3) observance of laws

and keeping dignity as faculty. The Korean government ordered every university and college to reappoint their faculty.

7. In 1990, in the case of Seoul City University, the faculty and governing body agreed that a student representative could be a presidential election committee member and elected a president. But the Korean government refused to appoint such a person as president because of student participation. And in 1990 Seojong University suffered very much because of the government's rejection of student participation on the presidential election committee.

8. In 1990, because the Korean government couldn't find an able translator, the government had a hard time when the Korean president and the Soviet president had a meeting in the Soviet Union. Without diversity, a society cannot adapt to rapid change.

REFERENCES

Berdahl, R. O. (1971). *Statewide coordination of higher education.* Washington, DC: American Council on Education.

Dressel, P. L. & Faricy, W. H. (1972). *Return to responsibility.* San Francisco: Jossey-Bass.

Giroux, H. A. (1985). Intellectual labor and pedagogical work: Rethinking the role of teacher as intellectual. *Phenomenology and Pedagogy, 3(1)*, pp. 20–32.

Goldschmidt, D. (1984). The university as an institution: present problems and future trends. *Higher Education in Europe, IX(4).*

Hanguk G. S. P. W. (1980). *Hanguk Gyoyuk Samsibnyeon* [Korean education for thirty years]. Seoul: Ministry of Education.

Joo, C. (1990). *The politics of implementing educational reform: A graduation quota system in Korean higher educational institutions.* Unpublished doctoral dissertation. Cambridge, MA: Harvard University.

Joo, S. et al. (1988). *Daehakaeseoui uisagyuljung hablihwa bangan yungu* [A plan for rational decision making in universities and colleges]. Seoul: Korean Council for University Education.

Kim, J. (1979). *Hanguk Godunggyoyuck Youngu* [Study of Korean higher education]. Seoul: Baeyoung Sa.

————. (1987). *Hanguk Gyoyuk Jungchek Yungu* [Korean educational policy study]. Seoul: Gyoyuk Gwahack Sa.

Kim, J. et al. (1989). *Hanguk Kodunggyoyucku Yuksajuck Byunchunae kwanhan Yungu* [The history of Korean higher education]. Seoul: KCUE.

Korean Council for University Education. (1989). *Statistical indicators of Korean higher education*. Seoul: KCUE.

————. (1990). *Korean higher education: Its development, aspects and prospects*. Seoul: KCUE.

Korean Federation of Education Association. (1977–78). *Hanguk Gyoyuk Yungam* [Korean education yearbook]. Seoul: KFEA.

Lee, C. et al. (1989). *Daehakui jayulgwa Dunglokgum chakjunggwajungae gwanhan Yungu* [University autonomy and tuition adjustments process]. Seoul: Korean Council for University Education.

————. (1990). *Hanguk Daehaku SungJang Yuhyunggwa Hakgwa Bunhwaae Gwanhan Yungu* [The research on Korean universities and college development and their differentiation of departments]. Seoul: KCUE.

Lee, G. (1989). Dahak gyosuui uisik gujo [Consciousness structure of university faculty]. *Daehak Gyoyuck* [Higher education], *41*, pp. 8–15.

Lee, H. (1990). Daehak seolibjaedo, gui tongjaewa jiwon [University founding system, its control and support]. *Daehak Gyoyuck* [Higher education], *45*, pp. 24–30.

————. (1992). *An Analytic study of the social dynamics determining higher education enrollment quota*. Unpublished doctoral dissertation. Seoul: Seoul National University.

Ministry of Education. (1965–1992). *Mungyo Tonggye Yunbo* [Statistical yearbook of education]. Seoul: MOE.

————. (1988). *Gyoyuck gaehyuckan jangdangi chugin gaehwek* [The short- and long-term plan for reformulation of education]. Seoul: MOE (unpublished).

Moos, M. & Rourke, F. (1959). *The campus and the state*. Baltimore: Johns Hopkins Press.

Park, N. (July 1989). *Higher education trends in governance and decision making*. Paper presented at the Sixth International Meeting of University Administrators, University of Maryland.

————. (1991). A study of the Korean faculty employment, promotion, and tenure system. *Korean Higher Education, 3(1)*, pp. 293–336.

Paterson, V. D. (1986). Government intervention and university autonomy in Guyana and Tanzania—A third world perspective. In Conference on Higher Education, *Governments and higher education—the legitimacy of intervention*. Toronto: Conference on Higher Education.

Polin, R. (1983). Freedom of the mind and university autonomy. In J. W. Chapman, *The western university on trial*. Berkeley, CA: University of California Press.

Public Corporation of Teachers' Pension Management. (1991). *Hangukui gyoyuk baljungwa sahak* (Korean education development and private schools). Seoul: PCTPM.

Salibhakgyo G. Y. G. G. (Ed.) (1992). *Hanguk Gyoyuck Baljungwa Sahak* [Korean education development and private schools]. Seoul: Salibhakgyo Gyowon Yungum Gwanli Gongdan.

Shin, H. (1990). What is the problem of new private school law? *Daehak Gyoyuck* [Higher education], *45*, pp. 75–80.

Song, B. (1990). The meaning of university founding in the light of Korean university development history. *Daehak Gyoyuck* [Higher education], *45*, pp. 75–80.

Trow, M. (1989). American higher education: Past, present, and future. In L. F. Goodchild & H. S. Wechsler (Eds.), *ASHE reader on the history of higher education* (pp. 616–26). Boston: Ginn Press.

UNESCO. (1990). *Statistical Year Book*. Paris: UNESCO.

CHAPTER V

State Legislatures and Public Universities
Changing Relationships in the U.S.

Paula L.W. Sabloff

Introduction

It is difficult to generalize about reform in higher education in the U.S. because it takes place at different levels—state and federal—and at different times in each state. However, certain trends for "reform" can be seen. This chapter will show that higher education reform in the U.S. is partly the result of changes in state legislatures. Increased regulation appears to be related more to changes in political pressure on legislators than to the actions or needs of the institutions. Whereas other chapters in this volume focus on the effects of reform legislation on higher education institutions, the emphasis in this chapter is on the process of political reform itself. By focusing on the process and implications of political change, this chapter complements the historical analyses of the other chapters, for changes in the U.S. parallel changes in other industrialized nations.

Higher education institutions in the U.S. operate on a continuum from public to private classification. If they are public, they derive their authority from the state government, for states—rather than the federal government—charter each institution. Public institutions often have state-appointed members sitting on their boards of trustees, and the general education mission of the institution is largely funded with state support. In most states, the faculty, staff, and administrators are state employees or civil servants. And in some states, the government sets the tuition rates.

If the institutions are private, they are not controlled by the state, but they must follow minimal state regulation; they have boards of trustees independent of the state; and their education component is largely funded through private means—tuition, endowments, investments, etc. Still, their actions are regulated by the state; that is, the laws passed affecting teaching, research, and administrative functions usually apply to the private as well as the public universities. These laws concern such issues as student assessment, publication of crime statistics and institutional budgets, use and treatment of animals in research and teaching, English language fluency of instructors, etc.

Within each category (private or public), institutions range from postsecondary vocational training centers to junior or community colleges that grant two-year degrees (associate degrees), colleges that grant four-year baccalaureate degrees, and universities that grant two-year and four-year degrees as well as graduate and professional degrees. This chapter will be limited to the public four-year baccalaureate colleges and universities. The term *university* will be used to refer to both colleges and universities.

Public universities have been described as being in partnership with state governments to accomplish mutual goals (Hines, 1988, pp. 103–4, 112–14). However, when the relationship between the two is focused on the allocation of resources and the regulation of institutional activities, the relationship fits the patron-client model better than the partnership ideal. The patron-client relationship has been defined as an asymmetrical relationship based on mutual support (Wolf, 1966, pp. 16–17). In the political system examined here, state legislatures are the patrons, for they are key players in allocating resources and setting policies that affect the public institutions. The public universities are the clients that receive from one-quarter to over half of their revenues from their resident state. Furthermore, legislative policies regulate the institutions' teaching, research, and administrative activities.

The patron-client relationship is not a new concept in U.S. politics. Studies of Tammany Hall in the 19th and 20th centuries reveal patterns of political bossism similar to those found in Latin America and elsewhere (Moscow, 1971; Riordan, 1963). Consequently, it is not unlikely that the pattern exists in American politics today. This chapter will show that just as public universities are clients to legislative patrons, so, too, are legislators clients to other patrons. In fact, the chapter hypothesizes that the shift in patronage for legislative clients (from political party organizations to special interest groups, legislative leaders, and constituents) may cause a concomitant shift in legislators' attitudes and actions when they act as patrons to their public university clients.

State-Level Politics Are Changing

The literature from higher education and political science indicates that the U.S. political system has been transformed over the last 20 to 30 years. New and revised laws, which sought to make the election of officials more democratic, inadvertently altered the players and the patronage system at every level of government, from the president to the town mayor. The changes affecting state legislatures' decision process may be grouped under three headings:

1. *Professionalization of State Legislatures*
   - Over the last 30 years, one-fifth of state legislatures evolved from part-time to full-time sessions (8–12 months). As a result, the legislative membership changed from part-time citizens who often treated their state service as a secondary job to full-time professionals. Now reelection meant job security rather than pride in continued service to the state (Rosenthal, 1989, p. 71). Therefore, legislators became even more anxious than their predecessors to please their constituents (ibid., pp. 70–78, 82–83, 92, 96).

- The level of education of state legislators rose so that to-day most are college-educated and some hold advanced degrees. Because they have been taught to think for themselves, they are less willing to follow the party line than were their predecessors. They want to understand the issues behind every bill before they vote for or against it. Therefore, their legislative leaders (speaker of the House, president pro tem of the Senate, the majority and minority leaders of both chambers, the whips, etc.) work with them differently than past leaders worked with their party caucus members (i.e., legislators in the same political party).

- State legislatures have formalized and streamlined the rules governing the process of a bill's passage (Rosenthal, 1981, p. 3). Senators and representatives have a greater ability to trace and influence a bill; they also have reduced the time to alter a bill between its intro-duction and final action. Thus their work has gained in stature and increased in pressure.

- State legislatures have increased the professional staffs who support the work of the members. As of 1988, it was estimated that nearly 20,000 people worked full-time for state legislatures, an increase of over 200% since the mid-1960s (Van Horn, 1989, p. 4). The principal growth has been in partisan staffing, which can supply the legisla-tors with information and studies as they request them.

   One consequence of the expansion of professional staff is that legislators are less likely to depend on infor-mation from people they do not trust (such as the gover-nor's office) or on hearsay than they have in the past. Staff support is another reason why legislators have been freed from control by their party organization, their governor, and their legislative leadership.

2. *Changes in the Political Process*

- Political party affiliation no longer guarantees the reelec-tion of a legislator (Salmore & Salmore, 1989, p. 189). Bibby et al. (1990, p. 100) write that the increased nomination of candidates by primary elections, or within-party elections, in this century

> has undercut the influence and control of political parties over nominations. With nominations ultimately in the hands of the voters, party organizations cannot unilaterally designate party nominees. Therefore, candidates have an incentive to set up personal campaign organizations to contest the primaries.

- The political party apparatus (i.e., the local and state party organization) no longer acts as patron to the legislators by providing necessary campaign funds and votes. State political parties' budgets have actually decreased over the past decades, once inflation is taken into account. The party with the weakest state organization and least financial support—the Democratic party—has elected more legislators than the Republican party. Thus there seems to be no correlation between party strength and ability to elect officials (Salmore & Salmore, 1989, p. 195).[1]

Political party organizations have altered their relationship to the candidates. In the 1980s the two parties added full-time staff to their offices and improved their services to candidates, namely, fund-raising assistance, polling, media consulting, and campaign seminars (Conlan, Martino, & Dilger, 1984, p. 7). But instead of *raising* the funds and getting out the votes for the candidates, the parties are now acting as consultants to and support for the candidates, who have to do the work themselves (Bibby et al., 1990, p. 105).

As a result of these changes in the role of the political party organization, the legislators' party ties, while extant, are not as strong as they once were. And legislators do not consistently vote the party line. Instead, legislators are turning to their legislative party caucus for help rather than the traditional political party organization (Salmore & Salmore, 1989, p. 195). To help fill the void created by the weakening of the political parties, legislative leaders are helping their party members get reelected.

- Legislative leaders have become patrons to legislators, providing campaign funds received from political action committees (PACs) and individuals and distributing key committee positions that give the legislators the visibility necessary to get reelected (Salmore & Salmore, 1989, p. 189). Hence, legislators became more beholden to their legislative leaders and their party caucus than to the party organization. Rosenthal (1989, p. 88) adds:

> The primary focus of the . . . legislative party lead-
> ership used to be governing. Now, they are dis-
> placing party organizations at state and local levels,
> taking over the electoral function as well. Thus, a
> major shift in political power is occurring, at least in
> a number of states.

Indeed, as of 1989, the legislative leaders raise and distribute funds in about half of the states (ibid.), and a
large percent of these funds are obtained from PAC
payments to legislators (Sorauf, 1988, pp. 267–68). Party
funding of campaigns "runs a poor third to individual
contributions and PAC expenditures" (Patterson, 1989,
p. 162).

Legislative leaders also provide professional and
nonprofessional staff to aid incumbents' reelection
(Bibby et al., 1990, p. 108). In short, legislators are pulled
into their party because of their dependence on the
goodwill and monetary support of their political caucus's legislative leaders. Thus, legislators' loyalty is to
their leadership, not to the political party organization.

- Legislators have entered into a symbiotic relationship with their constituents, exchanging services for votes. Because legislators are ultimately dependent on their constituents for tenure, they introduce bills that will benefit their districts and seek to get more than their fair share for their districts from state funds (Rosenthal, 1989, p. 95). They perform local services for their constituents, helping them navigate the vicissitudes of government agencies to get jobs, licenses, tax help, etc. Furthermore, they introduce bills suggested by their constituents in order to curry favor. Because legislators appeal directly to the voters, they are not as dependent on party support as they once were and therefore vote to please their constituents rather than their party.

- Legislators are becoming increasingly dependent on the support of PACs,[2] special interest groups (SIGs),[3] and temporary alliances between unrelated interest groups (ibid., p. 97). Republican legislators also receive considerable help from the national party coffers; Democrats receive a smaller amount from the national committee (Patterson, 1989, p. 163).

  The PACs primarily target incumbents, especially legislative leaders. But they also funnel campaign funds through the political parties (Bibby et al., 1990, p. 113). New legislators found that by serving on the right committees, they could attract PAC contributions. They also learned that more campaign funds could be obtained from SIGs by taking judicious stands on certain issues (Salmore & Salmore, 1989, p. 190).

  While legislators may not have started their term of office by wooing PACs and SIGs, their consistent support of these organizations' positions helps assure their reelection. Thus, many legislators maneuver themselves into position to gain PAC support.

- The governors have increasingly taken a leadership role in setting higher education policy, mainly by setting the agenda for action through the budget they send to the legislature (Van Horn, 1989a, p. 3). In 48 of the 50 states, the governors submit an executive budget to the legislature. Such budgets reflect planning and policy decisions as well as financial control of programs (Beyle, 1989, p. 37). Thus, legislators are often forced into the reactive rather than the proactive mode in policy formulation. Still, they strive for professional equality with their governor. Rosenthal (1989, p. 70) writes:

> The new generations of post-reapportionment legis-
> lators were not willing to settle for subordinate sta-
> tus. They believed that their branch [of govern-
> ment] should be independent of the executive, and
> they strove for coequality. . . . Legislators began to
> play a larger role in deciding on policy, allocating
> funds through the budget, and even controlling
> administration.

3. Changes in the Role of the States

- Reagan's New Federalism, whereby the federal government gave block grants to the states which then appor-
  tioned them to the various local units, increased the importance of the states at the levels of policy formulation
  and program planning. Thus, legislative positions became more attractive and legislative leaders more powerful in setting and implementing their party's policy
  (Nathan, 1989, pp. 25–26).

- The 1962 U.S. Supreme Court decision in *Baker v. Carr*
  enforced the concept of one-person, one-vote in state
  politics, thereby reducing the power of the rural sector
  and increasing general public support for strengthened
  state government (ibid., p. 18). Furthermore, support
  from a legislator's constituents gained prominence in
  his/her mind, for only the right number of votes could
  maintain the legislator's tenure.

The changes in the political process are summarized in
figure 1. In the past, the political party organization was the major influence on legislators' voting patterns, and interest groups
(e.g., public colleges and universities, labor unions, and local
constituents) could sway legislative decisions. The political party
organization acted as patron to the legislators, their leaders, and
their constituents. Today, the legislative voting pattern in many
states is influenced by several factors. PACs, SIGs, and political
party organizations are three factors. But legislators' major tension occurs between pleasing their constituents and pleasing
their legislative leaders, who control access to PAC and SIG
funding on the one hand and committee appointments on the
other. In short, today many state legislators act as clients to their

FIGURE 1. The Changing Patronage System in State Legislatures

Old System (Pre-1970):

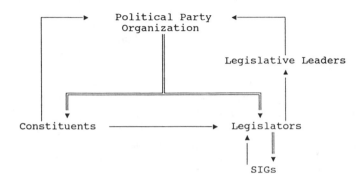

New System (Late 1980s-1990s):

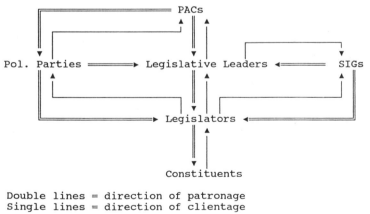

Double lines = direction of patronage
Single lines = direction of clientage

legislative leaders and patrons to their constituents while the political party organization acts as support for rather than patron to
the legislators.

Political Changes Affect the Regulation
of Public Universities

It is clear that the state legislatures have undergone significant change since the late 1960s. But are the present political processes and characteristics of state legislatures factors that affect
the passage of bills regulating public universities? To help determine whether or not the new legislative characteristics may be
related to legislative decisions, two different data bases have
been built. The first is a statistical analysis of all 50 states, a comparison of the number of laws passed by each state that restrict
university autonomy with characteristics of legislatures that reflect changes in the political process and some other traditional
indicators used by political scientists. This data base shows some
correlation between political trends and legislative regulation of
colleges and universities.

The second data base shows the considerable influence of
political changes on legislative decisions. This data base is a case
study of Pennsylvania, a state whose legislature has adopted the
federal political process and has passed a high number of laws
affecting universities, according to the first data base. It includes
interviews with state legislators, which reveal their concern
about recent political changes, and a comparison of the number
and type of bills passed in the 1969–70 legislative session with
those passed in the 1989–90 session, which shows that the more
recent Pennsylvania legislature passed more restrictive bills that
were signed into law than the earlier legislature.

The 50 States: Differences
in the Regulation of Higher Education

A statistical comparison of a number of laws regulating
universities with certain characteristics of the state legislatures

was made for the 50 states. The laws were marked passed or not passed (1, 0) for each state, and the sum of laws passed that restrict university autonomy—either in the research, teaching, or administrative function—was determined. The criteria for determining restriction of autonomy were based on a classic definition of the term: Universities maintain autonomy when they are free to make their own decisions regarding: (*a*) selection of their own staff; (*b*) selection of students; (*c*) development of curriculum for each degree awarded; (*d*) development of research programs; and (*e*) responsibility for the allocation of resources among the various units of the institutions where resources include space and equipment, capital funds, and recurrent operating revenues (James, 1965, p. viii).

The issues, or possible laws that restrict autonomy, are as follows (see table 1):[4]

1. The state requires that higher education institutions issue reports on the incidence of crime on their campuses (Chronicle of Higher Education Editors, 1991, pp. 20–21). This administrative chore is usually not supported by state funding; furthermore, it is designed to help students choose a school.

2. The state limits or taxes the business activities of universities (ibid.). This restricts the decisions of the university administration.

3. The state offers plans that allow parents to purchase prepaid tuition plans; i.e., they allow parents to pay a set sum of money, years in advance, for their children's education (ibid.). While this may help the parents, it limits the future income of the institutions.

4. The state requires that all faculty and teaching assistants be certified as competent to teach in the English language (ibid.). This law interferes with the universities' responsibility to hire and retain faculty and teaching assistants.

5. The state requires public universities to set up programs to assess what students learn (ibid.). This law imposes outside standards and means of assessment on the institutions.

6. The state requires prospective secondary-school teachers to major in a subject other than education (ibid.). This sets the curriculum for a university program.

7. The state restricts the use of animals for teaching purposes (National Association for Biomedical Research, 1991, pp. 6–7). This law affects teaching methods used in the universities.

8. The state does not grant exemption from the animal cruelty statutes to institutions that are using the animals for research purposes (ibid.). This law affects research.

9. The state governs the licensing and regulation of research facilities that use animals (ibid.). This law also regulates research.

TABLE 1. Higher Education Issues Voted by State

State	Issue 1 Camp/ Crime	Issue 2 Busns Actvs	Issue 3 Prepd Tuitn	Issue 4 Engl Comp	Issue 5 Stdnt Assmt	Issue 6 H.S. Tchrs	Issue 7 Anml Educ	Issue 8 Anml Crlty	Issue 9 Regltn Resrch	Total
AL	0	0	1	0	1	0	0	1	0	3
AK	0	0	1	0	0	0	0	0	0	1
AZ	0	1	0	1	0	0	0	1	0	3
AR	0	0	0	0	1	1	0	1	0	3
CA	1	0	0	0	0	1	1	0	1	4
CO	0	1	0	0	1	1	0	0	1	4
CT	1	0	0	0	1	1	0	1	1	5
DE	1	0	0	0	0	1	0	0	0	2
FL	1	0	1	1	1	1	1	0	0	6
GA	1	0	1	0	1	0	0	0	0	3
HI	0	0	0	0	0	1	0	0	0	1
ID	0	1	0	1	1	0	0	0	0	3
IL	0	1	0	1	0	0	0	1	1	4
IN	0	0	0	0	0	0	0	1	0	1
IA	0	1	1	1	1	0	0	1	1	6
KS	0	1	0	1	0	0	0	0	0	2
KY	0	0	0	0	0	1	0	1	0	2
LA	1	1	0	1	0	0	0	0	0	3

State	Issue 1 Camp/ Crime	Issue 2 Busns Actvs	Issue 3 Prepd Tuitn	Issue 4 Engl Comp	Issue 5 Stdnt Assmt	Issue 6 H.S. Tchrs	Issue 7 Anml Educ	Issue 8 Anml Crlty	Issue 9 Regltn Resrch	Total
ME	0	0	0	0	0	0	1	0	1	2
MD	0	0	0	0	1	0	0	0	0	1
MA	0	0	1	0	0	1	0	1	1	4
MI	0	0	1	0	0	1	0	1	1	4
MN	0	0	0	0	0	1	0	1	1	3
MS	0	0	0	0	0	0	0	1	0	1
MO	0	1	0	1	0	1	0	0	0	3
MT	0	0	0	0	0	0	0	1	0	1
NE	0	0	0	0	0	0	0	0	0	0
NV	0	0	0	0	1	1	0	0	0	2
NH	0	0	0	0	0	1	0	1	0	2
NJ	1	0	0	0	1	1	0	0	1	4
NM	0	0	0	0	0	0	0	1	0	1
NY	0	0	0	0	0	1	0	0	1	2
NC	1	0	0	0	0	1	0	0	1	3
ND	0	0	0	1	0	1	0	1	0	3
OH	0	0	1	1	0	0	0	1	1	4
OK	0	0	1	1	0	1	0	1	1	5
OR	0	0	0	0	0	0	0	1	0	1
PA	1	0	0	1	0	1	0	1	1	5
RI	0	0	0	0	0	1	0	1	1	3
SC	0	0	0	1	1	0	0	1	0	3
SD	0	1	0	0	1	0	0	0	1	3
TN	1	0	0	1	1	1	0	0	1	5
TX	0	0	0	1	1	1	0	0	0	3
UT	0	1	0	0	0	1	0	0	1	3
VT	0	0	0	0	0	0	0	0	0	0
VA	1	0	0	0	1	1	0	0	1	4
WA	0	0	0	0	1	1	0	0	0	2
WV	0	0	1	0	1	0	0	1	0	3
WI	0	0	0	1	1	1	0	0	0	3
WY	0	0	1	0	0	0	0	1	0	2

(*continued*)

Issue 1: Reports of Incidence of Campus Crime. These states require col-
          leges/universities to issue reports on the incidence of crime on their
          campuses.
Issue 2: Restrictions or Taxes on Business Activities. These states limit or tax
          the business activities of universities.
Issue 3: Pre-paid Tuition Plans. These states offer plans that allow parents to
          pay a set sum of money, years in advance, for their children's
          education.
Issue 4: Certification of Competence in English Language for Teaching Assis-
          tants. These states require public universities to certify that their
          teaching assistants are competent in English.
Issue 5: Requirements to Assess What Students Learn. These states require
          public universities to set up programs to assess what students learn.
Issue 6: Non-education Majors for High School Teachers. These states require
          prospective secondary-school teachers to major in a subject other than
          education.
Issue 7: Use of animals for education is restricted.
Issue 8: An exemption from the animal cruelty statutes is not granted if the
          animals are to be used for research. [Data are presented in reverse or-
          der from the original.]
Issue 9: State laws govern the licensing and regulation of research facilities that
          use animals.
Total: Sum of issues (absolute numbers).

These, then, are nine possible laws that any of the states
could have enacted by the summer of 1991. Each one impacts on
the teaching, research, or administrative autonomy of the universities in some way. The number of laws passed per state was
summed (see table 1 totals), and the range of the summed scores
varied from 0 (Nebraska and Vermont) to 6 (Florida and Iowa).
These sums were then compared with "indicators," or ranges of
behavior and demographic characteristics of state legislatures
that had been tallied by state in published research. The
indicators selected are those listed as reflecting changes in the
legislatures (as mentioned in the beginning of this chapter) or are
traditional indicators used to explain trends in the political
science literature (see table 2). Of course, the choice of indicators
was limited to the ones that have data bases in the political
science literature.

  1. Overall impact of interest groups, ranging from "interest
     groups are dominant" to "interest groups are subordi-
     nate" (Thomas & Hrebenar, 1990, p. 147).

2. Relative strength of the Democratic party, ranging from "a strong state and local party organization" to a "weak state and local party organization" (Cotter, Gibson et al., cited in Patterson, 1989, p. 161).

3. Relative strength of the Republican party, with the same ordinal scale as #2 (ibid.).

4. Authority of the state boards of higher education. Here, the indicators include a consolidated governing board or a coordinating board (Wirt & Gove, 1990, p. 472).[5]

5. Average number of months the legislature was in session for 1991 and 1992 (the average of the two years was used, as many states have two-year sessions; *State Legislatures*, 1991, p. 2 and 1992, p. 2).

TABLE 2. **State Legislative Indicators**

State	Total Issues	Ind. 1 Impact SIG/PAC	Ind. 2 Dem Prty Strength	Ind. 3 Rep Prty Strength	Ind. 4 State Boards	Ind. 5 Legis Session
AL	3	4	NA	3	3	3
AK	1	4	2	NA	2	4
AZ	3	3	1	4	4	3
AR	3	3	1	NA	3	1
CA	4	3	4	4	3	8.5
CO	4	2	1	3	3	4
CT	5	1	2	4	3	4
DE	2	1	2	NA	1	5
FL	6	4	4	3	2	2.5
GA	3	3	3	3	4	2
HI	1	3	NA	2	4	3
ID	3	3	2	1	4	2.5
IL	4	2	2	4	3	12
IN	1	2	2	4	3	2
IA	6	2	1	4	4	3
KS	2	2	1	3	4	3
KY	2	3	3	1	3	2
LA	3	4	1	1	3	3

(*continued*)

TABLE 2. *(continued)*

State	Total Issues	Ind. 1 Impact SIG/PAC	Ind. 2 Dem Prty Strength	Ind. 3 Rep Prty Strength	Ind. 4 State Boards	Ind. 5 Legis Session
ME	2	2	2	4	4	4.5
MD	1	2	2	NA	3	3
MA	4	2	1	1	4	12
MI	4	2	4	4	1	12
MN	3	1	4	4	3	4
MS	1	4	1	3	4	3.5
MO	3	2	1	3	3	4.5
MT	1	3	1	3	4	1.5
NE	0	3	3	3	1	3
NV	2	3	1	4	4	2
NH	2	2	2	3	2	4.5
NJ	4	2	NA	NA	3	12
NM	1	4	NA	4	3	1.5
NY	2	2	2	4	3	12
NC	3	2	2	4	4	3
ND	3	2	4	4	4	1
OH	4	3	2	4	3	12
OK	5	3	NA	3	3	3.5
OR	1	3	1	3	2	3
PA	5	2	4	4	3	12
RI	3	1	4	2	4	5
SC	3	4	1	3	3	5.5
SD	3	2	3	3	4	2
TN	5	4	2	4	3	8
TX	3	3	1	3	3	2
UT	3	3	2	1	4	1
VT	0	1	1	1	1	3.5
VA	4	3	3	3	3	1.5
WA	2	3	2	4	3	2.5
WV	3	4	1	2	1	2
WI	3	2	3	4	4	12
WY	2	3	1	2	4	1.5

(continued)

Total: Sum of issues passed into law by state.

Indicator 1: Overall impact of interest groups:

    4 = interest groups are dominant

    3 = dominant/complementary

    2 = complementary

    1 = complementary/subordinate

Indicator 2: Relative strength of the Democratic party:

    4 = strong state and local party organization

    3 = strong state party/weak local party

    2 = weak state party/strong local party

    1 = weak state and local party

Indicator 3: Relative strength of the Republican party:

    4 = strong state and local party

    3 = strong state party/weak local party

    2 = weak state party/strong local party

    1 = weak state and local party

Indicator 4: Authority of the state boards of higher education:

    4 = consolidated governing board

    3 = 2 + 4

    2 = coordinating board

    1 = planning agency

Indicator 5: Average number of months the legislature sat in 1991–92.

Each indicator was compared with the sum of the laws passed by the states. The first four variables were tested with the one-way ANOVA and Pearson's Correlation Coefficient; the fifth variable was tested using Pearson's Correlation Coefficient.

If changes in the legislature, especially changes in the political structure, took place, then one would expect that variable 1, impact of interest groups (political action committees and special interest groups), would be a factor in the number of bills passed that restrict public universities. In other words, the variable was used to test the hypothesis that the burgeoning number of interest groups would cause pressure on the legislators that would result in the passage of more restrictive bills. A sophisticated method to evaluate the impact of interest groups was devised by Thomas and Hrebenar; it classifies each state according to the relative impact of its special interest groups. In other words, the interest groups in a state may be dominant, complementary, or subordinate to "groups' impact on their respective state policy-making systems" (1990, p. 147). The authors define states as *dominant* if

> groups as a whole are the overwhelming and consistent influence on policy-making. The *complementary* column contains those states where groups have to work in conjunction with or are constrained by other parts of the political system. More often than not this is the party system; but it could also be a strong executive branch, competition between groups, the political culture, or a combination of all these. The *subordinate* column represents a situation where the group system is consistently subordinated to other participants in the policy-making process. The absence of any states in this column reveals that groups are not consistently subordinate in any state. The *dominant/complementary* column includes those states whose group systems alternate between the two situations or are in the process of moving from one to the other. Likewise the states in the *complementary/subordinate* column are in a process of transition. (ibid., p. 148)

One of the greatest concerns in the modern political arena is that special interest groups are determining policy. Yet the statistical comparison of the number of laws restricting higher education with the relative impact of special interest groups shows no correlation between the two variables. Both the one-way ANOVA and Pearson's Correlation Coefficient were used to search for any relationship between the variables, and both tests suggest that the correlation is low or nonexistent.

Variables 2 and 3, strength of the Democratic and Republican parties respectively, complement variable 1, impact of special interest groups. It is feared that as the special interest groups grow in power, the political parties will recede in their effective control of legislators' policy decisions. Recent scholarly research (Patterson, 1989, p. 158) concludes that the major political parties have not been strong for decades, yet they remain resilient to outside forces. The purpose of conducting statistical analysis of the two parties was to see if party strength correlates with the passage of laws restricting higher education institutions. Here the hypothesis tested is: either a Democrat-run or a Republican-run legislature has a greater tendency to pass restrictive laws.

The one-way ANOVA and Pearson's Correlation Coefficient found no significant correlation between the three variables (passage of laws compared with strength of the Democratic party and strength of the Republican party). Thus it appears that the organizational strength of the parties does not affect decisions regarding higher education.

Variable 4, authority of the state boards, refers to the three major forms of statewide organization of higher education institutions. *Governing boards* of all or a group of higher education institutions within a state (e.g., all four-year campuses) are given authority (by the state) over the governance of individual institutions, including the appointment of the campus president, the allocation of state funds within institutions, and the internal affairs of the institutions, e.g., defining institutional missions, approving admission standards, determining tuition and fees, and approving campus governance (Hines, 1988, p. 2). One of the responsibilities of governing boards is to "advocate institutional interests to the governor and legislature" (McGuinness & Paulson, 1991, p. 5). According to Hines (1988, p. 2), the relationship between legislatures/state government and governing boards is often problematic as legislators try to directly intervene in particular campuses, and the board may be unable to represent the needs of all institutions under its jurisdiction to the state government. On the other hand, governing boards can call on a statewide constituency for lobbying support.

Coordinating boards are more identified with state government than are governing boards. While coordinating boards lack management authority over individual institutions, they are usually responsible for "the preparation of a state master plan for higher education, approval and disapproval of new degree programs, and recommending state appropriations for operating and capital budgets" (ibid., p. 3). Coordinating boards are usually advocates for the state rather than the institutions; "they serve more as the intermediaries between the interests and priorities of the states on one hand and the institutions on the other" (McGuinness & Paulson, 1991, p. 6). Institutions under the aegis of a coordinating board have their own board of trustees which may act independently of the coordinating board. Thus the institutions may be found lobbying the government on their own.

Furthermore, the institutions maintain their own constituencies rather than coordinate lobbying efforts with one another. Thus, support for issues concerning higher education may be fragmented (Hines, 1988, p. 3).

Higher education *planning agencies* have limited authority, as the states in which they coordinate activity also have two or more governing boards (McGuinness & Paulson, 1991, p. 8).

Because coordinating boards and governing boards affect university access to legislators, it seems reasonable to expect that the type of board would influence the number of laws passed on higher education. However, a comparison of the sum of laws passed with the type of authority structure (governing board, coordinating board, planning agency), using the one-way ANOVA, again proved to have no statistical significance.

Variable 5, average number of months the legislature is in session per year, is the only variable that correlates with the number of bills passed by each state. Pearson's Correlation Coefficient suggested weak correlation at the 95% confidence interval. Thus the statistical analysis suggests that the longer a legislature sits per year, the more laws regarding higher education will be passed. Because variable 5 is one of two variables that reflects legislative changes (variable 1, impact of special interest groups, is the other), it is significant that this is the only variable that is even slightly significant statistically. It suggests that increased professionalization of state legislatures is related to increasing regulation of higher education.

Case Study: Pennsylvania

The statistical analysis described above suggests that correlation does exist between a legislature's level of professional and political sophistication and the degree of a state's regulation of its public universities' teaching, research, and administration. To learn whether or not the correlation is more than coincidence, a case study of one state was undertaken. Pennsylvania was selected for study because it has a highly professional legislature and a strong system of PACs similar to the ones operating on the national level. The entire Pennsylvania higher education system consists of:

- One-hundred nine private colleges and universities. Twelve are classified as state-aided, which means they receive some financial assistance from the state.

- Fourteen state-owned universities, which are the former normal schools, or teachers colleges. They have been extended to four-year colleges offering some master's-level programs. These institutions have been organized into the State System of Higher Education (SSHE), which is headed by a chancellor and governing board.

- Four state-related universities, which include 25 branch campuses. Formerly private institutions, the state adopted financial responsibility for them since the 1950s in order to prevent their bankruptcy. The governance of these universities is not organized into one administration; as a result, each institution lobbies the state legislature separately.

Interviews conducted in 1990 with several legislators from Pennsylvania[6] indicate that the political and professionalization pattern discovered in nationwide surveys fits the experience of Pennsylvania legislators. The five in-depth, semistructured interviews started with the question, "How has the legislature changed over your tenure?" (Three had entered the legislature by 1972, one began serving in 1974, and one in 1978). Of the five, only one was retired at the time of the interviews. In their interviews, all five listed the following changes.

First, the Pennsylvania legislators perceive that the role of the political parties has changed drastically since the early 1970s. Endorsement by a political party no longer guarantees one reelection. Several legislators referred to the 1978 election when ten new people were voted into the legislature; of those, eight overthrew incumbents even without the endorsement of the Democratic party. This election stands as a watershed in their minds; it symbolizes their concern that in order to maintain their legislative seats, they cannot count on their party apparatus. At the same time, less party control means they can maintain greater flexibility and autonomy. To these legislators, autonomy from the party means greater direct responsibility to their constituents. In fact, two legislators even described the demise of the state's party structure as the collapse of the patronage system. They said that political parties could no longer reward supporters as they had in the past because (*a*) jobs could no longer be distributed as payback, since they require specific skills and government jobs require that the applicant pass civil service examinations, and (*b*) the creation of welfare services precluded the need for handouts from the political parties.

Second, the Pennsylvania legislators believe that the stature of legislative leaders has grown vis-à-vis the party organization and the governor. These informants report that in the past the governor would tell the leaders how he wanted his party caucus to vote on every bill. The leaders would then inform their caucus members and deliver the votes. Leaders were also described as dependent on the political party organization to keep or replace incumbents if they did or did not vote the party line. Now the leaders are described as having the power to (*a*) stand up to the governor and persuade their party caucus to vote in opposition to the governor if necessary, (*b*) directly affect incumbents' reelection by distributing campaign funds, distributing choice committee appointments and chairmanships to their fellow party members, and by helping legislators get projects for their districts passed, and (*c*) improve their legislators' standing in their district by including in the budget money for each legislator to initiate projects in his/her district. These "legislative initiatives" provide each legislator with about $50,000 to distribute as she/he sees fit. In Pennsylvania, the slang name for this fund is WAM—"walking around money." Pennsylvania is not unique; other states provide such free funding to their legislators also.

Informants who have held leadership positions add that the leaders must relate to their rank-and-file legislators differently from their predecessors. In the past, leaders were perceived as strong personalities who could bully their underlings into following their decisions. Now, leaders are perceived as having to persuade the legislators to vote their way by using such tactics as co-optation, moral persuasion, rationalization, and even threats. Informants report that leaders gain legislators' loyalty by giving them what they want. And what they want is to look good in front of their constituents.

The third point is that the legislators interviewed perceive that the legislature and their colleagues have changed. Each informant reported that in the 1960s the Pennsylvania legislature was a body of part-time people who held other jobs and often had barely completed a high school education. Their impression is supported by the self-reported occupation list in the 1969–70 and 1989–90 histories of bills. The most frequent occupations reported by members of the House in 1969–70 were attorney (55 out of 203 members of the House) and legislator (45 out of 203); the most frequent occupations for senators were attorney (15 out of 50) and businessman (3 out of 50) (Commonwealth of Pennsylvania, 1969). In contrast, the 1989–90 *Final History of House Bills and Resolutions* lists the most frequent occupations of House members as legislator (145 out of 203) followed by attorney (8 out of 203); senators' most frequently listed occupations are state senator/legislator (30 out of 50), then attorney (8 out of 50).

In the 1969–70 legislative session, education levels were reported as follows: 42 representatives and 5 senators completed high school or attended public/parochial school without receiving a high school diploma; 75 representatives and 22 senators completed some higher education or received a baccalaureate degree; 12 representatives and 4 senators started or completed a master's, Ph.D., or professional degree; and 62 representatives and 16 senators started or completed a law degree (LL.B. or J.D.; Commonwealth of Pennsylvania, 1969). By 1989, education levels had changed to the following: 19 representatives and 4 senators completed high school or attended public/parochial school without receiving a high school diploma; 96 representatives and 22 senators completed some higher education or received a baccalaureate degree; 44 representatives and 8 senators started or completed a master's, Ph.D., or professional degree; and 36 representatives and 16 senators started or completed a law degree (LL.D. or J.D.; Commonwealth of Pennsylvania, 1989).

Fourth, those interviewed felt that the change in the relationship between legislators and their leaders appears to be related to a new relationship with constituents. Legislators' major motive seems to be their desire to report to their constituents that their vote on any issue is based on two concerns: their personal ideology/beliefs and their concern for the people who vote them into office. To keep their constituents happy with their performance, legislators propose bills that their constituents request (the Pennsylvania House processed over 2,800 bills in the 1989–90 session) even if they think the bills are useless, connect constituents to employment opportunities, recommend them for jobs, provide services that help constituents fill out their tax forms, help constituents process other state government paperwork, etc. Since the political parties no longer provide jobs to party regulars, the individual legislators have stepped into the breach to act as middlemen, or brokers, to state and federal agencies. When I suggested to one interviewee that the legislators themselves have now become the patrons to their constituents, his face lit up with recognition and he agreed with my analysis.

The result of the trends noted by the interviewed legislators has been a complete change in the political process in Pennsylvania. The hope of one legislator had been that such changes would result in a political body that is truly concerned with the needs of the state. But, he concluded, the result has been just the opposite: despite greater access to information through the proliferation of legislative staff and a greater ability to grasp policy issues (through the higher level of education of the legislators themselves), legislators have not become statesmen. Rather, their concern is even more deeply focused on their constituency, the population that will either vote them back into office or replace them.

The notion that constituents are of paramount importance in the eyes of the legislators is reinforced by a recent proliferation of regional/county delegations. These groups of legislators meet occasionally, with or without local elected officials, and set priorities for their region. They then vote as a block on the top-priority issues that come to the legislature.

In short, the trends in Pennsylvania reflect the general changes in many state legislatures. Legislators' time commitments and responsibilities have increased, and they are caught in creative tension between maintaining the favor of their leaders or their constituents. They appear to be loyal first to their constituents, second to their legislative leaders (who are members of their party caucus), and third to their party organization.

Regarding public universities, the interviewees felt that the best way for these institutions to gain legislative support is to join the legislators in their new relationship with constituents. That is, universities can best gain support and influence legislative decisions by serving legislators' constituents and then getting the constituents to advocate university positions. Thus the interviews with Pennsylvania legislators suggest that this state is definitely operating under new political conditions and that legislative decisions regarding universities are affected by the new political system.

Did Pennsylvania increase the regulation of higher education over the same period of time as professionalization and politicization of the legislature increased? A comparison of past and present bills regulating university activities in Pennsylvania shows that while the number of bills proposed and laws/resolutions passed has not increased, there is some shift in the kinds of laws passed. In the 1969–70 legislative session, 21 bills and resolutions were introduced into the Pennsylvania legislature; three were passed into law. These laws (*a*) exempted foreign teachers from taking the loyalty oath in order to teach, i.e., lifted a restriction; (*b*) provided alternative certification for teachers, i.e., increased flexibility; and (*c*) established a Senate committee to investigate student unrest, i.e., proposed to study a problem before making any decisions on what to do about it. The increase in university autonomy during this session is particularly interesting because it occurred against a backdrop of increased student unrest. While many bills were introduced to control student activities, none were passed.

In the 1989–90 legislative session, 11 bills and resolutions were introduced; two were passed. One was a resolution to establish a House committee to investigate racial relations on campuses, an approach similar to the 1969–70 Senate resolution; the second required public universities to certify the English proficiency of all faculty and teaching assistants on threat of being fined—$10,000 per course. Whereas it appears that the 1989–90 legislature passed fewer laws than the 1969–70 session, the laws passed by the former were restrictive rather than nonregulatory. Furthermore, the session was preceded by recent sessions that also passed restrictive laws. Within the last eight years the Pennsylvania legislature (in previous sessions) has also passed laws (*a*) forcing the public universities to publish statistics on campus crime, (*b*) requiring high school teachers to major in a subject other than education, (*c*) restricting animal research to conform to animal cruelty regulations, and (*d*) governing the licensing and regulation of animal research facilities.

Pennsylvania may be seen as a microcosm of the relationship between professionalized, "new political" state systems and the regulation of higher education institutions. Clearly, there is more than a correlation between the two, for the number and kinds of bills passed show increased regulation of these institutions. Furthermore, the legislators with long tenure note that the legislature has changed tremendously over the past 20 years and that these changes influence how they work with public universities.

Conclusion

People usually think of reform as change for the better. Clearly, higher education institutions do not view increasing government regulation of teaching, research, and administration as an improvement. But the legislators do. They see higher education reform as fulfilling their *duty* to their constituents, i.e., making sure that state and local citizens get what they pay for and protecting citizens from abuses, be they bodily harm, poor-quality teaching, or faculty who are not focused on teaching. State legislators also view increased regulation as a way of showing their constituents that they are responsive to constituent concerns and, therefore, are worthy of being reelected.

While statistical analysis for all 50 states suggests the possibility of correlation between the state-level political process and the kinds of laws passed that directly affect universities, archival and interview data from one state which operates under the new political system suggest that the correlation is not only strong but is also one of causality. That is, the development of a new patron-client relationship between legislators and both their leaders and constituents directly affects the patron-client relationship between legislators and public universities.

What can public universities in the U.S. expect in the next decade? As legislatures move toward increased professionalization and as political control continues to shift from traditional party organizations to caucus leaders who are, in turn, influenced by PACs and SIGs and to legislators' direct dependence on constituent support, public universities can expect increasing regulation of their teaching, research, and administrative functions. For while these institutions have always been *for* the people, they will increasingly become governed *by* the people, or at least their representatives.

Notes

1. One cannot, then, conclude that the political party structure is dormant in the U.S. As Bibby et al. (1990, pp. 85–86) point out, between 1950 and 1988 only one person has been elected governor as an independent, i.e., neither a Democrat nor a Republican; only one senator out of nearly 2,000 and seven state representatives out of over 5,000 were independents. And "state legislative chambers are normally organized on the basis of partisanship, with powerful leadership posts and committee chairmanships going to members of the majority party" (ibid., p. 86).

2. Bibby et al. (1990, p. 112) defines a PAC as "a subspecies of a 'political committee,' defined in the statute [FECA] and granted conditional rights to solicit and accumulate funds for distribution to candidates."

3. Thomas and Hrebenar (1990, p. 124) define a SIG as "any association of individuals, whether formally organized or not, which attempts to influence public policy."

4. Washington, D.C., and Puerto Rico were not included because of lack of data. While laws were used to mark legislative decisions, they actually mark legislative decisions that are signed into law by the governor of the state. Thus bills may be passed by a state's legislative body

and vetoed by a governor. Whereas the passage of bills reflects legislative decisions, there is no 50-state data base to trace them (apart from
the bills signed by the governors). Therefore, this chapter substitutes actual laws for legislative decisions.

　　5.　The states using only a planning agency were omitted from the
statistical analysis.

　　6.　Legislators in the author's geographical area were selected
based upon recommendations by university lobbyists and fellow
legislators.

REFERENCES

Berke, R. L. (September 25, 1990). Lawmakers accept PAC money while
　　urging finance changes. *New York Times*, p. 1.

Beyle, T. L. (1989). From governor to governors. In C. Van Horn (Ed.),
　　State of the states. Washington, D.C.: Congressional Quarterly, Inc.

Bibby, J. F.; Cotter, C. P. et al. (1990). Parties in state politics. In V. Gray,
　　H. Jacob & R. B. Albritton (Eds.), *Politics in the American states: A
　　comparative analysis* (5th ed.). Glenview, IL: Scott,
　　Foresman/Little, Brown Higher Education.

Blum, D. E. (1990). Scholars who see colleges in the thrall of politics
　　meet to plan a counterattack. *Chronicle of Higher Education*, pp.
　　A15–A16.

Blumenstyk, G. (July 25, 1990). State officials deplore higher education's
　　resistance to change. *Chronicle of Higher Education*, pp. A15–A16.

Brittingham, G. R., Jr. (Ed.). (1969). *The Pennsylvania manual 1968–69,
　　Vol. 99*. Harrisburg, PA: Department of Property and Supplies,
　　Commonwealth of Pennsylvania.

————. (Ed.). (1989). *The Pennsylvania manual 1989–90, Vol. 109*. Harris-
　　burg, PA: Department of Property and Supplies, Commonwealth
　　of Pennsylvania.

Brown, P. E. (1985). *The organization and management of state-level lobbying
　　efforts of different types of institutions of higher education*. Ed.D.
　　dissertation submitted to the Faculty of the Center for the Study
　　of Higher Education, School of Education, University of Virginia.

Chronicle of Higher Education Editors. (1991). Nine issues affecting colleges: A roll call of the states. In *Almanac of higher education*. Chicago: University of Chicago Press.

Commonwealth of Pennsylvania. (1985–90). *History of house bills and resolutions, final issue*. Sessions of 1985–86, 1987–88, 1989–90. Harrisburg, PA: Commonwealth of Pennsylvania.

Conlan, T.; Martino, A. & Dilger, R. (1984). State parties in the 1980s: Adaptation, resurgence and continuing constraints. *Intergovernmental Perspective, 10(4)*, pp. 6–13.

Cotter, C. P.; Gibson, J. L.; Bibby, J. F. & Huckshorn, R. J. (1984). *Party organizations in American politics*. New York: Praeger.

Crossen, P. H. (1988). *The study of public service in higher education*. Paper prepared for presentation at the 1988 Annual Meeting of the Association for the Study of Higher Education, St. Louis, MO.

Davis, W. E. (1977). How to work with state legislatures. In R. W. Heyns (Ed.), *Leadership for higher education: The campus view*. Washington, D.C.: American Council on Education.

Durenberger, Senator D. (1984). View from the commission. *Intergovernmental Perspective 10(4)*, pp. 2, 31.

Education Commission of the States. (1989). *New issues—new roles: A conversation with state higher education executive officers*. Denver: Education Commission of the States and State Higher Education Executive Officers.

Fisher, L. A. (1988). *External political traditions: Their development and continuing impact on the nature of two public systems of higher education*. Paper presented at the 1988 Annual Meeting of the Association for the Study of Higher Education, St. Louis, MO.

Gilley, J. W. & Fulmer, K. A. (1986). *A question of leadership: Or, to whom are the governors listening?* Report of the Center for Policy Studies in Education. Fairfax, VA: George Mason University.

Goodall, L. E. (Ed.). (1987). *When colleges lobby states: The higher education/state government connection*. Washington, D.C.: American Association of State Colleges and Universities.

Goodall, L. E.; Holderman, J. B. & Nowlin, J. D. (1971). Legislature and university: The uneasy partnership. *Educational Record, 52*, pp. 36–40.

Gove, S. K. & Beyle, T. (Eds.). (1988). *Governors and higher education*. Denver: Education Commission of the States.

Gove, S. K. & Stauffer, T. M. (Eds.). (1986). *Policy controversies in higher education*. Contributions to the Study of Education No. 19. Westport, CT: Greenwood Press.

Gray, V. (1990). The Socioeconomic and political context of states. In V. Gray, H. Jacob & R. B. Albritton (Eds.), *Politics in the American states: A comparative analysis* (5th ed.). Glenview, IL: Scott, Foresman/Little, Brown Higher Education.

Halstead, K. (1989a). *Higher education tuition*. Washington, D.C.: Research Associates of Washington.

———. (1989b). *State profiles: Financing public higher education 1978 to 1989*. Washington, D.C.: Research Associates of Washington.

Heftel, C. (1984). Out of the ivory tower and into the lobby. *AGB Reports, 26*, pp. 11–13.

Hines, E. R. (1988). *Higher education and state governments: Renewed partnership, cooperation, or competition?* ASHE-ERIC Higher Education Report No. 5. Washington, D.C.: Association for the Study of Higher Education.

Holmes, R. A. (1983). How to work with your state legislators. *AGB Reports, 25*, pp. 24–27.

James, F. C. (1965). Introduction. In *University autonomy: Its meaning today*. Papers of the International Association of Universities No. 7. Paris: International Association of Universities, 1965.

Jewell, M. E. & Patterson, S. C. (1986). *The legislative process in the United States* (4th ed.). New York: Random House.

Jones, D. P. (1984). *Higher-education budgeting at the state level: Concepts and principles*. Boulder, CO: NCHEMS.

Jones, R. S. (1984). Financing state elections. In M. J. Malbin (Ed.), *Money and politics in the United States*. Washington, D.C.: American Enterprise Institute.

Kerr, C. (1985). The states and higher education: Changes ahead. *State Government, 58*, pp. 45–50.

Kingdon, J. W. (1984). *Agendas, alternatives, and public policies*. Boston: Little, Brown and Co.

———. (1989). *Congressmen's voting decisions* (3d ed.). Ann Arbor, MI: University of Michigan Press.

Krotseng, M. V. (1990). Profiles of quality and intrusion: The complex courtship of state governments and higher education. *Review of Higher Education, 13*, pp. 557–66.

Layzell, D. T. & Lyddon, J. W. (1988). *The relationship between environmental factors and state appropriations to public universities.* Paper presented at the 1988 Annual Meeting of the Association for the Study of Higher Education, St. Louis, MO.

——. (1990). *Budgeting for higher education at the state level: Enigma, paradox, and ritual.* ASHE-ERIC Higher Education Report No. 4. Washington, D.C.: Association for the Study of Higher Education.

Likins, P. (1990). In an era of tight budgets and public criticism, colleges must rethink their goals and priorities. *Chronicle of Higher Education*, pp. B1–B2.

Marcus, L. R. & Hollander, T. E. (1981). The capital and the campus— Each in its proper place. *Policy Studies Journal*, pp. 19–32.

McGuinness, A. C., Jr. & Paulson, C. (1991). *State postsecondary education instructions handbook: State coordinating and governing boards.* Denver: Education Commission of the States.

Moscow, W. (1971). *The last of the big-time bosses: The life and times of Carmine De Sapio and the rise and fall of Tammany Hall.* New York: Stein and Day.

Nathan, R. P. (1989). The role of the states in American Federalism. In C. Van Horn (Ed.), *The state of the states.* Washington, D.C.: Congressional Quarterly Inc.

National Association for Biomedical Research. (1991). *State laws concerning the use of animals in research* (3d ed.).Washington, D.C.: NABR.

National Conference of State Legislatures. (1992). Partisan composition of the state legislatures: 1992 legislative session. *National Conference of State Legislatures*, November 6.

Patterson, S. C. (1989). The persistence of state parties. In C. Van Horn (Ed.), *The state of the states.* Washington, D.C.: Congressional Quarterly Inc.

Pound, W. T. (1989). The state legislatures. In *The book of the states 1988– 89.* Denver: The Council of State Governments.

Public Policy Center, SRI International. (1986). *The higher education-economic development connection: Emerging roles for public colleges and universities in a changing economy.* Washington, D.C.: American Association of State Colleges and Universities.

Riordan, W. (1963). *Plunkitt of Tammany Hall.* New York: E. P. Dutton.

Rosenthal, A. (1981). *Legislative life: People, process, and performance in the states.* New York: Harper and Row.

———. (1989). The legislative institution. In C. Van Horn (Ed.), *The state of the states.* Washington, D.C.: Congressional Quarterly Inc.

Salmore, B. G. & Salmore, S. A. (1989). The transformation of state electoral politics. In C. Van Horn (Ed.), *The state of the states.* Washington, D.C.: Congressional Quarterly Inc.

Sederburg, W. A. (1989). A legislator looks at academe. *Change,* pp. 31–38.

Sorauf, F. J. (1988). *Money in American politics.* Glenview, IL: Scott, Foresman/Little, Brown.

State Legislatures. (1991). 1991 Legislative Session Calendar, pp. 1, 2.

———. (1992). 1992 Legislative Session Calendar, pp. 1, 2.

Thomas, C. S. & Hrebenar, R. J. (1990). Interest groups in the states. In V. Gray, H. Jacob, & R. B. Albritton (Eds.), *Politics in the American states: A comparative analysis* (5th ed.). Glenview, IL: Scott, Foresman/Little, Brown Higher Education.

Van Horn, C. (1989). The quiet revolution. In C. Van Horn, (Ed.). *The state of the states.* Washington, D.C.: Congressional Quarterly Inc.

Wirt, F. & Gove, S. K. (1990). Education. In V. Gray, H. Jacob & R. B. Albritton, (Eds.), *Politics in the American states: A comparative analysis* (5th ed.). Glenview, IL: Scott, Foresman/Little, Brown Higher Education.

Wolf, E. R. (1966). Kinship, friendship, and patron-client relations in complex societies. In M. Banton (Ed.), *The social anthropology of complex societies.* A.S.A. Monographs No. 4. London: Tavistock Publications.

Zusman, A. (1986). Legislature and university conflict: The case of California. *Review of Higher Education, 9,* pp. 397–418.

CHAPTER VI

Higher Education in Turmoil
The Impact of Political Changes in East Germany on the Transformation of Higher Education*

Helmut de Rudder

Higher Education in the Context of the Peaceful Revolution in East Germany

Introduction

The fundamental changes in East German[1] higher education during the process of its integration into the West German higher education system is a case in point for a basic sociological assumption about the relationship between higher education and society: higher education, whatever the degree of its autonomy and self-regulation, and however self-referential it may be, is always a product of its society; it is determined by the social, cultural, political and economic system and by the conditions under which these systems operate. To understand and explain differences between national systems of higher education is to analyze their societal context. Higher education on the one hand is a semi-autonomous subsystem of society, driven by its imminent forces and its own dynamic. It is a multifaceted subculture with its particular norms. And it is a factor of social and cultural change. But at the same time, higher education is shaped by that change, and it is always dependent on society's needs, demands and problems. (This, of course, is true of any subsystem of society; they all oscillate between being dependent and independent variables of societal conditions.)

This view is particularly applicable to what has been happening to and in East German higher education since 1989: the revolutionary changes of the whole higher education system are a direct consequence of the breakdown of the German Democratic Republic (GDR) in 1989 and the reunification of Germany in 1990. The present challenges, problems and difficulties of change in East German higher education are largely due to the fact that after the division of Germany in 1945, the two parts, right at the borderline of the Western and the Eastern blocs, were integrated into two inimical political, economic and military systems and, for 44 years, developed into two increasingly different societies, separated by the Iron Curtain, which for more than 25 years (until the beginnings of political detente in the early '70s) became more impenetrable every year. These developments do more to explain the differences in the systems of higher education in the two German states than would an analysis concentrating on the internal forces and factors in higher education.

It should be noted that German reunification—as the decisive frame of reference also for the changes of higher education in East Germany—was not an act of two countries forming a common state on an equal basis. Instead, after the breakdown of the old regime, the GDR within less than one year dissolved itself and joined the Federal Republic of Germany, thereby adopting the West German system.[2] For higher education—as for all public institutions—this meant adopting the West German system more or less as it was. ("As in the West, so in earth" commented Dieter Simon, the chairman of the West German Science Council.) So far, West German higher education, on the whole, has remained unchanged in this process, whereas the East German system has had to undergo changes from top to bottom. This is happening at a time when in the old West German states higher education reform is becoming a political issue again—after the first reform movement in West Germany in the '60s and '70s.[3]

At first, the task of renewing and restructuring East German higher education seemed to supersede discussion of reforms in the existing West German system. The implicit motto seemed to be: integrate first, reform later. But under the pressure of increased instances of overcrowding, understaffing and underfunding of higher education in West Germany, and in the face of a general financial crisis due to the huge costs (much higher than expected) of funding the rebuilding and renewal of the new East German states, the necessity of changes in West German higher education is being pushed onto the political agenda.

Higher Education and the Political System

The present situation and problems of higher education in East Germany can only be properly understood if it is compared with the situation during the GDR regime until 1989. After 1945, the development of higher education in East Germany was part of the emerging totalitarian system under the virtual one-party rule of the communist Socialist Unity Party (SED) which, following the Soviet model, had set out to create the "first German state of workers and peasants" and to that end effected a thoroughgoing change of society, government, economy and—as a major instrument and safeguard of this change—education. The education system was to be aimed at creating the "all-around educated socialist personality." This plan also pertained to higher education, resulting, for instance, in compulsory courses in Marxism-Leninism as well as in athletics for all students, regardless of their field of study. Until the peaceful revolution of 1989, all sectors of organized education from kindergarten to the university were considered to be important elements of the continuous process of creating and re-creating the "new man" by disseminating the true doctrine and the worldview of the regime.

It is, of course, the function and an explicit responsibility of organized education in all societies to educate the young to be loyal citizens of their country and to identify with the system.

Education always transmits norms, values, beliefs and cultural patterns. But the fundamental difference between totalitarian and dictatorial systems—as in the old Eastern bloc, on the one hand, and what we have come to look at as "Western" systems, on the other hand—lies in their opposite value systems. These concern basic concepts of humanity and society, having to do with the value of individual liberty in relation to the exercise of power and authority in the organization of society. In short, though it is a function of education in all societies to integrate the young and to pass on to them norms and values and patterns of social action, it is the difference in ends and means between different systems that matters. This very general point proves to be important when comparing and assessing basically antagonistic systems of education, like East and West Germany before 1989. And it says something about the inevitable problems and difficulties which are bound to occur in a system of education when the established political and economic system breaks down and is replaced by the opposite one of the "other side," which—in the case of East Germany—for more than four decades has been denounced as the enemy. The basic changes in higher education in East Germany after the breakdown of the old GDR regime have to be seen in this context. This poses questions, some of which cannot be sufficiently answered, but remind us of uncertainties in some of our assumptions:

- To what an extent do values, norms and behavioral patterns really differ between East and West Germany after 40 years of opposite political systems? After all, it was one country, one culture and one society until 1945. In spite of what happened between 1945 and 1989 it might be a plausible assumption that the differences between East Germans and West Germans may not be as big as, for instance, those between Russians and Americans.

- Even if growing up—socialization—over the years has become quite different in East and West Germany and the totalitarian state did everything to educate the young in the spirit of the system, how deeply have the new values, beliefs and ways of thinking been internalized, or to what extent has the pressure to go along (with all its rewards) produced more or less superficial adaptation?

(Riesman's [1950, chap. 8] concept of "other direction" replacing "inner direction" as a mode of orientation in modern societies may be applicable here.)

The totalitarian state as a powerful exogenous force shaping higher education (in East Germany as well as other Eastern European countries) always mingled with endogenous factors of the academic system, which, to a certain degree independent of the political system, are driven by imminent forces of scholarship, research and teaching as has become typical for occidental (and today worldwide) science, of which Eastern Europe higher education and research institutions are also a part.[4] Thus, when we stress the tremendous impact of the bygone East German regime on higher education and research, we should also consider those forces and factors in higher education and research which, even under an all-encompassing totalitarian regime, to a certain extent still follow their inherent necessities and produce and perpetuate norms, attitudes and also institutional arrangements which are conducive to scholarship and scientific inquiry. Since any modern, highly industrialized society is dependent on the high-level research, scientific expertise and numerous services provided by academia, even a totalitarian regime cannot but grant academic institutions some leeway in acting according to their own patterns. This is augmented by the fact that academic institutions have become highly complex self-referential systems of experts which—to a limited extent—defy external political control.

The State of Research: Questions of Methodology

This chapter is not a result of completed research. The process of change we are concerned with began only two years ago and is still in full swing. While there have been quite a few studies—originating in East as well as West Germany—on problems and developments in higher education in East Germany and also comparative East German/West German studies before 1989 (Ashwill, 1991; Bundesministerium, 1990; Rudolf, 1984), research on recent developments is just beginning. Of particular interest are two studies taking stock of East German higher education

and reflecting on its perspectives; these were written in the tu-
multuous months between the overthrow of the old regime and
reunification (Zentralinstitut, 1990a; Goldschmidt & Schäfer,
1990). It is still too early for a comprehensive and in-depth study
of the ongoing complex and dynamic process of change. There
are, however, studies supplying data for planning and policy-
making such as surveys on the number and flow of students or
supply and demand of staff (Zentralinstitut, 1990b-g; Projektgruppe, 1990a-g, 1992a-c). Finally, there are the exercises by the
Science Council and by state higher education commissions to
evaluate higher education and research institutions (see below).

Any attempt to gain an overall view of the processes of
change and of their structures, directions, trends and outcomes—
intended as well as unintended—can only be provisional at this
stage. At best, it will be more the result of efforts at "explanatory
understanding" (in the sense of Max Weber's methodological
approach) than of strictly empirically falsifiable causal explanation. The general methodological problem of sociology—namely,
the sociologist always being part of his/her subject—applies to
our subject in a particular way: the perception an academic researcher develops of what is going on in East German higher education will almost necessarily be influenced by his/her own
position in this process.

Some Characteristics of East German Higher Education Until 1989—Compared to West Germany

Students and Studies

In both German states and in keeping with German tradition since the early nineteenth century, the comprehensive exam
(*Abitur*) at the end of either grammar school or a university-
preparatory branch of other secondary schools entitled one to
study at institutions of higher education. There were no university entrance examinations. But institutions of higher education
in both German states still had to select students when there
were more applicants than places. Whereas in West Germany

admission then depended on the grade point average of the Abitur exam (there is now a heated discussion about changing this), in East Germany "societal activity" and political reliability were major criteria for university admission (see below).

In 1989, when the old regime in East Germany broke down, 26.9% of the age-group (60,400 students) qualified for admission to higher education; in West Germany it was 32.0% (280,100 students). In 1989 there were about 134,000 students in higher education in East Germany—of a population of about 16.4 million (0.8%). In West Germany there were 1.5 million students—of a population of 62.7 million (2.4%). In East Germany, the 32,200 first-year students in 1989 were about 13.8% of the age-group. In the same year in West Germany, there were 252,600 first-year students, comprising about 25.7% of the age-group. In 1989 23,000 students graduated from institutions of higher education in East Germany, about 9.5% of the relevant age-group. The figure for West Germany was 147,600, which is 13% of the relevant age-group (Bundesminister, 1991, and own calculations).[5]

A comparison of these figures already hints at important differences between higher education in East and West Germany before reunification:

- The lower rate of transfer from secondary to higher education in East Germany (about 50%, versus 80% in West Germany) is a result of integrating higher education into overall economic planning: the number of admissions to the different programs and institutions depended on the planned demand for highly qualified manpower within the framework of five-year plans. In West Germany, on the other hand, the Federal Constitutional Court (Bundesverfassungsgericht) ruled that access to higher education must not be denied for reasons of perceived demand of the employment system.

- Retention and completion rates in higher education were much higher in East Germany than in West Germany, where, in turn, the dropout rate was much higher (overall about 25%, in some programs more than 50%) than in the East.

There are several reasons for these differences, which are indicative of quite divergent characteristics of the two systems:

- Academic study was even more regulated in East Germany than in the West (where the extent of regulation has also increased considerably over the last 30 years). In East Germany there were detailed compulsory curricula with very little individual choice.

- Classes in East Germany were much smaller. In 1989, the ratio of academic staff to students was 1:4.2—as against 1:12 at universities and 1:34 at vocational colleges (*Fachhochschulen*) in West Germany (Bundesminister, 1991, pp. 21, 25).[6]

- In East Germany, attendance in class was compulsory, and student performance was continuously monitored by tutors and advisers.

- East German students were organized into "seminar groups" of 20 to 25, which stayed together from the first semester to the last. Each group had a permanent tutor and a (party) "secretary." These groups certainly were instruments of political control and supervision, but they also were tightly knit frameworks for their members' academic work: it was hardly possible to drop out because informal social control was strong, as was mutual support. Studying was much more an organized collective enterprise than in the West.

The West German scene was (and is) quite different: though there are more regulations, requirements, prescribed curricula and instruments of control than before due to the implementation of mass higher education since the late '60s, there is still much more academic and individual freedom for students than there was in East Germany. In keeping with old German university traditions, it is basically not the responsibility of the university to put its students to work and to monitor their studies. Though there are many more prerequisites (e.g., papers, tests, intermediate exams) for admission to final exams than there were before, it still is the prime responsibility of the students to organize their studies and to decide how much time to devote to them and how many classes to take and attend per week. It is up to them to decide after how many semesters beyond the prescribed minimum they take their final exams. It is easy for them to dodge or neglect their studies and to mix them with other activities. In contrast to East Germany before 1989, studying in West Germany is an individual matter and not so much a group activity. Not more than 10% of the students (versus more than 75% in the East) live in dormitories; all the others are more directly integrated into the daily life of the town. By now, the large majority of West German students not only work between semesters but increasingly work part-time during semesters. (Housing has become very expensive—for students roughly one-third of their monthly income—and most students have to make money on their own to pay for part of their living expenses. Many do not want to give up the amenities of life in affluent West German society.) Thus, as part of daily life in general, the student subcultures had become quite different in East and West Germany.

The social composition of the East German student body changed over the last 40 years in a remarkable way. In the early times of the GDR, it was a definite policy of the party and the government to bring children of workers and peasants (who so far had been grossly underrepresented) to the university. Special preparatory schools were created for this purpose. This policy was very successful: by 1958 54% of all students in higher education came from working class families. Children from the old middle and upper classes were systematically excluded from higher education. (Every applicant had to prove his or her "proletarian descent.") One generation later, when the new "intelligentsia"—that is, graduates of vocational schools and higher education—had children of college age, the picture changed dramatically: the percentage of children of workers in the student body dropped from year to year, until, in 1989, it was down to 7–10%, as against 15% in West Germany (Geißler, 1992, p. 227). In 1990 the fathers of 47% of the students in East Germany had a higher education degree; the percentage for West Germany was only 23%. At the other end of the spectrum, only 0.5% of the GDR students had fathers who had not completed vocational training, as against 5% in the Federal Republic

(Geißler, 1992, p. 229). The new upper middle class of the GDR absolutely dominated the universities.

The great differences in the structure of studies and the ways of studying between East and West before unification are not only a result of the basic changes the GDR brought about since its funding in 1949. They are also due to the continued existence of some traditional features of the West German system which were functional at the time when less than 5% of the age-group received a university education, but which, arguably, have not really been adapted to the conditions of mass higher education as it developed only in the last 25 years. In Germany— East and West—and in other continental European countries there is no lower (bachelor's degree) and higher (master's degree) division at the universities. The German university degrees, conferred after a rather stiff exam at the end of a program designed to take five years, are—very roughly again— equivalents of American master's degrees. (In the GDR, students really finished in five years; in West Germany it actually takes them seven.) In the middle of a program of studies at a university—usually after five semesters—there is an intermediate exam, a purely internal affair and without a degree, dividing the program into "basic studies" (*Grundstudium*) and "main studies" (*Hauptstudium*). Consequently, the level reached at the intermediate exam could then be compared, with caution, to an American undergraduate degree (Naumann & Krais, 1991, pp. 686, 688).

In the GDR, the traditional German system of four years of elementary school, followed by nine years of a university-preparatory secondary school (*Gymnasium*) was changed—just to name the major types of schools—to a 10-year comprehensive school plus a two year "extended high school" (*Erweiterte Oberschule*) which prepared one for higher education. Thus, in all, it took one year less than in West Germany to reach the Abitur. In both German states there was compulsory military service, two years in the East, one year in the West, which had to be taken before entering higher education. In the GDR, it was more or less expected of male applicants for higher education institutions to complete a reserve officers training program before entering the university.

New Institutions

In the process of expanding higher education, the GDR took a distinctly different course from the Federal Republic. Though the old universities and technical universities still had most of the students, many new highly specialized university-level institutions were created, often offering one academic program only but having the right to grant Ph.D.s. Many of these new institutions had only several hundred students. In addition to the publicly accessible institutions of higher education, the party, the Ministry of the Interior and even the state security forces (*Stasi*) had set up special university-level (that is, degree-granting) institutions of their own. Most of the higher ranking functionaries and officers of these institutions would hold degrees (up to Ph.D.s) from these special political institutions of higher education which were not open to the public.

Following the model of the Soviet Union, the GDR had a policy of concentrating basic research outside of universities in central academies with numerous research institutes. The Academy of Sciences had about 24,000 researchers in a vast array of institutes. There were also academies for educational sciences, civil engineering and agricultural sciences, all of them with a huge staff and their own Ph.D. programs.

Until the '70s, there was a systematic policy of expanding higher education in the GDR, resulting—at the time—in higher participation rates than in West Germany. But then it was found that the system produced more graduates than the employment system needed. A policy of limiting the number of graduates to the planned demand of the economy resulted. The staff, however, was not reduced, leading to a better staff/student ratio than in most other countries. These planned reductions took place at the same time that West German higher education had its biggest expansion ever. From 1980 to 1989 there was a steady state in the number of students in the GDR, whereas in West Germany the number increased by another 50% (Bundesminister, 1991, pp. 20–21, 24–25).

Political and Ideological Control

After the division of Germany, the overriding phenomenon in the development of higher education in the GDR
was domination and tight control by the political regime. Marxism-Leninism became the official state doctrine. It penetrated
systematically the whole educational system from kindergarten
to the university. Universities—like schools, industry, agriculture, courts or the mass media—were centrally planned, controlled and administered as integrated parts of the socialist system under the undisputable leadership of the party and on the
basis of the theory and teachings of Marx, Lenin and, for a while,
Stalin. There was virtually no institutional autonomy for universities, and academic freedom was denounced as an individualistic relic of bourgeois society, the class enemy on the other side of
the Iron Curtain. The so-called "leading role of the party of the
working class" meant in higher education—as in all other public
sectors—two things: the party controlled higher education centrally from Berlin by policy decisions and planning, and the
party units in the university and in the departments controlled
policy and decisions on these levels, including staff appointments. As in factories, schools and administrations, there was
always a double structure at the institutional level: the administration as such and the party-group within the institution, which
had everything under control (Müller, 1953). In addition to that,
the state security police informants and functionaries operated
on all levels in all institutions (among the faculty, the students
and the office staff), only one did not know who they were. West
and even East Germans only learned after the fall of the regime
to what an unbelievable extent people in the GDR were spied on
in all walks of life, including the private sphere. And this information was used when it came to appointments, promotions,
approvals, privileges, etc. To top this, there were the so-called
Officers on Special Duty of the state security forces. They would
be, for instance, professors like any other professor, but they
would also hold a rank in the security police and be a permanent
member without anybody in the university knowing (Schell &
Kalinka, 1991).

Pressures to Adapt to the System

Admission of students to institutions of higher education was controlled by the party, too: to be admitted to the last two years of high school and then to an institution of higher education was a question not only of good grades but also of "societal activities" and political reliability. There were security police informants even among high school students.

The selection of teachers and academics and their further careers depended largely on their willingness and ability to adapt and go along with the system. Ever since the borders to the Federal Republic were hermetically closed by the GDR in 1961—it was not just the Berlin Wall, but the whole borderline from the Baltic to Czechoslovakia—there was no way of getting out of and no alternative to, the existing system. To expect that this could change in the foreseeable future was unrealistic. Somebody who had the potential and the interest to do academic work somehow had to make his or her peace with the regime and had to find a way to come to an arrangement with the system. Retreating into private life, participating in required public activities as much as was absolutely necessary, adapting (to whatever extent) to get along, not attracting attention in order to be left alone, to the extent that this was possible—that was one way of living under that system. Identifying, believing, seeing the final goal, internalizing the foe image of the West was another. What outsider could claim today to know what was camouflage and what was real? A third way was to forgo chances of an academic life by steadfastly refusing to adapt—and as a consequence, live, for instance, as a production worker or a janitor.

The socializing effects of being integrated into East German academe were intensified by the fact that most academics and researchers were cut off from the scientific world outside of the Eastern bloc. They had extremely limited access to Western books and journals. That also applied to students and the books they would find in their libraries. Of course, there were differences between disciplines; access to Western research findings and discussions in the natural sciences was not as strictly controlled as in the social sciences, economics and other ideologically relevant disciplines. Individual travel to Western countries

was virtually impossible. Participation in conferences and meetings outside the Eastern bloc was restricted to carefully selected
"travel cadres."

Academic Research

Research was rather tightly controlled. If a psychologist or
social scientist wanted to do a survey, the questionnaire had to
be approved—often as far up as Berlin. Questions which were
not in line with official policy would be deleted, and so would
unwelcome answers. Publications had to be approved before-
hand. There were no private publishing houses. As in literature,
East German academics developed to perfection their ability to
read and write "between the lines."

Technologically, the GDR was the most advanced of the
Eastern European countries—in spite of the disastrous state of
large parts of its production capacity and the low rate of productivity of its economy compared to the Federal Republic. Like any
highly industrialized society, it depended heavily on research
and big science. As in the West, the "knowledge industry" was
central and employed a steadily increasing proportion of the
highly qualified labor force. There was no lack of qualified researchers and scientists, and the state of the art in many specialized fields of research was comparable to West Germany
(Fischer, 1988; Krejci, 1976; Voigt et al., 1987). The problem was
cost-effectiveness and the translation of research into large-scale
advanced technology. Since everything had to go according to
rather rigid five-year plans controlled by huge bureaucracies,
there was no premium on innovative thinking as in Western science think tanks. Incentives and rewards (including personal
income) were largely lacking. There was too little flexibility to
pursue the unexpected and the unusual, too little freedom in
setting and changing one's own research agenda, too little real
competition inside the system and too little access to the competitive international research markets and to cooperation with
transnational scientific communities. Too much of researchers'
energy simply had to go into nerve-racking and time-consuming
quarrels with the bureaucratic systems that controlled and directed their work. In many fields, the results of scholarship and

research under these adverse conditions were truly remarkable, as the West German Science Council found out when it had to evaluate higher education and research institutions in East Germany. This judgement appears to be even more justified if one considers the often deplorable state of buildings, equipment, supplies, communication facilities and other working conditions (Bundesministerium, 1990, pp. 394–489).

Modelled after the Soviet Union, research—especially basic research—was concentrated in the numerous institutes of the central Academy of Sciences and in specialized academies and thus pulled away from universities. The traditional German principle of "unity of teaching and research" was given up, although the universities strove hard to keep or attract research capacities and projects, for instance by cooperating with collective industrial combines (Institut für Gesellschaft und Wissenschaft, 1979).

Changing Higher Education in East Germany

Higher education in East Germany is right in the middle of most radical changes, processes which have been going on for more than three years now and which are going to continue for a long time to come. But the gears have been shifted and major decisions taken.

Though the peaceful revolution of 1989 has spurred initiatives for changes at the institutional level, the restructuring and renewal of East German higher education was mainly top-down. There were individual academics and students among those who brought about that revolution, but it cannot be said that higher education or groups originating in higher education were instrumental in this process. Higher education as a whole was too much adapted to the regime and too much under its control to allow for the development of an oppositional or revolutionary potential. Furthermore, the mechanisms of selection and socialization of staff and students hardly encouraged the development of patterns of independent thinking. As a result, higher education in East Germany was confronted with the revolution and the breakdown of the old regime rather than being an active participant in these processes, even though many rank-and-file academics, especially those not in leadership positions, welcomed the end of the totalitarian regime.

The fundamental changes to the system of higher education in East Germany since reunification are mainly a result of adopting the West German system. Policymakers inside and outside of higher education in the East and West did not grow tired of stressing that (*a*) the West German system should not simply be copied, (*b*) one should learn from its shortcomings and undesirable developments, (*c*) the new freedom should be used to search for new solutions, (*d*) now there were opportunities for innovations, and (*e*) reunification was also a chance to evaluate critically the West German system of education and research (Wissenschaftsrat, 1990b, p. 6). But the imminent forces of integration; the financial situation; the dominance of West German experts, administrators and policymakers; the eagerness of some of the new Eastern politicians and officials ("wryneck" soon became a new household word) and—last not least—the pressure of time—all tilted the scales more toward copying the West German structures, ways and means.

The forces that had made the revolution (like the "New Forum" and groups originating within the Protestant Church) and that at the outset did not think of unification, lost their influence soon after the big "turn," as it came to be called in Germany, to the new East German outlets of the established West German parties.[7] This development further weakened attempts at creating something new, which would differ from the West German way. (After all, in 1989–90, the very large majority of the East German population definitely wanted to become part of the Federal Republic, which not only provided individual and political freedom but also held the promise of economic well-being and a high standard of living.)

Implications for Adequate Theoretical Approaches

Changes of and in higher education systems have always been a major topic of sociological theories of higher education, especially in a comparative perspective (Clark, 1981, pp. 182–

237). They are mainly concerned with evolutionary developments of higher education institutions and systems in long-range
interactive processes between higher education and the political,
economic, social and cultural system. Their analytical categories
also are useful for studying the present changes in higher education in Eastern Europe, including East Germany. What is happening there, however, differs radically from processes of
change in higher education we have known so far: the whole
system in all its elements and segments is being transformed (as
is the surrounding political and economic system) into the system of what until 1989 officially used to be called the "class enemy." Considering the long-sequences-of-time characteristics of
reforms in higher education, the transformation in East Germany
is taking place in time-lapse speed and is therefore almost
necessarily creating a cultural-lag effect (Ogburn, 1957) with all
its frictions and conflicts. It seems that what has been and still is
going on in East Germany and Eastern Europe—and higher education is an integral part of this—will make it necessary to recon-
sider theories of social and educational transformation and revolutionary change in order to arrive at satisfactory explanations.

Transformation of Structures

The structural transformation of East German higher education is taking place on three levels: (1) interrelationship with
government, (2) structures of the system as a whole and (3) institutional structures.

Interrelationship with Government

It was clear (and undisputed) from the beginning that
when it joined the Federal Republic, East Germany would have a
federal structure and that political responsibility for education,
including higher education, would basically rest with the five
new states. (The GDR in 1952 had abolished the states and created a centralized system of government and party rule. Institutions of higher education reported directly to their respective
ministry in East Berlin.) The new governments had to start from
scratch. New ministers of education and science and their staff

mostly were without any experience in this kind of business. Inevitably, there had to be "imports" from West German states on all levels, from ministers down to civil servants. Because of the power vacuum created by the dissolution of central government, the development of new state administrations had to be accomplished very fast. Consequently, relationships between ministries and institutions of higher education were structured the same way as in West Germany, and the West German discussion about deregulation and more institutional autonomy did not bear any fruits in the new administrations of the Eastern states. The dominance of ministries as against universities and colleges became even stronger than in West Germany because institutions were not yet granted the degree of autonomy of their West German counterparts as long as there were not enough newly appointed academics (see below), no governing bodies elected according to new higher education laws and no strong institutional leadership experienced in coping with ministerial power. The intricate patterns of power plays and policy-making—especially their informal mechanisms—between institutions of higher education, civil servants, state ministers, legislators, political parties and pressure groups, having grown in West Germany in four decades into a complex system of checks and balances, provided ways for institutional leaders to bring to bear the influence of higher education on higher education policy and on decisions concerning their institutions. This does not yet work in the new states, and therefore the weight of the new state administrations for higher education is not yet balanced by a corresponding weight of institutional leadership.

The basic relationship between higher education and government in the Federal Republic is regulated by the constitution and the federal Higher Education Framework Law (Hochschulrahmengesetz [HRG]). With the act of joining the Federal Republic, these regulations automatically apply to East German higher education.

Though the legal authority over higher education basically rests with the states, there are four important federal rights and responsibilities:

- The right to enact "skeleton provisions concerning . . . the general principles governing higher education" (Basic Law, Article 75).

- Concurrent with the states, legislative power to regulate student aid and the support of research (Basic Law, Article 74).

- The "joint task" of the federal government and the states to pay for the "extension and construction of institutions of higher education including university clinics" (Basic Law, Article 91a).

- Cooperation between the federal government and the states "in educational planning and in the promotion of institutions and projects of scientific research of supraregional importance" (Basic Law, Article 91b).

These provisions mean that:

- Higher education and research institutions in the new East German states fully participate in federally funded research grants administered by the German Research Society (Deutsche Forschungsgemeinschaft [DFG]);[8]

- Federal student aid is extended to the Eastern states (consisting of 50% grants and 50% loans);

- The federal government pays for 50% of capital investments in higher education (but only after the Science Council has evaluated every project and given a positive recommendation); and

- Federal funding for research institutes outside of universities, usually jointly with the respective state, is now extended to East German institutes, after they have been integrated into the Federal Republic's research structure.[9]

The structure and the organization of higher education in East Germany is most directly affected by the HRG. It is the binding legal basis for higher education legislation of the states. It:

- Contains mission statements for higher education institutions;

- Prescribes the different types of institutions;
- Regulates the rights and responsibilities of the state and the institutions and the relations between government and higher education;
- Regulates admissions;
- Provides general rules for exams;
- Prescribes the different types of staff and their rights and responsibilities, as well as the prerequisites for appointments;
- Prescribes the organizational structures of higher education institutions; and
- Regulates the organization, composition, election and authority of governing bodies, and the rights and responsibilities of chief executive officers, thereby defining the scope and limit of institutional autonomy (Hochschulrahmengesetz, 1987).

This list is not complete. It just shows how federal legislation regulates in minute detail the affairs and the organization of higher education institutions in Germany. This, of course, means that higher education in East Germany has to be restructured according to these regulations. In spite of states' rights, the new East German states cannot but accept this "framework" for higher education, which actually does not just set a frame but determines to a very large extent how higher education looks. Because of all of these detailed federal regulations, the higher education laws of the states are very much alike and differ only in—sometimes important—details. This goes for the East German states as well. What little variations there are depend more on the political composition of state legislatures and less on whether it is an East or West German state. To be able to act, the East German states needed their higher education laws fast. They did not have much time (and it was not their most urgent problem in regulating higher education) to develop their own particular profile in their higher education laws. Thus they more or less mirrored those of West German states.

Though in the GDR the influence of the party on higher education and the extent, intensity and kind of control and regu-

lation by government certainly went further than in any democratic Western system, it is obvious that the Federal Republic still
belongs to that group of Western states where government control of higher education is strong. Traditional institutional autonomy in internal affairs is more and more checked by state
control over allocation of funds, staff positions, contents of academic programs, examination requirements, statewide planning
and detailed administrative regulations by ministries.

This system of external control and increasing bureaucratization of higher education, as it has developed at the state level
in West Germany since the beginnings of the higher education
expansion in the '60s, is now being introduced in East Germany,
too, though there is mounting criticism of it in the West German
states because of inefficiency and inflexibility. But under the
pressure of having to create functioning state administrations of
higher education as fast as possible in order to implement the
existing higher education legislation of the Federal Republic and
to fill the power vacuum left by the dissolution of the GDR administration, the new administrators and decision makers were
not concerned with modifying the existing West German higher
education administration or the established relationship between
government and higher education institutions. There was no
time to lean back and think about a new order of things and to
devise new ways to administer higher education. To be able to
make decisions at all in that rather anomic East German situation
of transition, the only practical solution was to take over the established system of the West German states, with experienced
staff from the West. It was not possible to close down higher
education for a while or to reflect on and prepare all the changes
and then start anew. The institutions, the staff, the students were
there, and all changes had to be made with the system in full
operation.

Restructuring the System of Higher Education in East Germany

The major recommendations and decisions for restructuring East German higher education were made between the
summer of 1990 and the fall of 1992. The Treaty of Unification
(Einigungsvertrag) of August 31, 1990 (ratified September 23,
1990), between the GDR and the Federal Republic provided that

decisions on closing down institutions of higher education or sections (departments) of them would have to be made by the end of 1990. The treaty also decided that the numerous research institutions of the three central East German academies (the academies of Sciences, Agricultural Sciences and Civil Engineering), which were the backbone of the East German research organization, were to be discontinued in their present form by the end of 1991. In the summer of 1990, the governments of the GDR, the Federal Republic and the 11 West German states asked the West German Science Council (Wissenschaftsrat)[10] to evaluate the research institutions of the central academies as well as the structure and organization of higher education in East Germany and make recommendations as to their future structures. This task of the Science Council was then written into the Treaty of Unification (Die Verträge, 1990, p. 64). The council was not burdened with recommendations on closing down (the euphemistic term was "winding up") institutions of higher education or sections of them; this was a responsibility of the new state governments. One of the first measures was to close down all of the higher education institutions within the party, the unions and some of the ministries and other big government agencies. Also closed down were the central Academy of Educational Sciences (Akademie der Pädagogischen Wissenschaften), the East Berlin School of Economics (Hochschule für Ökonomie) and other institutions which were particularly close to the party and the old government. Within universities the new state governments "wound up" departments of law, economics, business administration, history, education and philosophy, i.e., departments that were directly geared to the political, economic and ideological system of the old GDR.

Most of the important structural changes the Science Council recommended for East German higher education and research institutions were accepted by the state governments and have been largely implemented or still are in the process of implementation. They may be summarized as follows (Wissenschaftsrat, 1992a, pp. 8–11):

1. The many small, highly specialized (one field or one branch of the economy only) institutions at the university level are not to be continued in their present form.

Some are to be integrated into the broader spectrum of a general or technical university; most of them are to be changed into polytechnic or vocational colleges (*Fachhochschulen*) combining several special fields.

2. About 20 of these polytechnic colleges are to be founded in East Germany, as a second sector of the system of higher education, either by combining existing specialized institutions (see above) or as new institutions—for instance, for social work, business administration, public administration or design. The level of polytechnic colleges did not exist in the GDR, but has grown in importance in West Germany (as in other West European countries) since the late '60s. They offer three to four degree programs, which are comparable to the programs of American four-year colleges. It is a goal of the higher education policy for all of Germany today (Wissenschaftsrat, 1991b) to expand this sector of higher education. Programs are shorter than at universities; the colleges are less expensive, since they are mainly teaching institutions, and are more directly geared to the needs and demands of the employment system in their teaching as well as in their applied research. In the new states it still seems possible to prevent this West German development; 70% of the students in higher education study in programs lasting (on the average) seven years, whereas only 30% are in three- to four-year programs of polytechnic colleges (Wissenschaftsrat, 1991c).

3. The former institutes of the central academies employed about 24,000 researchers. The Science Council recommended that most of the institutes should be continued—though with a smaller staff and in different combinations, partly with different or new research programs—either as institutions belonging to the major (West) German research organizations to be founded in East Germany, as state-related institutes or as parts of universities. According to the Science Council, this would amount to about 13,200 positions for researchers, 2,000 of them in universities (Wissenschaftsrat, 1992b, pp. 12–60). So far, these changes have only been partly

realized, but the process of implementation is still in full swing, especially as far as the founding of research centers by the big German research organizations is concerned. The Science Council wants to reestablish the function of universities as centers of research. The universities certainly do want to become centers of research again and restore the traditional German principle of unity of teaching and research, but they are not always interested in taking over central institutes of the Academy and especially their staffs.

4. The Science Council gives priority to renewing the existing system of higher education and research over founding new universities. Renewal alone will result in tremendous investments and high operating costs. New universities, according to the Science Council, should not be considered before the monumental effort of renewing the existing institutions is well under way. There may be exceptions, however, in the state of Brandenburg (the region around Berlin), which so far does not have any university. The council therefore approved the founding of a new university in Frankfurt on Oder, at the Polish border (the old university there was closed in 1811). It is to serve as an academic bridge to Poland. The Science Council also approved of the new University of Potsdam, in the outskirts of Berlin, which was founded by combining existing institutions of higher education and research. Reluctant and conditional approval finally came for a new technical university (based on a former engineering school) at Cottbus in the state of Brandenburg. The state government has gone ahead with all three new institutions.

As was to be expected, controversy arose over many of the recommendations of the Science Council, not only concerning details but also concerning basic principles. To what extent can Westerners, who have not lived under the regime in the East, really understand? And to what an extent would West German institutions of higher education and research, if evaluated in the same way, pass the test? How can institutions and their academics be judged by Western standards if they have never had a chance to prove themselves under the conditions of the Western system? These are some of the more general questions raised in academia and in the media in East and West.

Though there is general agreement that the role of universities in basic research should be strengthened, there is controversy as to how this should be achieved and what this means for those research centers and institutes which should be continued according to the Science Council's recommendations. Thus, the German Rectors Conference, representing all German institutions of higher education, criticized the Science Council for wanting to keep too many institutes of the central Academy outside of the universities. (For years there has been a controversial discussion in West Germany about the increasing tendency to establish publicly funded research centers outside of universities.)

Planning and restructuring of the state systems of higher education in East Germany has been taking place at three levels at the same time: while the Science Council was doing its evaluations and was working on recommendations, the new ministries and state legislatures made many decisions (for instance, about closing down departments or introducing new programs) on their own. At the same time, all of the new state governments had appointed Higher Education Structural Reform Commissions (Hochschulstrukommissionen)—with a majority of their members coming from West Germany—to evaluate their state institutions and make recommendations for restructuring statewide systems of higher education and every institution (Projektgruppe, 1992d, pp. 8–15). These concurrent activities have elements of organized chaos, but maybe it could not be expected to be otherwise after that revolution and under an often extreme pressure for fast decisions.

Changing Programs, Curricula, Courses and Contents

The radical changes most directly affecting students and academic staff are those concerning what is taught (and which of it is compulsory) and who teaches it. The first measure taken in all institutions of higher education all over the GDR after the fall of the old regime was to abolish compulsory studies in Marxism-Leninism, which every student regardless of his or her major had to take for six semesters several hours per week (Fischer, 1992, p. 116). The respective departments were closed down, the teachers dismissed. It is estimated that about 6% of all academic staff in the GDR were engaged in these studies. Also abolished were compulsory Russian language courses and compulsory participation in athletics. Before the revolution every student had to take one period of military service (civil defense for female students) and one period of working on a collective farm during harvest time. These, of course, were discontinued too.

After the establishment of new ministries of education in the five new states, the ministers closed down departments and discontinued programs and courses which were considered to be dyed-in-the-wool ideologically, e.g., political science, sociology, economics, education and philosophy. These decisions were usually taken without the participation of the institutions concerned and, as was to be expected, led to controversies between universities and ministries. In one case—at the Humboldt University in East Berlin—the courts did not uphold the ministerial decision to close down several departments. The controversy basically was about autonomy: whereas, for instance, the Humboldt University felt that it should and could manage the processes of transformation and fundamental change itself (Toro, 1991), it was the predominant position of ministers (and many academics) that departments and universities dominated by party-line academics would neither be willing nor able to really change the system and the contents. Therefore, autonomy as laid down in the federal higher education law—as the ministers saw it and decided accordingly—was to be withheld until after "purification." Renewal—that was the position of most of the political decision makers—could not be accomplished and, for reasons of principle, should not be left to those who held positions of responsibility under the old regime in academia. This point really touches on one of the basic problems and challenges of the process of unification—not just as a political but also as a societal issue.

To close down, discontinue, abolish is only one side of transformation, a preparatory stage and a precondition for renewal. By ministerial decision or approval (e.g., when proposals were made by the universities), new departments were founded and new programs and courses had to be developed. In fields like economics, business administration, political science and law, there were hardly any East German academics who would be able to teach that content which had not been taught previously and which had been "enemy territory" for Eastern researchers. Therefore, various programs were started to recruit academics—including retired ones—from West Germany to teach in former East Germany. This also pertained to disciplines that were mainly taught according to Marxist-Leninist theory and where "bourgeois science" had been largely excluded since the '50s: philosophy, psychology, history and education.

This transformation and renewal of institutions of higher education in Eastern Europe in general, and in East Germany in particular, was without precedent. It was therefore important to develop procedures for founding new departments and introducing new programs and to define the rules of the different actors in the institutions and in the ministries. In the first year after unification, a pattern and structure for founding and building up new departments and programs was developed—with variations from state to state and from case to case—which somehow resembles the founding processes for new universities, professional schools or departments that had become customary when many new institutions were founded in the Federal Republic in the time of the big expansion of higher education in the '60s and '70s. The minister appoints a "founding dean" (*Gründungsdekan*)—in a majority of cases, from West Germany—for a new department, professional school or graduate school and a mixed founding commission. This develops the new program, sets up rules and requirements for examinations, works out a budget and acts as a search committee for the "founding chairs," which are advertised nationally. The founding dean recruits visiting professors and lecturers—most of them from the West—to fill in the gaps until permanent staff is appointed (Klemm, Böttcher & Weegen, 1992, p. 130). This procedure is applicable only where the old units have been "liquidated" and new ones started from scratch. These are relatively clear-cut cases (though the normal chaos of reality differs from this scheme) in comparison to more difficult situations in which renewal has to be accomplished out of the existing structures and programs and with large parts of a faculty socialized under the old system. In principle, every program will have to be reviewed in the light of a changed and changing environment that the graduates will have to live and work in.

Renewal of Higher Education and the Old Staff

Overcoming the GDR past, renewal of higher education and integration into the higher education system of the Federal Republic have far-reaching and often existential consequences for East German academics. We may distinguish between three kinds of developments concerning the staff of higher education institutions in East Germany: (1) dismissing functionaries, (2) winding up departments and (3) evaluating staff.

Dismissing Functionaries

- Academics who held responsible positions in the party (e.g., party secretaries at the department or university level) or who owed their positions to the party without adequate academic qualifications were dismissed or resigned. The same applies to undercover informants and members of the state security forces.

- Rectors, deans and most directors of institutes lost their positions but not necessarily their chairs.

- Lecturers for compulsory courses in Marxism-Leninism were dismissed as their departments were closed down.

These were mainly rather clear-cut cases, and there was a widespread consensus about them among the new political decision makers: after the totalitarian regime had been overthrown by a broad revolutionary movement, the functionaries, higher ranking representatives of the regime and those who had spied on their colleagues or harmed them in their careers or their private lives could not expect to be kept in office.

Winding-Up Departments

All members (including nonacademic staff) of "wound up" departments lost their jobs collectively because their workplace no longer existed, even if they were fully qualified and not politically incriminated. In that case they could reapply for a position if there was a follow-up institution (like a new department in the same field).

Evaluating Staff

All members of departments and institutes that were not closed down are "evaluated" as to their political past by "personnel commissions" appointed by the ministry and consisting of members from the university and representatives of the public (for instance, local or state legislators). If the outcome is negative, they are dismissed. These procedures are regulated by "higher education renewal laws" (*Hochschulerneuerungsgesetze*) in all of the new states. It is still too early to assess the work of personnel commissions (Webler, 1992). But it is apparent that they work under a self-imposed pressure to prove they can manage the painful process of "purification."

East German academics who are "positively evaluated"—another one of the new terms—still cannot be sure they will be kept in their positions. The new state governments are still in the process of developing new staffing plans for every institution of higher education, containing considerably fewer positions than there were before. Compared to West Germany, East German institutions of higher education were overstaffed. Given the misery of public finances in Germany since and because of reunification and taking into account the extent of overcrowding and understaffing in West German higher education, and furthermore considering that most of the funding of higher education in the new East German states has to be provided by West Germany, it is not surprising that the new staffing plans have to be adjusted to this situation and thus to the West German staff/student ratios. And this is where the problem of the human costs of integrating East German higher education comes up: even after all dismissals for political reasons have taken place and all possibilities of early retirement have been exhausted,[11] the remaining number of academics and nonacademic employees will still be higher than the number of positions in the new staffing plans according to West German index figures and the ability of the East German state governments to pay. Thus, even many of those who have

been cleared politically and who have been found to be academically qualified will finally be let go. When the new budgets and
staffing plans come out, even those academics whose old positions are identical with those in the new staffing plan have to
reapply. In many cases they have to compete with applicants
from West Germany.

There is considerable criticism of these policies in both
parts of Germany (Gardner, 1991), both as to the methods used
and the extent to which academic staff is reduced. Assuming that
after a couple of years the participation rates in higher education
in East Germany become the same as in the West and taking into
account the high rate of early retirements, it has been forecasted
that there will be a considerable shortage of academic staff
within less than ten years. Though the number of academic staff
positions needed around the turn of the century and until 2010 is
lower than the number was in the GDR in 1989 (Burkhardt,
Scherer & Erdner, 1991), the demand will be much higher than
the number of positions the new state governments are presently
planning for (Klemm, Böttcher & Weegen, 1992, pp. 168–79).

A tentative balance of old and new academic staff, taking
into account that most academic positions in the new programs
(law, economics, business administration, social science, education, etc.) are being filled with applicants from West Germany,
shows that in the end probably not more than 40% of the old
academic staff will be retained in East Germany.[12] Thus, renewal
of higher education has come to mean redundancy for roughly
half of the East German academics.

Influences of West German Problems
of Higher Education

The problems of renewing higher education in East Germany in the process of integrating it into the system of the Federal Republic cannot be properly understood without considering some of the problems of West German higher education and
their—partly indirect—effects on higher education policy for and
in the new states. The unprecedented rise in the number of stu-

dents during the last decades in West Germany (Der Bundesminister, 1991, pp. 140–41) has not been met by a corresponding increase in staff. The ratio of academic staff to students went down to 1:22 at universities and 1:31 at vocational colleges (*Fachhochschulen*). On the basis of statistical index figures, there are almost twice as many students in West Germany as there is room for them. The situation of higher education in West Germany has been analyzed and documented both by the then West German Rectors Conference (Westdeutsche Rektorenkonferenz, 1988) and the Science Council (Wissenschaftsrat, 1988). The Rectors Conference recently stated that there was a shortage of 30,000 positions for academic staff and that an investment program of 6 billion Marks was necessary to meet the most urgent needs of higher education (Gardner, 1992). On the other hand, the federal government just decided to cut the projected funds for investments in higher education by 20% and decreed that no new investment projects for West German higher education would be started because of the necessity of focusing on the East German states. The problem thus seems to be that higher education renewal in the East apparently can only be funded by neglecting—to a certain extent—the needs of higher education in the West, where a huge funding deficit has accumulated over the years.

This financial crisis of higher education is undoubtedly overshadowing the process of transformation of higher education in East Germany. These difficulties, however, have not prevented close cooperation between institutions of higher education in both parts of Germany. From November 1989 on, a steady stream of visiting professors and lecturers flowed into East German universities, especially in fields and disciplines which had to be built anew. New programs and courses were planned and set up in close cooperation between East and West German academics and with massive support from West German university departments. Every university in East Germany developed links with more than one university in West Germany. The flow of ideas and support went mainly in one direction, and it was inevitable that tensions would develop in these highly sensitive relationships; there were tensions also between those East German academics and students who had welcomed the revolution and those who had not and subsequently tended to view it more like a defeat than a liberation. In the general context of the unification process, the unequal relationships were almost bound to create feelings in the East of being dominated. On the other hand, the fact that West Germany had become the model for the East also influenced attitudes of West Germans toward East Germans. In higher education, as in other walks of life, it turned out (as sociologists might have expected) that becoming one people again would be a long and difficult social process.

Conclusion

The direction of change and the contours of the evolving system of higher education in East Germany are clearly visible if we take a long-term perspective. The present turmoil in East German higher education, however, will continue for quite some time. This concerns structural changes and, even more so, the development and implementation of the new staffing plans. Material renewal will take at least another decade or longer. Funding will remain a critical issue, and investment programs are going to be "stretched," as finance ministers say euphemistically when they allot less money per year. To the extent that the process of transformation is also a matter of values and norms and thus of socialization, the time span will be more in the order of a generation. Therefore, the new liberties—in connection with new existential problems—are often experienced not only as freedom and self-determination but also as a straining uncertainty concerning norms, values, ways of life and behavioral patterns—notwithstanding continuities and East/West similarities—reinforced by the turmoil of changing the whole system of higher education, with the very high risk that many will be made redundant.

There are no indications that people in East German academia want the old system back. There seems to be a very broad consensus among academics and students that academic freedom and institutional autonomy are imminent necessities for academic study, scholarship and research, and that they are integral elements of Western democracies. Even though East German higher education was not part of the avant-garde of the 1989 revolution, it is, from what a particular observer can see, definitely "going West." It remains to be seen to what an extent and in which ways institutions and state systems of higher education in the East German states will develop their own identity, corporate culture and specific characteristics within the federal system of Germany or whether in the end they will fall in line with the West German states.

NOTES

* This chapter is an expanded and updated version of the author's article, "Transforming Higher Education in East Germany," which appeared in the *Review of Higher Education*, Vol. 16, No. 4, pp. 391–417.

1. Throughout this article the term "East Germany" stands for the territory which until the day of reunification (October 3, 1990) was the German Democratic Republic, GDR (Deutsche Demokratische Republik, DDR), and since then has been part of the Federal Republic of Germany, FRG (Bundesrepublik Deutschland, BRD). East Germany consists now of five federal states, which are usually referred to as "the five new states." Geographically, these states are the eastern part of the Federal Republic, often called "the East."

2. This was preceded by the treaty creating a "currency, economic, and social union" between the Federal Republic and the GDR (May 18, 1990), by an "elections treaty" for all-German elections (August 3, 1990) and, finally, by the famous Treaty of Unification (*Einigungsvertrag*) (August 31, 1990) and its supplements. Complementing these treaties between the two German states was the "Two-Plus-Four Treaty" between the four powers (U.S., U.K., France, Soviet Union) and the two German states (September 12, 1990), formally ending all rights and prerogatives of the former allies concerning Germany, giving their approval to unification, and restoring the full sovereignty of Germany (*Die Verträge*, 1990).

3. Within the framework of a general educational reform movement between, roughly, 1966 and 1978 there were reforms in higher education concerning mainly the structure of the system, introducing the participation of students, junior staff and office staff in the governing

bodies; creating planning mechanisms for higher education on the state and federal level; introducing new types of institutions (comprehensive universities and polytechnic colleges); reforming the structure of academic programs; regulating access and exams, etc. All of these measures paved the way to mass higher education. For a general and comparative account, see Teichler, 1988. The process of democratization in West German higher education is analyzed by Pritchard, 1990.

4. In the discussion of external and internal forces shaping higher education, many social scientists concentrate on the influence of social, political and economic change. It is the merit especially of Burton R. Clark to have stressed and analyzed the importance of the internal factors determining higher education systems in a broad comparative perspective (Clark, 1983).

5. It does not seem possible to get exact figures on students and staff in the GDR. The figures of the Science Council differ from those of the Federal Ministry of Education, which I have used. As to comparing participation rates, my calculations differ slightly from the figures given by the ministry because I have used an average yearly age-group of the 19- to 22-year-olds (instead of 19–20) as a basis.

6. These figures somehow distort the real picture; for an East/West German comparison, it should be taken into account that East German academics have to take care of many students in further education, which is not shown in these statistics. The number of students in East Germany is more or less equal to those really attending courses and seminars, whereas the West German student/teacher ratio is, in reality, not quite as bad because it usually takes students about two more years than it is supposed to to finish the number of courses they have to complete, and they usually do not take as many courses as are expected of them. The number of students actually attending classes is probably considerably smaller than the number of enrolled students. But even considering all of these factors, the student/teacher ratio in East Germany is still much more favorable than in West Germany.

7. Whereas the Social Democratic Party had to be founded anew in East Germany, because in 1946 it was involuntarily "joined" with the Communist Party, the Christian Democrats and the Liberals formally continued to exist in the GDR, though they were without influence and there were no free elections. They were part of a more or less unified "democratic bloc" and thereby were allotted a limited number of seats in the legislature, where they could not in any way play the role of an opposition party as in Western countries.

8. The German Research Society is the biggest institution promoting academic research in Germany. In 1990 it spent about 1.2 billion Marks for research grants, fellowships, promotion of doctoral students, institutional support of research institutes, etc. It is funded jointly by the federal (60%) and the state (40%) governments but is completely independent of both. All decisions are made by nationwide elected academics. Grants, etc., are subject to strict peer review.

9. In Germany, there has been a strong tendency in the last decade to create and expand research institutes and centers outside of universities. Most institutions belong to one of the umbrella organizations of research centers, but federal and state governments also operate research institutes of their own. Universities are increasingly concerned about this "emigration" of research.

10. The Science Council is the most important advisory body for the federal and state governments in all matters of higher education and research. Its influence goes far beyond mere advice. It was founded by an agreement between the federal government and the states in 1957. Of its 54 members, 32 are appointed by the federal president (24 academics and 8 representatives of the public, all with an academic background) and 22 are high-ranking representatives (ministers, permanent secretaries of state or their deputies) of the federal government and of all the state governments. Because of this composition, there is always a great deal of government consent worked into the recommendations of the council, which tends to increase their impact on political decision makers as well as academia. The Science Council evaluates research institutions and programs funded by public grants; it is responsible for assessing all plans of the states for capital investments in higher education. The federal government will only pay its 50% share if there is a positive recommendation by the council. Such a recommendation is always based on an evaluation of the activities for which the building investments are to be used. In that way, the Science Council, de facto, decides about academic programs, research institutes, libraries, etc. The council publishes recommendations and opinions on all major issues concerning higher education and research in Germany and therefore is a major factor in German higher education policy.

11. There are no exact figures about these early retirements. Burkhardt and Scherer have calculated that between 1991 and 2000 about 9,400 academic staffers will qualify for retirement in East Germany. It can be assumed that most of these—instead of being dismissed—will "voluntarily" take early retirement now, which is possible from the age of 55 on (Burkhardt & Scherer, 1991, pp. 218–19).

12. There are no exact figures, because it is not yet known how many positions will be in the staffing plans of the East German states for higher education, how many of the *new* positions will go to West German academics (from what we know so far, it is the large majority) and what the difference between the planned number of positions and those really available will be. The following figures are taken from statistics (not yet published) by the Standing Conference of Ministers of Education (Kultusministerkonferenz [KMK]) and Burkhardt/Scherer (see above):

	12/31/89	12/31/91	Planned for 1992
Academic staff	30,945	22,432	16,458 (53.8% of 1989)
Nonacademic staff	36,746	25,274	17,410 (47.4% of 1989)
Total higher education staff	67,691	47,706	33,868 (50.0% of 1989)

The number of positions in 1993 will be lower than the planning figures for 1992. The figures for 1989 do not include the staff of those institutions and sections which have been closed down in 1989; also not included are institutions within the party, the unions and some of the ministries.

REFERENCES

Ashwill, M. A. (1991). German democratic republic. In P. G. Altbach (ed.), *International higher education: An encyclopedia* (pp. 671–83). New York & London: Garland Publishing, Inc.

The basic law of the federal republic of Germany. (1986). Bonn: Press and Information Office of the Federal Government.

Der Bundesminister für Bildung und Wissenschaft. (1991). *Grund- und Strukturdaten 1991/92.* Bad Honnef: Verlag Karl Heinrich Bock.

Bundesministerium für innerdeutsche Beziehungen. (ed). (1990). *Vergleich von Bildung und Erziehung in der Bundesrepublik Deutschland und in der Deutschen Demokratischen Republik.* Köln: Verlag Wissenschaft und Politik.

Burkhardt, A. & Scherer, D. (1991). Personal an Hochschulen in den neuen Bundesländern—Ausgangspunkte und Perspektiven. *Beiträge zur Hochschulforschung 3*, pp. 185–225.

Burkhardt, A., Scherer, D. & Erdner, S. (1991). *Personalbestand an Hochschulen der ehemaligen DDR 1989 und 1990*. Projektgruppe Hochschulforschung, Projektberichte 3/1991. Berlin.

Clark, B. R. (1983). *The higher education system: Academic organization in cross-national perspective*. Berkeley, Los Angeles, London: University of California Press.

Fischer, A. (ed.) (1988). *Deutsche Demokratische Republik. Daten, Fakten, Analysen*. Freiburg/Würzburg: Verlag Ploeta.

———. (ed.) (1992). *Das Bildungssystem der DDR. Entwicklung, Umbruch und Neugestaltung seit 1989*. Darmstadt: Wissenschaftliche Buchgesellschaft.

Gardner, M. (1991). Professors and students in Eastern Germany protest "restructuring" of universities by Western officials. *The Chronicle of Higher Education*, pp. A31–A32.

———. (1992). Budget blues hit German rectors. *The Times Higher Education Supplement*, p. 9.

Geißler, R. (1992). *Die Sozialstruktur Deutschlands. Ein Studienbuch zur Entwicklung im geteilten und vereinten Deutschland*. Opladen: Westdeutscher Verlag.

Goldschmidt, D. & Schäfer, H. D. (eds.) (1990). *Aktuelle Probleme der Forschung über Hochschulen. Bildungsökonomische, bildungssoziologische und internationale Aspekte der Entwicklung in der DDR*. Berlin: Max Planck Institute for Human Development and Education, Contributions from the Center for School Systems and Instruction No. 34/SuU.

Hochschulrahmengesetz (HRG) (1987). (p. 1170). Bonn: Bundesgesetzblatt I.

Institut für Gesellschaft und Wissenschaft Erlangen. (ed.) (1979). *Das Wissenschaftssystem in der DDR* (2d revised ed.). Frankfurt/New York: Campus Verlag.

Klemm, K., Böttcher, W. & Weegen, M. (1992). *Bildungsplanung in den neuen Bundesländern. Entwicklungstrends, Perspective und Vergleiche*. Veröffent-lichugen der Max-Traeger-Stiftung. Weinheim/Müchen: Juventa Verlag.

Krejci, J. (1976). *Social structure in divided Germany*. London: Croom Helm Ltd.

Müller, M. & Müller, E. E. (1953). ". . . stürmt die Festung Wissenschaft!"—
Die Sowjetisierung der mitteldeutschen Universitäten seit 1945. West
Berlin: Colloquium-Verlag.

Naumann, J. & Krais, B. (1991). German Federal Republic. In P. G.
Altbach (ed.), International higher education: An encyclopedia (pp.
685–707). New York & London: Garland Publishing, Inc.

Ogburn, W. F. (1957). Cultural lag as theory. Sociology and Social
Research, 41(1/2), pp. 167–74.

Pritchard, R. M. O. (1990). The end of elitism? The democratization of the
West German university system. New York/Oxford/Munich: Berg.

Projektgruppe H. (1991a-g). Berlin-Karlshorst. Projektberichte, 1(7).
Berlin.

———. (1992a-c). Projektberichte, 1(3). Berlin.

———. (1992d). Zur Hochschulerneuerung in den neuen Bundesländern—
Situationsbericht. Berlin.

Riesman, D. (1950) The lonely crowd: A study of the changing American
character. New Haven: Yale University Press.

Rudolf, H. & Husemann, R. (1984). Hochschulpolitik zwischen Expansion
und Restriktion. Ein Vergleich der Entwicklung in der Bundesrepublik
Deutschland und der Deutschen Demokratischen Republik.
Frankfurt/New York: Campus Verlag.

Schell, M. & Kalinka, W. (1991). Stasi und kein Ende. Die Personen und
Fakten. Frankfurt/Berlin: Ullstein.

Teichler, U. (1988). Changing patterns of the higher education system: The
experience of three decades. London: Jessica Kingsley Publishers.

Toro, T. (1991). A university in the former East Germany struggles to
sweep away the influences of its communist past. The Chronicle of
Higher Education, pp. A37–A38.

Die Verträge zur Einheit Deutschlands. (1990). München: Verlag C. H.
Beck (Beck-Texts im dtv 5564).

Voigt, D., Werner Voß, W. & Meck, S. (1987). Sozialstruktur der DDR:
Eine Einführung. Darmstadt: Wissenschaftliche Buchgesellschaft.

Webler, Woff-Dietrich. (1992) Eine Schlacht für den Rechtsstaat
gewonnen? Personalkommissionen an ostdeutschen
Hochschulen. Das Hochschulwesen. Forum für Hochschulforschung,
-praxis und -politik 40 No. 2, pp. 52–62.

Westdeutsche R. (1988). Die Zukunft der Hochschulen. Bonn.

Wissenschaftsrat (West German Science Council). (1988). *Empfenlungen zu den Perspektiven der Hochschulen in den ioer Jahren.* Köln.

———. (1990a). *Press releases 8/90, 13/90, 14/90.* Köln.

———. (1990b). *Perspektiven für Wissenschaft und Forschung auf dem Weg zur deutschen Einheit.* Köln.

———. (1991a). *Press releases 2/91, 4/91, 5/91, 7–19/91.* Köln.

———. (1991b). *Empfehlungen zur Entwicklung der Fachhochschulen in den 90er Jahren.* Köln.

———. (1991c). Empfehlungen zur Errichtung von Fachhochschulen. *Den neuen Ländern vom 5(7)*, p. 91. Köln.

———. (1992a). *Empfehlungen zur künftigen Struktur der Hochschullandschaft in den neuen Ländern und im Ostteil von Berlin—Teil 1.* Köln.

———. (1992b). *Stellungnahmen zu den außeruniversitäten Forschungseinrichtungen in den neuen Ländern und in Berlin— allgemeiner Teil.* Köln.

Zentralinstitut für Hochschulbildung. (1990a). *Lehre, Forschung und Weiterbildung im Hochschulwesen der DDR: Ausgangspunkte und Wandel. Ein Gutachten des Zentralinstituts für Hochschulbildung zum Prozeß der Vereinigung Deutschlands.* Berlin.

———. (1990b-g). *Hochschullandschaft Berlin, Hochschullandschaft Brandenburg, Hochschullandschaft Sachsen-Anhalt, Hochschullandschaft Mecklenburg-Vorpommern, Hoch- und Fachschulen in Sachsen, Hochschullandschaft Thüringen.* Berlin.

CHAPTER VII

Equality of Higher Education in Post-Communist Hungary and Poland
*Challenges and Prospects**

Kassie Freeman

Introduction

Regardless of the culture, the word *equality* invariably evokes discomfort. No matter the context of discussion—whether it is education, employment or politics—it is one of those subjects that causes people to feel the need to defend their views and classify their position. Somehow, people tend to think that the word *equality* means that they have to choose between status in society (rich or poor), ethnicity or gender. In other words, the very idea of equality leads people to believe that something is being taken away from one group and given to another. Yet, education is one commodity that benefits everyone. It is through equal educational opportunities that everyone benefits. As Thurow says, "I can't afford to live with my neighbors' children ignorant because if they are ignorant my income is going to be lower than it otherwise would be."

Countless Western economists and educators have demonstrated the benefits of education to individuals and societies (Becker, 1975; Blaug, Preston & Ziderman, 1967; Bowles & Gintis, 1976; Carnoy & Levin, 1985; Cohn, 1979; R. B. Freeman, 1976;

Lynton, 1984; Psacharopoulos, 1985; Schultz, 1961; Solomon, 1980; Thurow, 1972). These human capital (economics of education) theorists have concluded that individuals and society benefit directly from education, either monetarily or non-monetarily. Direct monetary benefits to individuals are usually measured by increased earning potential after completion of an educational program. Society benefits directly from increases in taxes paid by individuals and indirectly from increased productivity of future generations of children of educated individuals.

In the U.S., the average layperson tends to think of equality of higher education in terms of color (black or white), whereas in former Communist countries, the issue of equality relates more to class in society (professional, semiskilled or manual worker). Regardless of the basis of inequality in higher education, the effects are devastating for individuals and society. The groups that are not privileged to participate in higher education are often relegated to lower status in society, holding less prestigious, dead-end jobs, participating less in the political process, and becoming victims of a permanent underclass (which tends to mean crime, drugs and other social problems). Obviously, the more people participate in the labor market, the more individuals have disposable income and the more society reaps in increased taxes. That means that countries have to spend less on social services.

As conflicts over territories shift to economic competition, higher education in former socialist countries will play a major role in how competitive these countries will become in the global marketplace. The Center for Educational Competitiveness (1992) states, "A strong human resource development is essential to the economic growth of every country." The new economies (those which compete successfully in a global marketplace) will be information- or knowledge-based, where people will be working in professions involving processing and distribution of information. While technological advancement is forming the basis for the information age, higher education will provide the quality training and education needed.

Among higher education planners and economists, it is widely accepted that it will be necessary for post-Communist countries to gear the relevance, efficiency and capacity of their educational programs to meet the demands of a market economy (Sadlak, 1990; Kozma, 1990; World Bank, 1991). In Hungary and Poland, higher education officials have indicated the need to radically transform higher education establishments (Hungarian Draft Concept for the Legal Regulation of Higher Education, 1992; Kwiatkowski, 1990). Kwiatkowski (1990) has indicated that increasing higher education participation is particularly important in newly democratic countries for three reasons:

1. Forming values and ideas needed for sustainable democracy.

2. Fostering inter- and intra-national links, since it creates an elite needed for sustainable cultural and economic development.

3. Providing service functions needed for economic and educational development.

Both Hungary and Poland recognize the importance of ensuring equality of educational opportunities in order not to create a social drain on their fragile economies. It would further strain their economies to create a permanent underclass, people who are uneducated or undereducated for a market economy and need unemployment benefits (a system only recently created in these countries) and other social services. The Preamble of the draft of the proposed Hungarian act for higher education (1992) states their commitment to equality:

> In accordance with the principles of the Constitution and the international agreements sanctioned by Hungary, the Act wishes to guarantee to every qualified applicant the admission to institutions of higher education, irrespective of their social, linguistic-cultural, or regional ties. The institutions of higher education should at the same time pay special attention to the realization of the principle of equal opportunities, to the positive discrimination of the socially disadvantaged, and to the careful guidance of the outstanding talents.

The issue of equality of higher education is not new in Hungary or Poland. In fact, Poland and Hungary have experimented with "positive discrimination" (providing extra points for students of semiskilled and peasant origin) long before the change in their economic systems. Why has equality of higher education been a problem to achieve in Hungary and Poland in the past? What will be the prospects for achieving equity in higher education in the future?

Equality of Higher Education under Communist Rule

There are at least three reasons why it is important to understand how Hungary and Poland attempted to achieve equality of higher education under Communist rule. First, it is important to understand the rationale for admission and selection for higher education participation under the Communist regime. Under Communist rule, admission and selection criteria in higher education were controlled for political, economic and social reasons. Lukacs (1989) said that the rationale for this was twofold: first, manpower was one of the fundamental resources of the national economy, and second, reproduction of the manpower structure also represented a reproduction of the social structure (i.e., the system of social positions and the relationship between the particular classes, strata and groups).

For political reasons, according to Kozma (1990), "a strongly selective higher education system helped to control the recruitment and limit the 'production' of intellectuals" (p. 383). In other words, the State attempted to control education as a means of reshaping the social structure. Policies to ensure youths from worker and peasant classes access to higher education were implemented to break the "ruling classes" (Dobson, 1977). By controlling the qualification system and the school system, the government sought to keep the market free from spontaneous influences (Lukacs, 1989). As Lukacs said, the idea was to maintain the existing social structure and to prevent those unfit from becoming members of the ruling elite class. Therefore, access to higher education institutions in these countries is still difficult because they are traditionally classic, i.e., very academic, elitist and closed. There is no community college system, for example, which in the U.S. serves as a division between the classes.

Manpower forecasting was one of the most powerful arguments against increasing the participation in higher education.

The idea was to prevent unemployment. Therefore, manpower planners developed mid-term and long-range plans (5-year and 15-year) in an attempt to determine the exact number of professionals needed in each occupation (i.e., engineers, teachers, doctors, etc.). In addition to determining the number of individuals needed in each profession, the political authorities determined the social background and what social group these individuals should represent. The availability for higher education, then, was based on projected socioeconomic demands. It is for these reasons that entrance to higher education has been highly selective and competitive. In Hungary, for example, Kozma estimates the ratio of applicants to admissions to be 3:1, and the ratio is roughly the same in Poland.

Second, an understanding of the "flow" of graduates from secondary to higher education, their perception and attitudes about higher education versus the needs of the State under Communist rule, is important for reformulating strategies for equal access to higher education. Admission to higher education in these countries is a three-step process. Applicants complete secondary schooling, have good marks in secondary school and pass an entrance examination. Noteworthy is the fact that students must determine after eight years of schooling (ages 6–14) whether to continue in a track of schooling that will enable them to be eligible for access to higher education. Should students choose apprenticeship training, for example, they would not be prepared to take the entrance examination.

The flow of students from secondary schooling to higher education was hampered by entrance examinations, manpower planning objectives and students' perception of the value of schooling. In a 20-year (from 1965 to 1985) Polish experiment to increase the tertiary participation of students of worker and peasant classes, Wnuk-Lipinska (1985) indicated that not only did the percentage of working class students not increase, but the proportion of peasant students participating in higher education actually declined from 17% to 5%. Her findings were confirmed in an earlier study by Najduchowska (1978). Lukacs (1989) reported similar findings in Hungary, i.e., the number of students from homes of manual workers increased from 1972 to 1978 but declined after then.

Students' and parents' perceptions of the value of higher education played an even greater role in students' decisions to attend higher education. The perception of the worth of schooling is typically class-based, i.e., the higher is the parents' level of schooling, the higher their aspirations for schooling for their child.

Finally, it is important to review equality of higher education under Communist rule to understand the obstacles Hungary and Poland will encounter in trying to equalize access to higher education in the future. Although under Communist rule attempts were made to equalize access to higher education, participation by students from lower classes was greatly limited. For example, in Poland in the early 1980s, working class and peasants comprised approximately 65% of the population while less than half of the students in higher education came from these two classes (table 1). Students of working class origin comprised 31.1% of the students accepted to higher education while 10.8% students of peasant origin were accepted. Sadlak (1991) listed

TABLE 1. **The Social Background of Students Accepted for Higher Education in Poland in 1974**

	Total Number	Percentage of Social Background		
		Workers	Peasant	Intelligentsia
Entered for examination	145,587			
	(100%)	32.0	11.3	55.0
Accepted for studies	65,987			
	(100%)	31.1	10.8	56.4

Source: Najduchowska, H. (1978). Higher education and professional careers: Students' perception. In B. C. Sanyal & A. Josefowicz (Eds.), *Graduate employment and planning of higher education in Poland* (p. 156). Paris: International Institute for Educational Planning.

similar figures for the social composition of higher education participation in Poland: 32% from working class, 9.3% from peasant families and 55% from intelligentsia. Hungary faces similar circumstances (figure 1). In Hungary, the percentage of children of manual workers attending regular courses at higher

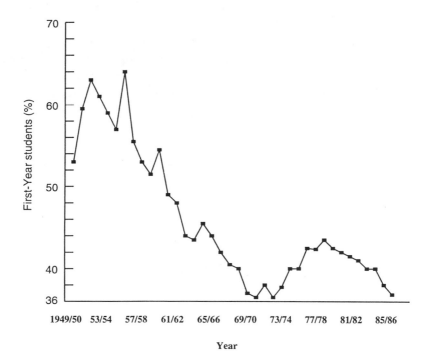

FIGURE 1. The Percentage of Children of Manual Workers among First-Year Students Attending Regular Courses at Institutions of Higher Education in Hungary

Source: Lukacs, P. (1989). Changes in selection policy in Hungary: The case of the admission system in higher education. *Comparative Education, 25* (2), 219–28.

education institutions in 1985/86 was approximately 37%. Najduchowska (1978) lists the following as reasons for the discrepancy in applications to higher education between the different social classes:

1. Inequalities resulting from hereditary and contemporary differences in the economic and social position of the various groups and classes.

2. Unequal upbringing and cultural levels acquired at home in different social and occupational groups and regions.

3. Uneven opportunities of admission to secondary and high schools, due to disparities in the geographical availability of secondary education.

4. Difference in patterns of career expectations predominant in various social classes. (pp. 154–55)

How to overcome these inequities will pose great challenges to these two countries as they make the transition to a market economy. Despite attempts of Communist countries (all countries for that matter) to equalize access to higher education, inequities still exist. How they overcome these challenges can be instructive for other countries (such as Western Europe and the U.S.) that are grappling with the same problem.

Challenges Confronting Hungary and Poland in Achieving Equality of Higher Education

By all accounts (Sadlak, 1990; Lukacs, 1989; World Bank, 1991; and Wnuk-Lipinska, 1985), post-Communist countries face at least five major obstacles in equalizing access to higher education: selectivity, tracking, motivation and aspiration, market value of education, and lack of resources. Sadlak and Lukacs raise the question, what should be the criteria for selectivity? Should higher education admission be collective- or individual-based, i.e., preferential or meritocratic, or both?

Selectivity Criteria

The first problem, then, is defining an inclusive basis of selectivity for higher education participation. Defining admission criteria and solutions to equalize access to higher education is extraordinarily difficult, since positive discrimination, tuition-free education has not increased the participation of underrepresented groups. As Sadlak (1991) has indicated, additional points for social background have apparently had marginal effect on applicants from underrepresented groups gaining admission to higher education, especially the more prestigious institutions. However, if, as Sadlak also suggests, admission to higher education were based purely on meritocracy, that would raise doubts about the sincerity of Hungary and Poland to achieve equal access to higher education. Equality and meritocracy are contradictory by definition. By meritocracy, it is assumed that all conditions are equal throughout life (e.g., socioeconomic status, environmental conditions, etc.) and, therefore, all students have an equal chance to be selected for higher education. There can never be a pure meritocracy because parents in the upper class pass on their influence to their children, thereby, in effect, continuing the creation of classes for each generation (Bell, 1977).

In Hungary, where the political mood can be described as conservative, there are two lines of thinking about the criteria for selectivity for higher education admission. One idea is that no immediate steps will be taken to develop or define a policy for equal access. The individuals who hold this view favor a policy based on meritocracy. They believe that the Communist policy of positive discrimination should be abandoned. Their views towards positive discrimination can be described as similar to conservative views in America toward affirmative action. They believe to add extra points for students from underrepresented groups would mean taking away opportunities from "much better prepared" individuals. The other line of thinking is that the conservative view will be short-lived. Their thinking is that the higher education system must be made broad enough to create real opportunity and give way to a more social democratic policy. They predict that one selection criterion that Hungary's equality of higher education policy might incorporate will resemble that of the Swedish model, where a number of predetermined slots will be reserved for students from underrepresented classes. In this model, students selected to fill these spaces will be judged on the usual criteria (entrance examination and academic background), plus they would be interviewed and judged on such criteria as motivation, creativity and work experience.

Poland, too, according to Sadlak (1990) favors discontinuing positive discrimination. However, several years ago, a number of Polish educators suggested a different method of testing students for entrance to higher education. For example, they proposed in the 1970s developing a biographical questionnaire to evaluate the all-around characteristics of an applicant and/or averaging the grades received in the top two years of secondary school, which would provide a much broader appraisal of an applicant's knowledge base (Najduchowska, 1978).

Without a concrete policy to increase higher education participation, it is doubtful that early progress will be made to equalize access for underrepresented groups. What is needed is a coherent policy with short- and long-term direction. Most researchers will agree that the decision about higher education participation is made long before students sit for an entrance examination.

Tracking System

It is the preselection process from lower secondary (primary) to upper secondary that poses a second challenge (and pehaps the biggest) in equalizing access to higher education in Hungary and Poland. A 1991 World Bank report on Hungary's transition to a market economy refers to the preselection process as "too early specialization." Students at too young an age (typically age 14) are required to make essentially lifelong career choices.

In Hungary and Poland, eight years of compulsory schooling (primary) are required, ages 6–14. At age 14 students select which track of schooling to continue. Students can select between basically three types of secondary schooling: (1) academic secondary schools (grammar schools) prepare students in general academic subjects; (2) technical professional or secondary professional schools provide general specialized or professional vocational training, e.g., for students interested in becoming engineers; and (3) apprenticeship or lower vocational schools provide students with training for specific occupations. Approximately 25% of Hungarian students attend academic secondary schools, 30% enter technical professional schools, and 45% attend apprenticeship training (World Bank, 1991). The percentages of students participating in each track of schooling in Poland is similar: 20% enter grammar school, 20% enter vocational secondary schools and 60% attend lower-level vocational schools (Wnuk-Lipinska, 1985).

While the smallest percentage of students attend grammar schools (these are typically the children of the elite), by far the highest percentage (70%) enter higher education institutions. Children from the upper class disproportionately have the best opportunity of attending grammar school (table 2) and, therefore, have the best chance of passing the entrance examination. As noted in table 2, in Poland in 1985, the higher the father's level of education, the more likely is the child to attend grammar school.

TABLE 2. Secondary School Graduates in Poland According to the Type of School and Educational Level of Father (Percentage)

Type of School	Father with Elementary Education N = 439	Father with Higher Education N = 662
Grammar School (Lyceum)	64[x]	31
Vocational School of Higher Level	12	33
Technical School	24	35

Note: [x] in Warsaw equals 82.

Source: Wnuk-Lipinska, E. (1985). Dilemmas of The Educational System in Poland. Unpublished paper. Warsaw, Poland.

There are even differences in the prestige of the grammar schools that students attend. The upper-class students attend more prestigious grammar schools, which have the best teachers and the reputation for a higher percentage of students passing the entrance examination to universities. For example, in Pecs,

Hungary, at one of the top grammar schools, where students have access to the best courses and teachers, 75% of the students came from upper-class families, while only 1% of the students came from manual workers' families (Schadt, 1992).

The ability of the upper class to hire tutors also works to the disadvantage of students from lower classes. Families pay large sums of money to have their children tutored in courses such as foreign languages, particularly English, which now provides extra credit towards points needed to gain entrance to university (ibid.). Location also has implications for who passes the entrance examination. In table 2, note that even when the fathers' educational levels are equal, Warsaw had a higher percentage of grammar school graduates. The same is true in Hungary. According to Schadt (1992), high-quality village schools need to be reestablished in Hungary to provide better opportunities for rural children.

Although graduates from general vocational schools have the opportunity to take the national entrance examination, as Wnuk-Lipinska (1985) points out, the "generally low level of teaching and poor curriculum in theoretical subjects give them almost no opportunity of being admitted" (p. 3). Approximately 30% of students from technical vocational schools are admitted to higher education. In Hungary, there are experimental schools (13), vocational secondary schools, which began operating in the fall of 1992 and were designed to blur the distinction in the quality of teaching between the grammar schools and vocational schools. The directors of these schools will have a freer hand in selecting and dismissing teachers who are not meeting the standards. The directors will have available the necessary resources for increasing the number of students capable of passing the entrance examination for higher education participation. The selected sites are throughout Hungary, not just the larger cities. One school site selected to participate will be in Komlo, a town of approximately 30,000, where the main industry has been mining.

These selected schools will emphasize general subjects such as cultural arts, active foreign language studies, computer techniques and other subjects, to enable these students to have a better chance of passing the entrance examination to higher education. The schools will also emphasize flexibility so that students will be able to make more informed career choices. The idea is to provide higher-quality vocational schools (which are similar to magnet schools in the U.S.) that will prepare students to choose between higher education or employment following secondary school (Rendeki, 1992).

In Poland, Najduchowska (1978) and Wnuk-Lipinska (1985) concluded that universal secondary schooling (where students would not select tracks after eight years of schooling) might be one of the most important factors in achieving equal access to higher education. In that way, students from different social classes would not have to determine so early which "track" of schooling to pursue. They also found that higher education participation went beyond accessibility; i.e., tuition-free and positive discrimination have not been enough to increase participation.

Motivation and Aspiration

At least three conclusions can be drawn about students' aspirations and motivation to attend higher education. First, the higher the father's educational level, the higher the child's aspiration and motivation. Children who come from a home where at least one parent is educated are more likely to aspire to attend higher education. That is because, says Najduchowska (1978), decisions concerning children's education are often made by parents. In Poland, she says, the advice of teachers and school psychologists plays only a small role in the choice of education for children. It is widely accepted that the value children place on learning is based on their social and cultural background. Therefore, to merely make higher education spaces available is not enough. Methods have to be developed that somehow generate student interest in higher education in the absence of a supportive family background.

Second, students' aspirations are associated with their academic achievement. The aspirations of culturally disadvantaged children are derived, in large part, from their ability to earn high grades (Dobson, 1977). Children who do not perform well academically are obviously more prone to drop out. Lower grades tend to be class-based across cultures. In Hungary and Poland academic performance has been linked to which track of schooling students select. Dobson (1977) described a survey which revealed that, in the former Soviet Union, students whose fathers had completed higher education were twice as likely as their classmates to get higher grades. Clearly, the students who are performing well academically in primary school are more likely to select grammar school and thereby stand a much better chance of passing the entrance examination. Thus, secondary school graduates who have high grades and come from the upper class have a better chance of attending higher education institutions.

The third conclusion that can be drawn about students' motivation and aspirations is that the more individuals of the same status (class and/or race) there are who are not participating in higher education, the more unmotivated individuals from that group become. This phenomenon seems to be the case across cultures. In the U.S., for example, the percentage of African Americans participating in higher education increased in the late 1960s to the mid-1970s; following that period, the participation rate began to decline. The same occurrence happened in Hungary and Poland during the same period. During the 1970s and 1980s, the percentage of students from lower classes participating in higher education in Hungary and Poland began to decline.

For many students from underrepresented groups, as they begin to perceive the decline of the prestige of higher education (the worth of higher education schooling), their motivation begins to decline. Minority and/or culturally disadvantaged youth necessarily need to perceive a more immediate return on their investment in higher education. More often they are investing more in resources, direct and indirect (Freeman, K., 1988 & 1989). Typically, underrepresented groups in higher education have less in resources, so it requires a higher percentage of their capital (e.g., in the U.S. minorities usually have to borrow more to attend higher education institutions). Even when students are receiving grants or when (in countries such as Hungary or Poland) the State provides tuition-free schooling, students from lower classes have a higher cost because their resource base is substantially lower. Indirect costs to underrepresented groups are also higher. If, as Davis and Morrall (1974) estimated, the major cost of education is the indirect cost (i.e., the amount of earnings students forgo while attending higher education), minority (underrepresented) groups pay a much greater cost. The earnings that minorities forgo while attending higher education are typically earnings that they would share in the total family income and are therefore a substantially greater loss for minority families (Freeman, K., 1988).

Market Value of Higher Education

It is the perceived lack of prestige and value of university degrees that pose another challenge for Hungary and Poland in equalizing access to higher education. In a market economy, labor market conditions play a much greater role in individuals' decisions to participate in higher education. In a market economy, much to the chagrin of educators, the worth of higher education is evaluated more in monetary terms. For example, Boyer (1987) reported that in the U.S. approximately 88% of the students and parents surveyed indicated that finding employment following graduation was one of their top priorities. Najduchowska (1978) found that in Poland students' interest in their value of higher education differed by social class. The children of university-educated families attached more importance to the interest and satisfaction of their future job, whereas students from lower socioeconomic backgrounds were concerned about the match between their job and qualifications, the ability to gain recognition and appreciation for their work, and assistance in finding accommodations quickly.

Even before the change to a market economy, the value and prestige of higher education degrees had begun to decline. The results from a survey in Poland (Wnuk-Lipinska, 1985) of youth from working-class and peasant backgrounds revealed that these youths did not think that it was worth studying if, after obtaining the degree, they were not going to get a well-paying job matching their skills and having high prestige. More of these students have begun to ask if there is a balance between the costs and benefits of higher education. It will be much more difficult to encourage students from these groups to participate in higher education now that even higher education graduates are unemployed. The unemployment rate for higher education graduates in 1992 has been predicted to be between 1–4% in Hungary, depending on location (the lowest rate is in Budapest, and the higher rates are in other locations, such as Debrecen). In Poland, in November 1990 Barbara Kunta, Manager of Career Centers, Ministry of Labor and Social Affairs, reported that approximately one-third of college graduates were without employment. In such a climate, it will be even more difficult to demonstrate to students from underrepresented groups that higher education is worth the cost. One way most countries have tried to increase student motivation to participate in higher education is through increased student aid. It is lack of financial resources that poses the most important challenge to increasing the participation of underrepresented groups in higher education in Hungary and Poland.

Lack of Resources

It is widely accepted that there are costs associated with increasing the participation of underrepresented groups in higher education. There are those direct costs (such as free tuition and waiver of fees) associated with attending universities, and there are also additional costs (such as stipends) which are necessary for students who have less resources. All of these costs are difficult for Hungary and Poland because of the current level of funding resources for higher education institutions. In Poland, according to Kwiatkowski (1990), universities have less power and money from the central government. Higher education in Hungary, on the other hand, has maintained good relations with the government; however, that does not mean that extra funding will soon be available for special programs. In fact, students will soon begin paying a share of the cost of attending higher education institutions. That is likely to further deteriorate the participation of underrepresented groups, although Hungary has indicated its commitment to continue funding the participation of lower classes.

Inevitably, when the issue of equality of higher education is mentioned, the question of quality is also raised. Cerych (1990) raises this question when discussing increasing the level of higher education participation in Central Europe. Increasing participation, he suggests, might lead to other social problems, such as large-scale unemployment of graduates. But, like most other educators, his main question about increased participation focuses on the issue of maintaining excellence: "Can the goal of excellence be pursued at the same time as the objective of a vigorous expansion" (p. 354). There, of course, are reasons for concern, but other questions about quality versus equality have yet to be raised: (1) Are quality and equality mutually exclusive, or is quality a rationale for maintaining elitism? (2) What are the real costs of increasing the participation of underrepresented groups? (3) Is it more feasible to increase funding for increasing participation in higher education or to spend more for attending social problems?

There are several ways to view the quality of higher education. Some educators and economists view quality of higher education in terms of the product produced (e.g., number of graduates employed and where they are employed). Others view quality in terms of the educational process itself (e.g., faculty/student ratio). In either case, it has been difficult to determine whether the quality of higher education of all deteriorates when underrepresented groups are admitted. That is, how many students would have to be admitted to a higher educational institution in order for the quality to begin deteriorating? "Educators and economists have been unable to identify dimensions of institutional quality which have consistent and persistent effects on student changes in knowledge and attitude," says Solomon (1987). There is not anyone who would argue that if all unprepared students were admitted to any higher education institution, the quality would diminish. That is a different argument from one that states that equality and quality necessarily have to be in conflict.

Economists and educators have discussed whether there is a higher economic return to individuals and society in providing higher education to the most gifted in a society. It is becoming increasingly clear, however, as some others have argued, that the social benefits would be higher if more resources were diverted to the less represented groups in society. More and more countries have begun to recognize the high cost of not including more groups in the higher education process. For example, the European Community (of which Hungary and Poland would eventually like to become members) has specifically indicated that opportunities for underrepresented groups to participate in higher education should be increased. This is necessary, they have indicated, because there will be an increased demand for highly skilled workers and higher education will have an increasingly important role to play in meeting this need. The U.S. also has recognized the importance of equalizing opportunities for minorities to participate in higher education, since minorities will play an increasingly important role in the labor market in the 21st century.

Meeting these challenges, then, leaves Hungary and Poland to ponder whether it is to their advantage to begin to increase the participation of underrepresented groups at this point in their transition to a market economy or to wait until the groups are so solidly divided that they will require even greater resources to motivate these students to participate in higher education. Nevertheless, while these are difficult issues to consider, there are lessons to be learned from the West, particularly the U.S. Also the West can learn valuable lessons from the research conducted in Hungary and Poland over the years regarding equality of higher education.

Reciprocal Lessons

Since the U.S. and Central Europe had such different economic systems in the past, the question could be raised, What can the U.S. possibly learn from Central Europe, and vice versa, regarding equality of higher education? Dobson (1977) reported that the degree of inequality of higher education in the U.S. was closer to that of the Scandinavian countries and the former Eastern European countries than to that of West European countries. According to him, while access to higher education in the U.S. and Eastern Europe has not been without fault, it has been considerably better than access to higher education in Western Europe. Although there were differences in the economic systems, included among the similarities in the egalitarianism in higher education in the U.S. and Central Europe was—at least in principle—a belief in opportunities for achievement through the educational system and high levels of aspiration. That is, although "tracking" occurred (and still occurs) in both systems, it was thought to be to a much less degree than in Western Europe. Finally, Dobson (1977) lists similarities in percentage of cohorts completing secondary school (a necessary condition for continuing on to higher education) as an indication of commonalties of equality of access to higher education in former Eastern Europe and the U.S. There exist today similar obstacles to achieving equal access to higher education, e.g., attitudes about positive discrimination and affirmative action.

One lesson that is clear for all countries concerning increasing the participation of underrepresented groups is that the problems are much deeper than positive discrimination or affirmative action. It will require more than merely making spaces available. It is ironic that people in the mainstream of societies are so resistant to providing additional assistance to increasing the participation of underrepresented groups in higher education and, yet, so few members of these underrepresented groups are interested in taking advantage of this assistance. But when societies recognize the importance of providing access to education for all its citizens, it looks to positive discrimination first, a system that educators and economists know has failed over the last 20 years. There have to be new ideas, new research about ways to increase participation, and that research needs to focus on the return side of investment in higher education. Students have many questions about the worth of higher education: Is it worth the cost? What if I do not get a job? McMahon (1987) says very few studies of labor market expectations of racial minorities exist in most countries. Unfortunately, educators still only think of education in elitist terms, education for the sake of education, while more and more students and families are beginning to think of it in terms of prestige and income.

Inequality of higher education is a problem that requires alliances to resolve. Therefore, relationships between secondary school and higher education and between industry and higher education are necessary. As educators realize, interest in higher education does not begin, nor can it be instilled, as late as the last years of secondary schooling, particularly for students who are coming from homes where neither parent is educated. As research has shown in Poland (Najduchowska, 1978; Wnuk-Lipinska, 1985) and in the U.S. (as far back as the Coleman report, 1966), schools have to play a much greater role in cultivating students' interest in participating in higher education, especially students from homes where education is not stressed. That simply means that schools from primary to higher education have to work in partnership to devise strategies for increasing students' aspirations and motivation to, first, perform well academically and, second, to continue with schooling beyond the secondary level.

Industry is one of the primary recipients of higher education services, whether through research and development or graduate employment of graduates. Particularly since the 1980s, industry has developed major alliances with higher education throughout the West for many reasons, including developing strategies to curtail the decline in minority students' participation at all levels of education. It is only natural that they should have a stake in increasing the skill level of all groups. As the U.S. has found, it is better to invest in the educational development of the work force incrementally than to wait and have to invest more later when the labor force skill level is not keeping pace with the technological advancement of the country. Industry can work in partnership with higher education in Central Europe to invest monetarily in increasing the participation of underrepresented groups. They can also provide much needed professional models of what various occupations entail and what is necessary to prepare for different types of positions. While to the typically educated person these ideas might seem too vocational in their orientation, it has to be remembered that higher education is not a naturally assumed process for students who do not come from educated homes.

Finally, most will agree that to increase participation of underrepresented groups requires a sincere commitment from all actors: politicians, educators, economists, industry leaders, etc. It is a complicated problem that requires resources, monetary and nonmonetary (new ideas, new solutions), to resolve. It has to be an aggressive approach and cannot simply be left to chance. It is reasonable to assume that the countries of Central Europe, at the moment, have an agenda of important items to attend to regarding higher education; equalizing access to higher education is probably—understandably—low on their list. The past decades, however, have shown across cultures that if concrete policies are not set to deal with this important agenda, it can cost economies more in the long run.

Prospects for Increasing Participation

Since the issue of increasing participation in higher education has been such a dismal failure in most countries, to be optimistic about Hungary and Poland achieving this in light of all the challenges they face is almost like denying the inevitable. In the short term, there is certainly reason for concern, almost pessimism. The generally conservative mood in these countries and the feeling that they have had enough of special arrangements for underrepresented groups make it even more doubtful that equity in higher education will have a high priority. Based on the experiences of other cultures, the conservative mood is likely to persist for some time. The financial constraints under which these countries are operating would make it appear that equalizing access to higher education will be even more difficult to accomplish.

In spite of these obstacles, however, there is reason for optimism, particularly in the long run. They are fully aware of the effects of inequality of access to higher education from the experiences of other countries, e.g., the U.S. and, increasingly, Western Europe. This is one of the reasons they are continuing with strategies to make higher education more accessible. Experimental programs such as the newly created vocational schools, as described earlier in this paper, are already underway. The stable size of the populations in these countries makes developing a strategy for increasing access to higher education a much more manageable process than it would in larger countries.

Economic necessity will be a driving reason for these countries to increase access to higher education. Mobilizing and developing efficient human resources is essential for economic development. The demand for a highly skilled work force will require that more previously underrepresented groups have the opportunity to participate in higher education.

The best reason to be optimistic, though, is the rich and excellent cadre of researchers and centers of research in Hungary and Poland. Researchers in these countries have over the years developed a body of research on this topic, so they are not starting from scratch. In fact, some of their research findings can be useful for the West. In the short span of three years, the researchers in these countries have defined the educational problems they will face in a market economy, including inequality of higher education, and have begun to devise methods for resolving these issues. It is the deliberate speed at which they are moving which gives much hope for positive results. While they have established contacts and cooperative agreements with scholars in the West, they are deliberately and carefully evaluating what is most appropriate for their own cultures. That does not mean that there is unanimous agreement on each decision regarding how to solve issues facing higher education, but it does appear that there is agreement on the importance of equalizing access to higher education.

Researchers in Central Europe have the best opportunity to see from the East and West some of the pressing issues and obstacles facing higher education administrators in their attempts to equalize access. They are in position to see what has worked and what has failed. Their continuing collaborative arrangements with educators in the East and West could enable Hungary and Poland to develop new ideas and new research for dealing with this very important topic.

NOTE

* The Hungarian Institute for Educational Research (HIER) provided the support for the writing of this chapter.

REFERENCES

Becker, G. S. (1975). *Human capital* (2d ed.). New York: Columbia University Press.

Bell, D. (1977). On meritocracy and equality. In J. Karabel & A. H. Halsey (Eds.), *Power and ideology in education*. New York: Oxford University Press.

Blaug, M., Preston, M. & Ziderman, A. (1967). *The utilization of educated man-power in industry*. London: Oliver and Boyd.

Bowles, S. & Gintis, H. (1976). *Schooling in capitalist America*. New York: Basic Books, Inc.

Boyer, E. L. (1987). *College: The undergraduate experience in America*. New York: Harper & Row.

Carnoy, M. & Levin, H. M. (1985). *Schooling and work in a democratic state*. Stanford, CA: Stanford University Press.

Center for Educational Competitiveness. (1992). *Knowledge for all Americans*. Arlington, VA: Knowledge Network for All Americans.

Cerych, L. (1990). Renewal of Central European higher education: Issues and challenges. *European Journal of Education, 25(4)*, pp. 351–58.

Cohn, E. (1979). *The economics of education*. Cambridge, MA: Harper & Row.

Coleman, J. (1966). Equal schools or equal students. *Public Interest, 4*, pp. 70–75.

Davis, R. J. & Morrall, J. F., III. (1974). *Evaluating educational investment*. Lexington, MA: D. C. Heath.

Dobson, R. B. (1977). Social class and inequality of access to higher education in the USSR. In J. Karabel & A. H. Halsey (Eds.), *Power and ideology in education*. New York: Oxford University Press.

Freeman, K. (1988). The returns to schooling: Comparative analysis of Black-White MBA starting salaries—a pilot study. Unpublished empirical study. Atlanta: Emory University.

———. (1989). The returns to schooling: The impact of career counseling on Black-White MBA starting salaries. Unpublished dissertation. Atlanta: Emory University.

Freeman, R. B. (1976). *The overeducated American*. New York: Academic Press, Inc.

Hungarian Ministry of Higher Education. (1992). *Draft act of Hungarian higher education*.

Kozma, T. (1990). Higher education in Hungary: Facing the political transition. *European Journal of Education, 25(4)*, pp. 379–90.

Kunta, B. (1990, November). Interview with Ms. Barbara Kunta, Manager, Career Centers, Ministry of Labor and Social Affairs, Warsaw, Poland.

Kwiatkowski, S. (1990). Survival through excellence: Prospects for the Polish university. *European Journal of Education, 25(4)*, pp. 391–98.

Lukacs, P. (1989). Changes in selection policy in Hungary: The case of the admission system in higher education. *Comparative Education, 25(2)*, pp. 219–28.

Lynton, E. A. (1984). *The missing connection between business and the universities*. New York: Macmillan.

McMahon, W. W. (1987). Expected rates of returns to education. In G. Psacharopoulos (Ed.), *Economics of education: Research and studies*. New York: Pergamon Press.

Memorandum on Higher Education in the European Community. (1991). Higher education on the eve of the year 2000. *Education & Training, II–V*.

Najduchowska, H. (1978). Higher education and professional careers: Students' perception. In B. C. Sanyal & A. Josefowicz (Eds.), *Graduate employment and planning of higher education in Poland*. Paris: International Institute for Educational Planning.

Psacharopoulos, G. (1985). Returns to education: A further international update and implications. *The Journal of Human Resources, 20(4)*, pp. 583–97.

Rendeki, A. (1992, July). Interview with Rendeki Agoston, igazogato, Kazinczy Ferenc Egeszsagugyi es Kezgazdasagi Szakkozepiskola, Komlo, Hungary.

Sadlak, J. (1990). The Eastern European challenge: Higher education for a new reality. *Educational Record*, pp. 29–37.

————. (1991, March). *A return to the democratic society: Is there need for the redefinition of equity in higher education in East and Central Europe—Polish experience?* Paper presented at the meeting of the 35th Comparative and International Education Society, Pittsburgh, PA.

Schadt, M. (1992, July 21). Interview with Dr. M. Schadt, sociology professor, Janus Pannonious University, Pecs, Hungary.

Schultz, T. W. (1961). Investment in human capital. *American Economic Review, 51*, pp. 1–17.

Solomon, L. C. (1980). New findings on the links between college education and work. *Higher Education, 10*, pp. 615–48.

————. (1987). The quality of education. In G. Psacharopoulos (Ed.), *Economics of education: Research and studies.* New York: Pergamon Press.

Thurow, L. C. (1972). Education and economic equality. *Public Interest, 28*, pp. 66–81.

Wnuk-Lipinska, E. (1985). Dilemmas of the educational system in Poland. Unpublished paper. Warsaw, Poland.

World Bank. (1991). *Hungary: The transition to a market economy, critical human resources issues.* Washington, D.C.

CHAPTER VIII

Restructuring Higher Education in the Czech and Slovak Republics
An Institutional Perspective*

Daniel S. Fogel
James E. Mauch

Introduction

For those living outside of the Czech and Slovak Republics, it is difficult to fully understand the current situation in higher education in these countries. Yet, through recording a detailed description of the countries' historical landscape and information on the present situation, one can become informed and gain some understanding to create a personal experience. This overview will aid in the understanding of higher education in these republics which, until a few months ago, were combined into one country.

The purpose of this chapter is to outline the antecedents and directions for change in one higher education system in Central and Eastern Europe. The chapter describes the historical context of the Czech and Slovak Republics' higher education systems, the two republics' present systems, and an analysis of possible future changes. At the moment, the economic and social transformation in the republics has had a negative impact on higher education. The key point here is that several actions can be taken within each institution to mitigate this impact.

The Historical Context

The rich traditions reflected in European higher education, reaching back almost a millennium, provide historical legacies that are important factors in the present restructuring of the Czech and Slovak Republics' higher education.[1] Following upon the founding of the universities at Salerno, Bologna, Paris, and Oxford, Prague became the site of a great university system which persisted for many centuries. The system followed the structure and organization of the ancient university models of its predecessors.

Two profound and contemporary influences on Czech and Slovak higher education were the Austrian-German and the Russian systems.

Austrian-German Higher Education

The Austrian-German university tradition forms one part of the background of the Czech and Slovak educational systems. The tradition linked the university to the national political structure. This tradition evolved to promote the ideals of freedom to teach and freedom to learn, but these freedoms were always the state's, which founded universities and established the legal structure within which they would operate. Professors became civil servants, drawing their salaries and privileges from the state and accepting its control, yet using it as a buffer from nongovernmental social and economic pressures.

By the end of the nineteenth century, institutions throughout the world were emulating German universities. Lord Ashby called the German university model "the nineteenth century idea of a university." The model influenced the development of modern universities in Japan, the United States, and much of Eastern and Central Europe. German became the language of scholarship; scientists emulated German scientific and teaching methods and degrees; and German laboratories became the world standard (Ashby, 1967).

When the former Czechoslovakia was founded in 1918, it had a university system almost exactly like that of the universities in Austria. Thus, the Austrian-German model pervaded the former Czechoslovak higher education system.

Soviet Higher Education

Soon after the end of World War II, Soviet higher education was imposed as a dominant model for the former Czechoslovakia, as Eastern and Central Europe was drawn into the sphere of world communism. While it is too early to analyze the entire legacy of the Soviets, some negative features of the system are clear: the failure of central economic planning, the priority given to heavy industry over consumer goods, the bureaucratic control of human rights and freedoms, the ever present internal security forces and use of informants, an arrogant and powerful bureaucracy, the constant attempts to suppress dissident thinking and activity, the use of groups and organizations in service of the State (including universities and mass media), and the use of Marxism-Leninism as the rationale for actions.

The negative features of communism affected higher education. Government-run science academies (imposed by the communists in emulation of Soviet higher education) did most of the research while the government limited universities to instruction.[2] The academies and universities were under strict government (party) control. For example, communist officials were afraid of politically unreliable faculty members who might affect students. These faculty members were often dismissed and suppressed; top scientists were allowed to work at the science academies so that they would be prevented from teaching classes. These past practices have led to present-day dilemmas. There is currently an uneven distribution of research skills among scholars, and it is unclear whether certain faculty members are capable of making the transformation to teaching a new curriculum or participating in the reemergence of teaching and research within one institution.

As Kallen (1991, p. 54) points out, "In several countries . . . higher education had deteriorated as a result of direct
and often brutal political interference in the universities and colleges. This interference often led to massive dismissal of many of
the best teachers and researchers."[3] The bureaucracy was all too
successful in destroying individuality and isolating faculty from
their colleagues throughout the world. University personnel,
among others, saw the state as punishing risk taking, initiative,
or creativity and positively reinforcing conformity to Marxist
dogma, following directions, and supporting the collective over
individual achievement (Kallen, 1991). The insecurity that the
State inspired also had an effect on political, social, and cultural
creativity and on freedom of any kind. The intensity of these
negative effects varied throughout the region. Educators in the
former Soviet Union, Romania, and Bulgaria felt the most severe
impact while educators were less affected in Hungary and the
former Czechoslovakia.

Along with isolation, politically correct curricula, and the
loss of outstanding teachers, East European universities were
characterized by a widespread system of rote learning, conformity to prescribed programs, and a few widely prescribed texts.
Isolation and controlled content resulted in an education that
was more and more remote from reality.

This legacy has had positive aspects, although they may be
difficult to describe objectively so soon after the collapse of the
hated and repressive communist regimes. The state offered free
public education from early childhood to the university level
and eradicated widespread illiteracy. The educational level of
the adult population in much of the region was comparable to
that of Western Europe. Educators designed some innovative
approaches to adult training. A substantial increase in female
participation in education has also been very positive (Kallen,
1991).

Some individual creativity and initiative managed to survive over forty years of repressive party and state control. This
resiliency is testimony to the courage of the citizens and to the
persistence of the ideal of common human rights and values
even in the worst of times. It is the persistence, courage, and
rededication to national history that is now coming into the fore-

front in the restructuring of higher education. In the former Czechoslovakia the development of higher education has paralleled economic and political history. The Austrian-German tradition and the effects of decades of communism on academic institutions provide the bases for understanding not only the past but also the present attempts of Czech and Slovak higher education reform.

Development of Higher Education Institutions

To 1918

Universities from the 1300s to 1918 had highly specialized curricula. An example of an early institution, the first mining academy in Europe, was founded in 1763 in Banska Stiavnica, Czech Republic. After the founding of Charles University in 1348, other institutions were established during the next 200 years, but the subsequent history of the Czechs and Slovaks led to a somewhat separate development, and during the nineteenth century some institutions split apart or ceased cooperating with one another across national boundaries.

This separate development led to tensions between the Czechs and Slovaks. The Kingdom of Bohemia and the Margaviate of Moravia united under the crown of St. Wenceslaus while the Hungarian monarchs wearing the crown of St. Stephen ruled the Slovaks. Even after the early sixteenth century, when the Habsburgs effected a personal union of the kingdoms of Bohemia and Hungary, the regions retained their local administrative agencies (Daniel, 1992).

The formulation of an absolutist monarchy resulted in the forcible Hungarianization of Slovakia, much harsher than the Germanization of the Czech lands. As a result, before 1918 there was not a single Slovak higher education institution in Slovakia (Hrabinska, 1992).

1918–1948

The former Czechoslovakia was founded on October 28, 1918. By 1936, it had 13 higher education institutions with 52 faculties, over 23,000 students and more than 3,450 professors, docents, and teaching staff (Hrabinska, 1992).

Comenius University was established in 1918 and quickly became a premier education facility. This was the only Slovak institution of the 13 existing institutions, housing more than 2,000 students. The 1939 occupation of the Nazis devastated Czech higher education. After November 17, 1939, the Nazis closed all education institutions within the territory of the Nazi Protectorate of Bohemia and Moravia. Nine representatives of student organizations were executed, and 1,200 students were deported to concentration camps (Harach et. al., 1992). The institutions remained closed for almost six years, after which time universities slowly reopened. In Slovakia, institutions remained open and grew during this period. For example, the Nazis permitted the formation of the Slovak Technical University (1939) and the Bratislava School of Economics (1940).

The Communist Period: 1948–1989

The Communist Party spent forty years attempting to remold the former Czechoslovak higher education in the image and likeness of the Soviet Union and the principles of international communism. The Party not only controlled all levels of higher education; it also used institutions as instruments for controlling and reeducating student minds to create the "new communist man" (Koucky, 1990, pp. 361–77).

The communist regime tried to create totality and uniformity with the following characteristics:

1. Uniform ideological education on the basis of Marxist-Leninist ideology;

2. Uniform, compulsory curriculum including textbooks;

3. State monopoly of schools, with a few exceptions in some church schools;

4. Uniform school structures; and

5. Party control of school management (Szebenyi, 1992, p. 20).

The government rigidly centralized and politicized higher education in terms of access, curriculum, staffing, resource allocation, and planning. Each successive five-year plan was designed to provide the planned state economy with personnel to meet the needs of the state. State planning affected university plans for student enrollment and discipline-specific decisions.

This administrative structure created a decrease in the former Czechoslovakia's international recognition and the reputation and position of higher education in research and science. The Communist Party controlled, in particular, the humanities curricula to ensure that information was consistent with Party dogma. Membership in the Party was a distinct criterion for the highest academic posts. Conforming to the planned system was the paramount means for evaluating the effectiveness of each institution (Koucky, 1990).

Another result of the communist period was the construction of the academies of science, with generous funding, the latest in equipment, and direct control by the party at the highest levels, bypassing the ministry bureaucracies. The former Czechoslovak Academy of Sciences emerged as the primary organ for establishing and administering research programs throughout the country (Daniel, 1992). New universities took on pragmatic missions, such as the technical curriculum[4] and the agricultural curriculum.[5]

In the process, pedagogical faculties lost status by being subjected to consistent subversion and monitoring. Because they trained teachers, and thus were seen as instruments of political indoctrination, teacher training institutes were the most heavily politicized and controlled. Politically correct but otherwise inadequately trained persons were given jobs and, at times, leadership positions in the institutes.

The "normalization" following the suppression from the Prague Spring caused many leading scholars and researchers to exchange their teaching positions for menial jobs or to choose emigration. The higher education system was poorly developed because the central government controlled institutions which were unable to exercise academic prerogatives within their schools (Cerych, 1990, p. 27; Koucky, 1990).

Nearly 50,000 students were studying full-time at the 15 universities in the Czech Republic, and over 9,000 students were studying in the three universities in the Slovak Republic, when the Communists took over in 1948. By 1990 the number of full-time students was about 149,000, of which 96,400 were in the Czech Republic and 52,600 were in the Slovak Republic. The number of students as a percentage of the population increased from 5.1% in 1948 to 10.9% in 1989.

The State has created few new universities during the last 40 years, and the few created were considered less prestigious than the older ones. Despite their troubled past, the universities have carried on teaching and have retained some traditional independent academic values. This perseverance has enabled the universities to maintain some degree of freedom of thought and independent scholarship.

Despite decades of repression and control, universities have remained an important part of Czechoslovak society. Given the brief liberalization period between 1966 and 1968 and development period between 1945 and 1948, the higher education institutions remained surprisingly vital to society. They have retained a certain status despite outside invasions, the near destruction of the system in World War II, and the communist state's use of them as instruments for controlling and reeducating student minds to create the "new communist man" and to provide the planned state economy with personnel to meet the State's needs (Koucky, 1990).

The Present Structure of Czech and Slovak Higher Education

Economic changes in the former Czechoslovakia in the last two years have been pronounced. These changes have shown a movement away from political control of institutions. Decentralized decision making and curriculum reform are now realistic goals for education leaders. Yet, a large degree of uncertainty still exists with respect to reorganizing the system (given the split between the Czech and Slovak Republics) and defining its role in the country's social and economic changes.

Widespread educational reform in the former Czechoslovakia is most likely to occur within the next decade. Czechoslovakia's economic restructuring puts pressure on existing ideological and structural arrangements, which must cope with change. Existing institutions will probably be redefined and newer ones will evolve to support the reforms. This evolution and coincidental change in educational systems have been well documented in studies of other educational systems (Ginsberg, ed., 1991).

We have chosen to analyze six forces within the Czech and Slovak education systems. We view these forces as having the greatest impact on educational reform. The goal here is to better understand the strategic decisions facing institutional leaders who want these higher education systems to become more competitive.

Legal Framework

There have been many recent changes in the law on higher education. On May 4, 1990, the federal assembly of the Czech and Slovak Federal Republic passed Act No. 172/1990 on higher education institutions, thus abolishing Act No. 30 of 1980, which reflected the ideology and control of the Marxist regime. The new act guarantees basic academic rights and freedoms, prohibits political parties from setting up their organizations on university premises, renews university self-governing bodies, and establishes a new body, the University Council, as the self governing body of each higher education institution.

The law also establishes accreditation commissions as advisory bodies to both government and institutions. The primary responsibility of the commissions is to evaluate higher education institutions. The new law allows differentiation of studies and introduces new degrees.

The federal legislation placed the executive power for education in the hands of the respective republican ministries. Thus, the split of the country had little impact on higher education. Financing, accountability, and general policies are set at the republic levels. The law has helped to create the new higher education structure. It lowered barriers to entry for new institutions or those that wanted to restructure institutions. It put more power in the hands of individual institutions. It also gave more power to students and faculty members.

Access

Access to higher education today is uncertain, given the extensive changes in curriculum, the possible change in the number and types of institutions, the overcrowded conditions in existing institutions, and the attempts to increase admissions standards.

What is certain is that student access to higher education has been low compared to other comparable countries. In the early 1900s Czechoslovakia enjoyed one of the top rankings in the world in student enrollments in higher education. Now only about 16% of the 20- to 24-year-olds are enrolled (OECD, 1992, p. 21). Enrollments in higher education as a percentage of the traditional college-age population are typically low in Central and Eastern Europe. The nine countries within Central and Eastern Europe have an average of 1,389 students per 100,000 population while West European countries (16 in total) enroll over 2,400 students per 100,000 population. In 1990 the former Czechoslovakia had about 190,000 students, or about 1,188 per 100,000 population, which represents 15% of the 19–24 age-group (see table 1).

TABLE 1.   Higher Education Enrollments per 100,000 Inhabitants

Hungary	938
Poland	1,306
Czech and Slovak Republics	1,188
Central/Eastern Europe (average of 16 countries)	1,389
Bulgaria	1,677
U.K.	1,913
Western Europe (average of 16 countries)	2,405
France	2,655
U.S.	5,142
Canada	5,024

Sources: Encyclopedia Britannica 1991; UNESCO Statistical Yearbook 1990.

Low participation rates in higher education do not surprise educators. These low rates are a result of low levels of student participation in the gymnasia and technical schools, which provide higher education preparation for students, and the universities' reliance on traditional selection criteria such as good secondary school grades and entrance examinations. After 1989 institutions removed the political and ideological exclusions. The dean and senate of each faculty of each higher education institution now have full authority to admit students and select the criteria for those admissions. Despite this freedom, educators are not considering many alternatives to the traditional standards (Koucky, 1990; VonKopp, 1992, pp. 101–13).

The Czech and Slovak Republics have primary levels of education followed by three divisions at the secondary level: gymnasia, technical schools, and vocational or apprenticeship schools. Attendance at each type of secondary school typically lasts four years. The vocational schools, previously under the supervision of industry groups, are now under the supervision of the Ministries of Education. This change was taken to avoid massive closings of vocational schools due to financial problems in companies (VonKopp, 1992, p. 106).

The existing system lacks consistent standards of educational attainment. Graduates of individual schools leave with certificates showing their performance in final examinations, but the achieved standard varies with each school. Some schools, notably the gymnasia, are more successful than others in promoting graduates to higher education. The three-tier secondary school system limits access to higher education. Almost half the graduates of academic and technical secondary schools in the Czech Republic continue on to higher education during the next year; in Slovakia the corresponding figure is 35%. Still, only about 45% of secondary school enrollments in the two countries are in the academic and technical secondary schools. Only these students can compete effectively for university places. The rest of the students are in vocational schools, which do not prepare students for the higher education entrance examinations. Therefore, only a small percentage of the population graduating from secondary schools has the preparation for higher education (Czech and Slovak Ministries of Education, 1990).

Educators' considerations for not developing new criteria, keeping unified standards, or providing special access to increase rates of admission are understandable. The communists managed the old systems by special arrangements for different privileged groups who did not meet the "normal academic criteria." Therefore, reformers are reacting against these special privileges and against any type of admission that discriminates beyond clear and standard processes.

Enrollments in higher education remained steady in the 1980s in the Czech Republic but declined in the Slovak Republic. Table 2 shows the enrollment figures for the two countries according to curriculum areas. This table shows interesting structural characteristics of the higher education system. Almost half the college students are in the general area called "technical sciences," a curriculum designation encompassing a variety of disciplines including, oddly enough, economics and business but mostly engineering. Contrast the percentage enrollments in the two countries with all degree programs in the United States. The U.S. shows over 41 categories of degrees, with business and management curricula representing 22% of enrollments, social sciences 8%, education 13%, and visual and performing arts 3%.

TABLE 2. Enrollments in Higher Education by Curriculum (1987–1988)

Curriculum	Number of Fields of Study	%
Natural Sciences	24	3.4
Technical Sciences	94	45.1
Agriculture, Forestry, Veterinary	14	9.9
Medicine, Pharmacy	8	8.3
Economics	16	12.9
Law	1	2.9
Humanities & Social Science	27	3.4
Teaching	7	12.9
Arts	8	1.3

Source: International Higher Education: An Encyclopedia. Oxford, U.K.: Pergamon Press, 1992.

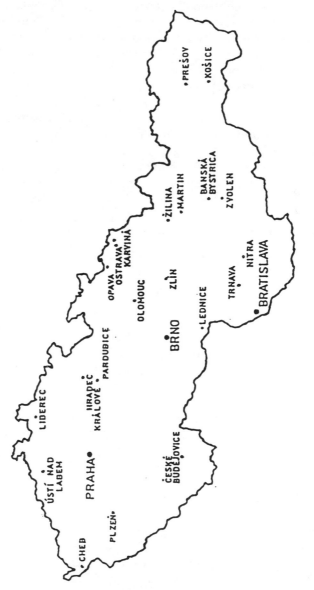

Figure 1.   Regional Structure of Czechoslovak Higher Education
Source: OECD, 1992, p. 70.

The universities with business and economics curricula have an especially small proportion of enrollments in the areas of accounting, auditing, marketing, etc. Under Communism, the discipline of economics included many diverse fields, which embraced topics related to business and management. Educators differentiated between some curricula, such as theoretical economics versus applied economics. Students view the Prague School of Economics and the Bratislava School of Economics as having applied economics curricula and schools such as Comenius and Charles University as offering more theoretical curricula.

Another reason for low enrollments in certain curricula and in higher education in general is the lack of relationship between wages and level of education. In developed Western societies, for example, salaries in general vary substantially according to one's educational qualifications. In Hungary, the variation was about 12%, and in the former Czechoslovakia it was less than 8% (OECD, 1992, p. 22).

Institutions

All Central European countries, except for the Czech and Slovak Republics, have both a university and a nonuniversity sector of higher education. The prestige is low at the nonuniversity level and not considered in most government reform policies. This condition contrasts with Western countries that have extensive, prestigious nonuniversity institutions. For example, consider the German Fachhochschulen, the French IUTs, the British further education colleges and the American community colleges. These all have strategic roles to play in economic development and meeting the social demand for higher education.

At present, 23 institutions (82 faculties) are in the Czech Republic and 13 (50 faculties) in Slovakia (see table 3). Five of these institutions are classical multidisciplinary universities, and the rest are specialized according to disciplines. Approximately 20,500 professors teach in both countries, 75% of them in the Czech Republic. Charles University is the largest institution in the two countries, with 16 faculties and 25,000 students. The smallest institutions are those with arts curricula.

TABLE 3. The Czechoslovak Higher Education
Institutions, Faculties, and Students

	Czech Rep.	Slovak Rep.	Total
Establishments	23	13	36
General University	6	3	9
Pedagogical University	4	2	6
Technical University	7	3	10
Economic University	1	1	2
Agricultural University	2	2	4
Fine Arts Institute	4	2	6
Faculties	83	50	133[*]
University	36	21	57
Technical	26	15	41
Economic	5	5	10
Agriculture	9	5	14
Arts	7	4	11
Students	129,777	69,095	198,872
Full-time	96,379	52,669	149,048
Foreign	3,122	1,681	4,803
Postgraduate (all nat'l)	7,285	3,875	11,160
Part-time (CSFR)	18,693	9,434	28,127
Others	4,298	1,436	5,734

[*] In 1990/91 the country employed 6,814 professors or associate professors and 12,536 other teachers in higher education.

Source: Harbison, 1991; Hrabinska, 1992; Harach et al., 1992.

New institutional entrants are rare in the higher education system. The recent changes from the 1990 Higher Education Act have resulted in six new universities, yet these are mostly reconfigurations of State-run institutions and newly acquired Communist Party property. The reconfigured institutions have received new missions but few new resources. Thus, the number and types of institutions have not changed dramatically despite the rapid political and economic changes.

The country has substitutes for higher education. For example, the Czechoslovak Management Center was founded in 1989. This center offers an American M.B.A. degree program, executive courses, consulting, and access to research comparable to Western standards. The faculty salaries are two to three times higher than those at any Czech or Slovak university, with opportunities for faculty to study abroad, earn extra pay, and work with foreign colleagues (Fogel, 1992, pp. 18–32).

Teaching Staff

Data shows that many faculty do not have Ph.D.s or the equivalent. The percentage of full professors in Czech universities is 7%, compared to 30% at American universities. In contrast, 60% of all Czech faculty are assistant professors, compared to only 24% in American universities. In addition, at American universities, for all professorial ranks, faculty members are required to hold a Ph.D. or equivalent degree. This is not the case for Czech universities, where 70% of full professors and less than half of all assistant and associate professors hold Ph.D.s or equivalent degrees (Harbison, 1991, 1987).

The Czech and Slovak DRSC degrees equate loosely to the Western Ph.D., and the Czech and Slovak MCSC degrees equate to a Western master's degree. The Czech and Slovak Ing. degrees relate to a special designation of the Western undergraduate degree with an additional year not equivalent to a Western master's degree. Most Czech and Slovak education reformers are anxious to change the degree system to one roughly equivalent to either the German or U.S. system.

Table 4 shows the student/teacher ratios for six of the more important universities. The ratios in 1989 in all higher education institutions are about 8.5. This ratio has declined steadily.

TABLE 4. Student*/Teacher* Ratios for Select Universities

Charles University	28,000/3,100	9.03
Prague School of Economics	11,340/620	18.29
Technical University of Prague	14,150/1,448	9.77
Bratislava School of Economics	5,268/634	8.31
Comenius	13,248/1,994	6.64
Masaryk	3,150/955	3.30

* Full and part-time.

Source: USIA Directory of Institutes of Higher Education in the Czech and Slovak Federal Republic 1991.

These ratios compare favorably to West European and U.S. universities. The higher education sector was the beneficiary of social employment. Thus, the labor force probably will decrease, as enrollments are not likely to increase as needed to absorb the costs of the teacher/student ratios.

Faculty training has not changed either. Most of the new university teacher training is occurring outside the two countries because of money available from programs such as PHARE, the U.S. Agency for International Development, the U.S. Information Agency, and TEMPUS.[6] All indications show that the supply of qualified professors will decline as market opportunities compete with university employment. This decline is noticeable, particularly in the social sciences.

An average base salary for a full professor in a Czech or Slovak university is approximately 8000 Kcs./month ($264.00 US) for 12 hours of teaching per week, whereas the average salary for a consultant is 2000 Kcs. per day ($66.00 US). At these rates, one cannot expect a dramatic increase in faculty desiring full-time university employment, especially those in business management areas.

Resources

Czech and Slovak students generally pay little in tuition or fees and only nominal amounts for the room and board provided by the universities. In addition, many students receive stipends. Institutions charge fees for special programs and to foreign students attending degree and nondegree programs. Thus, four sources of funds are:

1. Government (block grants and research grants);

2. Sale of academic and other services (special program tuition, paid courses, and room and board);

3. Fund-raising;

4. Unrelated business income (e.g., conferences, seminars, and book sales).

The budgets of the two republics finance higher education. Higher education consumes 17% of the total education budget. This budget is 1.7% of the total government expenditures and 0.8% of the two countries' GDP.

Expenditures in 1990 by the institutions of higher education totaled 6.3 billion *koruna*, which is about 18% of the total education expenditures for all levels of education. Of this amount, 40% of costs were attributable to personnel, 30% to goods and facilities, 11% to research, and 19% for student welfare and fellowships (Harbison, 1991). The expenditures were generally higher in Slovakia than the Czech Republic in both absolute and relative terms. For example, universities in the Czech Republic spent about 29,900 Kcs. per student in 1989–90 while in Slovakia the amount was about 36,800 Kcs.

The per-student expenditures vary widely between institutions. The lowest expenditures are for economics and the highest for music and arts. Economics and pedagogical universities spend about half as much per student as the general and technical universities.

Governance

The new Higher Education Act set up two new governance bodies, the Council of Higher Education Institutions and
the Accreditation Commission. The Council has become a powerful body in the Czech and Slovak Republics, taking on the responsibility of providing a forum for rectors and government
officials to discuss policy development. The Commission was to
provide unbiased assessments of the level of educational and research performance of higher education institutions. With the
Ministry of Education these three bodies represent the key elements in the country's official governance structure. The split of
the countries leaves in doubt how the ministries will restructure
these governing bodies. However, more decision-making power
now belongs to the academic senates and rectors of higher
education institutions and the academic senates and deans of
faculties. A university's teachers, staff, and students elect the
university's academic senate. Each faculty has to be represented
equally on the senate. In addition, each faculty has its own
senate, which considers issues related to specific faculty groups
and curriculum. The university's academic senate controls many
major internal decisions. For example, the senate can establish or
abolish faculties, nominate the rector and prorector, and vote on
the status of the university and its faculties. Scientific boards
complement the senates at the university and faculty levels. The
boards' activities are confined to pedagogical issues, scientific
research, and the nomination of professors.

At the Prague School of Economics, for example, the university senate has three staff senators, eight faculty senators, and
six student senators. For a vote to pass, a majority of the staff and
professors must vote for a particular choice. A majority of students must vote for the choice as well. In the Prague School of
Economics, therefore, four students must vote for a given choice
for it to pass. This system is changing rapidly, however, to provide power to those most informed on a given decision.

Recently, the rectors also formed an informal body they
call the "Rectors' Council." This group creates unified responses
to proposals generated by the Ministry of Education or any other
group that attempts to prescribe policy for higher education.

The key governance issue facing all institutions of higher education is how to balance the power bases with the need to act efficiently and effectively. For example, the involvement of students must be balanced by academically sophisticated judgments of the faculty.

Conclusion

In sum, higher education in the two countries is changing but suffers the remnants of its past legacies. The legal framework for change provides the basis upon which improvements can be made in access to higher education, new curriculum, and the ability of institutions to act autonomously in response to market demands. Major improvements are still needed in faculty training, the identification of new revenue sources, and the institutionalization of governance structures.

Themes of Present Changes

Reformers have implicitly or explicitly written about their visions of a new higher education system (Koucky, 1990; Harbison, 1991; Hrabinska, 1992). Five central themes are recurrent in reformers' visions. They result from a combination of market forces or perceived outcomes of market forces, historical traditions, the reformers' attitudes, recent accomplishments, and expectations for changes in the education system or from comparisons with other education systems. These themes (we have labelled them "institutional autonomy," "institutional development," "democracy," "external linkages," and "new financing methods") are discussed below.

Theme 1: Institutional Autonomy

As a result of reform, the responsibility and authority within the structure of the higher education system will be different. This change in power will be caused primarily by an increase in institutional autonomy and greater independence from state control. Reformers perceive this increased autonomy as indispensable for creating new curriculum, for hiring the best trained faculty, and for educating the next generation of students. The power shift also will force a reallocation of resources. The new Higher Education Act of 1990 made great strides in restoring autonomy to institutions. The Act enables institutions to decide on their own internal structure, the division of fields of study, the content and organization of studies, hiring of staff, the numbers and criteria for the admissions of students, and the distribution of financial resources (Act #172, May 4, 1990).

This type of restructuring is not uncommon in transformations such as that of Central and Eastern Europe (Estrin et al., 1991). Before reform, organizations were dependent upon the State for decision making and financial accountability. State planners determined student enrollments and job placements (Koucky, 1990).

Reform brings with it far greater autonomy and widens the range of permitted activities, and thus redistributes power among competitors, new entrants, suppliers, and buyers (Porter, 1980). Higher education managers will also be given more responsibility as a result of this autonomy because they must be financially responsible for their organizations and probably have to meet new standards for the privilege of offering degrees.

The universities' autonomy will also reduce access to guaranteed placements of students. While some established universities will have a competitive edge, new entrants to the system may quickly gain recognition. For example, new M.B.A. programs are placing students in prominent jobs more rapidly than are existing institutions (Fogel, 1992). The hiring firms trust the newer programs to provide students with the skills needed by these firms.

Government policy may help these autonomous universities by creating barriers to the offering of degrees by new universities and institutes. The government may also change policy to favor existing institutions. Still, the government's incentive is to encourage new universities that can take on the financial burdens provided by the government.

Initially, students will view certain curricula as inter-changeable and have little judgment about quality and useful-ness. For example, students now enroll in new programs for international business or international diplomacy expecting they are interchangeable in terms of content and job prospects. Student shifts will probably be rapid from institution to insti-tution as institutions offer new curricula or attractive prices for degrees.

In sum, the entire higher education system will change. New players will enter. Competition will increase among exist-ing universities. Autonomy from the government will give an advantage to the universities with prestigious names, financial resources, and quality faculty.

Theme 2: Institutional Development

Higher education may see new institutions enter the mar-ket, bringing with them new capacity and new resources. This influx of new institutions means that the barriers to entry will probably decrease as more existing institutions become au-tonomous from the government. New institutions will probably be formed initially as small specialized institutions such as those offering management education (Fogel, 1990, pp. 14–19; Fogel, 1992).

The search for economies of scale is inevitable. Some exist-ing universities will probably join together to take advantage of common facilities, administrative support, and faculty. This merging of activities has already begun with the recent intro-duction of six new universities that were reformulations of exist-ing institutions (*Concerning Institutions of Higher Education*, 1990).

The established universities may have a competitive edge because they have name recognition within Czechoslovakia. For example, students view the Bratislava School of Economics as a vocational type of school and not as a prestigious institution of higher learning like Comenius University in Bratislava. There-fore, the Bratislava School's adoption of a new image will be costly compared to that of their more prestigious competitors. Comenius could introduce new curriculum and market this cur-riculum more easily than its neighboring school.

Certain suppliers to the university will gain power by threatening to raise prices or by reducing the quality of their input. Faculty members are one supplier group. Qualified faculty members' power will increase because they can teach the new curriculum, especially in social sciences. Also, the quality faculty members have new opportunities such as employment in joint ventures, at foreign universities, or at private consulting firms.

To respond to this need for faculty, reformers expect higher education managers (1) to strengthen the personnel function, including extensive faculty evaluation systems; (2) to shift from benefit to cash compensation; (3) to set up new payment systems, including differential pay for highly valued faculty and incentives to join organizations; (4) to widen earnings differentials between skilled and unskilled labor and between those faculty members with many employment alternatives and those with few alternatives for employment; (5) to provide training and skill enhancement for faculty and administrators; (6) to tighten labor discipline, by allowing less absenteeism, making substantial layoffs, and allowing fewer voluntary separations.

Theme 3: Democracy

A third theme of the reform is that educators support the value of democracy within institutions. The democratic process now influences the ways in which faculty members are hired, the governance of the institutions, and the means by which educators begin to institute new curricula.

The democratic process will probably mean a drastic shift in who runs the organizations. Student groups, faculty, administrators, and government representatives are redefining their roles in this new democratic environment. Most reformers advocate this development, since it reflects the attitudes of the larger society. However, some balance is sought to ensure rapid, informed decision making.

Theme 4: External Linkages

A fourth theme involves the creation of linkages within and outside the region. These linkages influence the acquisition of new resources, develop a new community of scholarship, and increase the credibility of the universities.

We would expect these linkages to be visible early in the reform process and continue to grow as the transformation occurs. We would expect those universities with extensive linkages to be stronger than those without linkages. These linkages would serve many functions including financing, the acquisition and training of faculty, and increased strategic planning and management expertise (Fogel & Madhaven, 1992, pp. 4–10).

Theme 5: New Financing Methods

Reformers know that new financing methods must supplement the State's budget for higher education. The core financing for higher education institutions has been automatic increases for operational budgets. The capital budgets are handled separately. One of the problems with the budgets has been the lack of connection to the number of students attending a university. There is a sense of arbitrariness to funding. Thus, the government has too little room to steer the higher education system in a different direction because there are no instruments regulating output.

Reformers are looking at funding mechanisms to change or enhance the funding basis, i.e., the ways in which the amount of the institutional allowance are provided. For example, many reformers are considering the introduction of a tuition system (Jongbloed, Koelman, & Vossensteijn, 1992, chap. 1).

The basis of funding is to cover basic costs including faculty, staff, and materials. The institutions typically propose a budget and the government approves it, or the government provides a budget to the institution. The institutions have little discretion in spending the money. The amounts of money available to institutions, the budgetary process, and the allowed institutional discretion are in flux. Thus, reformers are searching for new and clear mechanisms.

The most active proposals are those advocating a tuition system. We would expect that the more institutions offer practical, market-oriented courses, the more likely they will be to attract tuition-paying students. This is a danger for higher education, since institutions may lose sight of their other two missions: to strengthen citizenship and to discover new knowledge. A penchant for practical skills may erode the philosophical basis of higher education.

The system's transformation is also a highly political process. It entails a fundamental redistribution of actual and effective rights over income and wealth. In particular, a class of individuals whose effective wealth stemmed from their bureaucratic position has to be replaced with those who are competitive and judged by market forces.

The politics of the reformation may have some unexpected results. Many researchers found that significant proportions of industries in Poland, the Czech and Slovak Republics, and Hungary have had decreasing value throughout the last few years (Estrin et al., 1991). In principle, these organizations should be closed; in these politically uncertain times, they may be kept open despite their absorption of valuable scarce resources. The link of this reasoning to higher education institutions is direct.

Conclusion

These five themes (institutional autonomy, institutional development, democracy, external linkages, and new financing methods) will be implemented within an environment of uncertainty. System reform involves fundamental change. The character of decision making changes because of the new, competitive environment and the pressures to be financially and academically capable according to world standards.

In summary, the history of the region has developed in a manner that has caused Czechoslovak higher education to stagnate, particularly in the social sciences. The separation of research and teaching, the lack of well-trained faculty, low student participation rates, and the lack of funding for new curriculum are indicative of this stagnation. The five themes that have been mentioned help formulate some possible directions for higher education reform.

Possible Directions: A Response
to the Reformer's Themes

Our response to the five themes present in higher education reform is based on the assumption that the primary goal of higher education reform is to increase the quality of instruction and research according to the world standards and the needs of the new economic, social, and political structures. Thus, higher education reform will support three education goals: (1) to contribute to the development of Czech and Slovak citizens, (2) to develop individual skills, and (3) to provide for the discovery and dissemination of knowledge.

Here are some ideas for consideration at the institution level. The ideas are organized according to the five areas discussed in the previous section of this chapter.

Institutional Autonomy

Institutions will compete with one another for students, faculty, and financial resources. This competition may define the number, size, and structure of specific higher education institutions. This competition is a positive sign for the new market economy. Yet, at the initial stages of the country's change, the competition may be wasteful in terms of resources. Thus, some planning mechanism may be needed to set a strategic course.

Both republics appear to have no priority-setting system for higher education. Nothing has emerged to replace the past central planning system. For understandable reasons, the mere mention of coordination of policy and programs, especially at the federal level, evokes a negative response. Yet, the role of the Higher Education Council has been a positive step toward creating a meaningful dialogue with the government and may be the mechanism for long-range planning and priority setting. We expect the Czech Republic will make more rapid progress in planning, since their higher education infrastructure is more established and well developed than the Slovak Republic.

Many countries have a high-level council or other form of consultative mechanism by which public authorities pay close attention to economic and academic matters without government intervention. These councils are sponsored by the government or by institutions. For example, the United States has several associations that act as accrediting bodies. These associations serve to set standards, provide policy advice, and act as a coordinating mechanism for related institutions. The quality of education is under the purview of educational institutions and their academic accreditation boards. An independent accreditation association should be formed in the two republics to set standards in admissions, degrees, faculty quality, and curriculum. This association would replace the ministries in terms of monitoring the quality of education. This association would act similarly to a Good Housekeeping seal of approval rather than as a regulatory agency.

All impediments to achieving administrative autonomy for all institutions of higher education should be removed. Administrative autonomy is particularly important in budgetary, personnel, and curriculum matters. One major problem is the existence of the Ministry of Education and their strong hold on degrees and curriculum. The government and higher education should not be separated totally; the roles of each should be defined in terms of value added to the system. The Ministry should function as a funnel for government aid and national research funding and as a means of strengthening universities according to federal goals. The institutions and government should create a dialogue on funding priorities and national interests. Thus, higher education institutions will be asked to compete for resources and students. This competition will create higher-quality institutions and a means by which reformers can make resource allocations. The competition will be coordinated in such a way that the government can achieve its goals of social reform.

Institutional Development

Several steps would be needed to develop the institutions and help them achieve the status of world-class higher education organizations.

The separation of research and teaching caused a certain sterility and unresponsiveness in the former system. The universities will need to develop the research agenda for their faculty now that they can combine research and teaching. Educators can facilitate programmatic research to facilitate the faculty's ability to engage in research. One mechanism is to create well-funded competition for those working in universities, which would enable them to compete for research funds through the preparation and submission of grant proposals.

Institutions are also very specialized and differentiated. Substantive domains within institutes are narrow. Republics duplicate efforts in this manner. This fragmentation and the resulting artificial boundaries may create a rigidity and narrow education experience for students. Faculty members are also less inclined to engage in interdisciplinary activity or to value research if they teach.

These artificial separations of activities and curriculum should be reviewed and changed to reflect the new social realities. For example, economics training should be available to all students. Faculty should engage in and be rewarded for teaching and research.

Certain curricula should get more attention. The social sciences (especially economics), management subjects (especially accounting and marketing), and world languages are the areas requiring the most strengthening. Some areas of physical and engineering sciences are below world standards and need strengthening as well. As a general matter, the theoretical disciplines and the theoretical foundations for hard sciences are nearly comparable to European levels. The Czech and Slovak Republics fall short on practical, hands-on experimental and empirical techniques supported by equipment such as contemporary computers and lab equipment.[7]

Universities may be overstaffed, and many faculty members may have become obsolete as a result of their isolation from the exchange of world-class information. Few opportunities exist within Czechoslovakia to develop new faculty. Thus, educators need a massive reeducation program during which faculty members would travel abroad to study and learn modern techniques. New disciplines are going to demand that some faculty change their specialties.

The challenge is to find legitimate ways to dismiss the weaker faculty and to keep those who are or could be productive. This process can be helped by well-designed faculty evaluation techniques and the reduction of faculty sizes. This reduction in staff would also allow rectors to reorient the curriculum.

The existence of two academic bodies—the academic senates and the scientific councils—with vague and sometimes contradicting powers results in a complicated and lengthy decision-making process. Their existence also decreases the power of the rectors and deans. Institutions must develop more efficient decision-making processes. These efficiencies should be supported legally, if in no other way than to provide permission for institutions to design their own governance structures.

Only 16% of age-eligible people are enrolled in higher education; the proportion of higher educational opportunity the two countries provide their citizens is roughly half that of most OECD countries. A change may be needed to open universities to more people and to expand the number and types of curricula offered to them. The three-cycle French system may be considered (i.e., a two-year A.A. degree plus two years to get a B.A. and another two years for a master's). Also, national examinations should be reconsidered and possibly eliminated to get a wider range of students into schools.

Reformers must be cautioned. The very notion of helping more people to get ahead by giving them more education is flawed. Higher education as a credential is a positional good, whose supply has to be limited to be of value. Thus, great care should be exercised before degree requirements are changed.

Democracy

The implementation of democracy within higher education institutions is fundamental to institutional success. In a free country, democracy is both a right and a responsibility. This responsibility demands informed judgment, not just the entitlement to participate in the educational system. Student participation may be appropriate in providing information to decision makers. However, few well-run organizations would give an equal vote to students. Democracy is most appropriate in decisions related to process rather than in outcomes.

External Linkages

External linkages are critical to the reform process. Each institution will need to develop these linkages during its reform process. At present, linkages tend to be made with the five or six key universities. The universities located outside large population areas tend not to receive as much attention.

Three ideas should guide the development of linkages. First, linkages must be made with credible Eastern institutions willing to make a long-term commitment. Western governments can help to give information on Western institutions so that informed decisions can be made. Second, linkages are relationships that need to be managed for mutual benefit. For example, some linkages have failed because they were viewed as sources of aid to the host institution without a mutual relationship. Third, linkages take time to develop. Too much emphasis is being placed on short-term commitments.

New Financing Methods

Funding should be based on performance criteria and the need to invest in curriculum and faculty development. The primary issue facing higher education reformers is how to replace state budget allocations with other sources.

Higher education institutions should fund portions of their budgets through tuition, revenues from payments by students for food and lodging, service contracts, etc. These funds should be controlled by the institution. This independent funding was beginning to be developed in 1991, but few administrators knew how such a financing system would work.

One system that should be tried is to fund students directly. In this way, students can have the freedom to choose faculties and institutions perceived as having quality. For the period of reconstruction of the higher education system, state funding should be based on the number of students taught and the number of staff, which is set by an agreed-upon norm. The Ministry can determine the number of staff from the number of students and then reimburse the universities for personnel costs and related material costs according to a set of rules. The staff/student ratios should be appropriate for the discipline.

This method of direct student funding is often called a "voucher system." Vouchers give students more freedom to choose institutions. A voucher represents a certain amount of money that is handed over by the Ministry to the student in the form of a coupon. This coupon would be used only for education.

Some researchers feel voucher success would be difficult in the short term (Jongbloed et al., 1992) for the following reasons:

1. Introduction of a voucher system presupposes a well-functioning, client-oriented system of higher education. Clearly, in Czechoslovakia, such a stage of development has yet to be reached by the higher education systems.

2. Mobility of students is a key to a successful voucher system. Considering the housing problems and the conflict between Slovaks and Czechs, the level of needed mobility is unattainable.

3. The introduction of vouchers involves high administrative costs, especially if the voucher scheme is income-linked.

4. As an alternative, students could be allowed to utilize transfer credits. Students could take part in universities of their own choice, and credit could be accepted throughout the two countries.

In summary, the above strategies are from an institutional perspective and show how a university could respond to the present conditions in both countries.

Conclusions

The reformulation of the Czech and Slovak higher education system is important in its own right. The wise reformer can have a profound impact on the Czechoslovak society and can lead some economic and social reforms.

We also can learn many lessons from other higher education systems and their reforms. At least four key lessons can be learned by watching these two countries as they progress through their changes in higher education.

First, reformers in other systems will have an unprecedented opportunity to study the interaction between major macroeconomic and societal changes and changes within the education system. The opportunity to observe this type of rapid and sweeping change does not occur often. All competitive forces will be changing rapidly. New entrants will compete with existing institutions, students and faculty will become more powerful, and higher education will alter the way it is financed. These changes will be occurring at the same time as the emergence of new financial markets, new political leaders, and the reformulation of other institutions throughout society.

Second, emulating foreign education systems is very complicated. For example, in the Czech Republic, we may see the usefulness of choosing other systems as a basis for comparison. They may learn a great deal from Portugal and the way that country's higher education system changes along with its economic changes. The comparison can be very instructive for other countries.[8]

Third, we should not underestimate the importance of outside influences for system changes. New linkages, outside funding, and new people working within higher education will have a profound impact on the speed and direction of change. These linkages are important and, if chosen carefully, can create a smooth transition. We can learn from these interactions and determine how and what linkages create system change.

Fourth, the changes in the two countries could be unique from the perspective of who initiates the changes. Our view here is that meaningful change will only come from the institutions. The key challenge is to understand the motivation for change and what the government can do to stand out of the way so that this change may occur. We still do not know if the private sector will play a major role in the changes, as it does in Latin America, or if new, private universities will evolve "alongside" existing institutions. These developments could prove unique, especially in the Czech Republic, and instructive for other higher education reforms.

NOTES

* We would like to acknowledge the support of the United States Information Agency 1991–1993 grant, entitled "Educational Institution Program in Business Management in Central and Eastern Europe," to the University of Pittsburgh Joseph M. Katz Graduate School of Business.

Many Czech and Slovaks provided valuable comments on earlier drafts of this chapter. We became aware of the emotional impact of some of the words and phrases we used. We realize that some of our colleagues in the Czech and Slovak Republics will not agree with some of our phrasing, yet we hope we have created an accurate picture of higher education in Czechoslovakia.

1. We will discuss the two countries. The two republics were united under the name Czechoslovakia until January 1, 1993. Given the similarity of their traditions structure, economies, and general conditions, we chose to discuss them together in this chapter.

2. Some commentaries on higher education specified that this split between research and teaching was most common for experimental natural sciences and was not as complete a split for other sciences.

3. See also P. Szebenyi. (1992). Change in the system of public education—East Central Europe. *Comparative Education 28*, p. 20.

4. The universities and the dates they were created are: Pilsen, 1950; Pardubice, 1950; Kocise, 1950; and Liberec, 1953.

5. The universities and the dates they were created are: Nitra, 1952; Zvolen, 1952; and Prague, 1952. See Daniel, 1992, p. 7, for a further discussion of the creation of universities.

6. PHARE stands for Poland-Hungary Assistance in Reforming Economies; TEMPUS stands for Trans-European Mobility Scheme for University Studies.

7. While some institutions have excellent equipment, their availability is not widespread.

8. This comparison to Portugal may be deemed unfair by some Czechoslovaks. However, the observation of another system can be very instructive. Portugal is just one example of a system worth observing. The country is experiencing transformations similar to those in Czechoslovakia and is also reforming its higher education system. Austria, Australia, Spain, the Netherlands, and Hungary may be others to observe.

REFERENCES

Ashby, E. (1967). The future of the nineteenth century idea of a university. *Minerva 6*, pp. 3–17.

Concerning institutions of higher education. Act #172. (May 4, 1990). Translated July 1991.

Czech and Slovak Ministries of Education. (1990). *Federal statistics from World Bank report*. Durham, England: Birks Sinclair & Associates, Ltd.

Cerych, L. (1990). Renewal of central Europe higher education: Issues and challenges. *European Journal of Higher Education, 25(4)*, pp. 351–59.

Daniel, D. P. (1992). *National higher education and research systems of Central Europe*. Unpublished manuscript of the Slovak Information Agency, Czechoslovakia.

Estrin, S., Gelb, A. & Singh, I. J. (1991). *Socialist enterprises in transaction: A framework for case studies*. Unpublished paper from the World Bank.

Fogel, D. (1990). Management education in Central and Eastern Europe and the Soviet Union. *Journal of Management Development, 9(3)*, pp. 14–19.

———. (1992). Approaches to management education in reforming economics. *International Education Forum, 12(1)*, pp. 18–31.

Fogel, D. & Madhaven, R. (1992). In support of reform: Western business education in central Europe. *Review of Business, 14(4)*, pp. 4–9.

Ginsberg, M. (Ed.). (1991). *Understanding educational reform in global context: Economy, ideology, and the state.* New York: Garland Publishing, Inc.

Harach, L., Kotasek, J., Koucky, J. & Hendrichova, J. (1992). *Higher education in the Czech and Slovak republic.* Report to the OECD. Prague-Bratislava.

Harbison, R. W. (1987). Unpublished report to the Czechoslovak Government. U.S. Department of Education.

———. (1991). *Education and training in Czechoslovakia.* Unpublished report to the Czechoslovak Government. Durham, England: Birks, Sinclair & Associates, Inc.

Hrabinska, M. (Ed.). (1992). *Higher education in the Czech and Slovak republic.* Bratislava, Slovakia: The Institute of Information and Prognosis of Education, Youth and Sports.

Jongbloed, B., Koelman, J. & Vossensteijn, H. (1992). *Challenges for the Hungarian system of higher education.* Unpublished report for the Center Higher Education Policy Studies, University of Twente, Netherlands.

Kallen, D. (1991). *Academic exchange in Europe: Towards a new era of co-operation.* Bucharest, Romania: UNESCO European Centre for Higher Education, pp. 10–80.

Koucky, J. (1990). Czechoslovak education at the cross-roads. *European Journal of Education, 25(4)*, pp. 361–77.

OECD. (1992). *Reforming the economies of Central and Eastern Europe.* Paris: OECD.

Porter, M. (1980). *Competitive Strategy.* New York: Free Press.

Szebenyi, P. (1992). Change in the system of public education—East Central Europe. *Comparative Education, 28(20)*, pp. 9–31.

VonKopp, B. (1992). The Eastern European revolution and education in Czechoslovakia. *Comparative Education Review*, pp. 101–13.

CHAPTER IX

Governmental Reforms in Hungarian Higher Education
Historical Traditions and New Actors

Peter Darvas

Introduction

Hungary is in a period of dramatic political and social transition. The political system has been reshaped as a constitutional democracy, and the socioeconomic system is moving towards a market-based economy. The process which brought about the fall of Communism serves as an impetus for broad changes in the whole society. This chapter will focus on the changes in higher education during the course of the nation's political transformation, providing an analytical foundation for research on the influences of recent political changes on higher education.

The analysis of how the political transition affects higher education aspires to determine the degree to which the state remains the dominant actor in the decision-making process. Further, it seeks to observe the degree to which democratization has created a political arena in which higher educational institutions, professional organizations, politicians and leaders of public opinion outside the government play a major role in defining and instituting changes in the substance and organization of higher education.

Higher education as an institution may be observed from different analytical angles: as a sphere of political manipulation for the state administration or other political actors, as an integrated part of the larger educational system, as an autonomous institution with its independent internal structure and power relations, and partly as the primary institution for preparing the elite for prestigious professions and other positions which require advanced training.

Among many qualities in the process of educational change, two seem most significant:

1. Traditional patterns in the relationship between higher education and its social, political and economic environment: Persistent traditions in the higher educational institutions of a nation influence the patterns of specialization, diversification and administration. One may not have a comprehensive understanding of recent reforms without an overview of how higher education is traditionally embedded in social and economic relations, trends of expansion and changes in admission policies, in the regulation of the examination system and in curriculum policy.

2. Actors and political participants in the decision-making, political negotiations and reform process: Higher educational policy-making in Hungary is in the process of being released from its tight monolithic structure as new actors appear and old actors introduce new strategies and ideologies in the higher educational policy arena. Examples of new actors include, among others, associations and councils of the professorate, university administrators and independent student organizations. Political parties, instead of dominating the entire decision-making system, are sometimes representing partial interests and following democratic strategies instead of old-style bureaucratic control. The democratically elected government has an urgent need to consolidate its power, which brings about renegotiation of participation, reform and administration.

Theoretical Background

In analyzing the traditional patterns and the emergence of new actors in the political arena, I will attempt to use Margaret Archer's concept and terminology designed to analyze the emergence and expansion of educational systems (Archer, 1979, 1982). Archer distinguishes crucial temporal phases in the development of educational systems.

Two distinct integrative strategies can be observed in the dynamics of educational systems: substitutive and restrictive ones. The substitutive strategy is typical when educational control is challenged by market-type competition. The restrictive strategy is typical when the aim of policy actors is the legal transfer of control. Internally, the restrictive strategy results in quick unification and systematization of the education system, whereas the substitutive strategy first results in differentiation and specialization. The outcome of the different patterns of emergence are traditionally centralized and decentralized educational systems. Furthermore, Archer distinguishes between different patterns of educational expansion according to the agents that initiate the growth. External transactions indicate the interests of newly emerging groups (emerging professions, active minority groups, newly emerging stratas, etc.) who aim at additional educational services; internal initiations manifest internal educational groups (teachers, administrators, etc.) who aim at increasing the extent (length) of instruction; and political manipulation takes place when powerful outside political groups (parties) put pressure on the system to increase enrollment. As these patterns suggest, each strategy results in distinct patterns of expansion. This terminology has the advantage of going beyond the simple notion of ideological determination and shows the potential of endogenous change within the system, without cutting education off from its social origins.

Burton Clark's (1983) typology, applied to the Hungarian higher educational system, classifies it as a single public system with multiple sectors. Apart from a few church-owned institutions, all are controlled by the state. Furthermore, the system is two-tiered, distinguishing between universities on the one hand

and "colleges" (also known as "higher schools") on the other. The latter are lower-level institutions of the postsecondary educational system. Nineteen of the 52 public institutions are called universities, although only four have programs in more than one disciplinary field. The remaining 15 are specialized: four in medicine, four in technology, six in agriculture and one in economics. The other public institutions consist of 35 colleges: 14 teachers' training colleges, seven colleges of technology, five art colleges and seven other institutions. Higher education is very selective; less then 10% of the 18–22 age-group is enrolled, which is very low by international comparison.

Although the traditions of the universities are different from those of the colleges (postsecondary training for technicians and teachers), both have been organized to provide specialized training for positions in different sectors of the economy.

The possible consequences of the political transformation of higher education may be better understood if we focus on the following issues:

1. The persistence of historical patterns.
2. The traditionally politicized character of higher education, and the political manipulation of admission policies and the pattern of growth.
3. The centralized nature of administration and planning.
4. The technical nature of institutions and programs.

Historical Patterns

According to Archer's terminology, the Hungarian educational system was historically centralized. Its emergence followed a restrictive pattern that was politically manipulated.

Before the Second World War Hungary had one of the highest proportions of theological (10.5%) and legal training (37.9%) programs and one of the lowest proportions of engineering (8.0%) and economic or business programs (4.6%) in Europe. The number of students between 1935 and 1939 was 153 per 100,000 population, one of the lowest in Europe. The structure reflected the continued existence of the Habsburg traditions of higher learning (Ladanyi, 1992).

These traditions go back to the 17th century. Before that, a few academies existed under the supervision of the Roman Catholic and the Protestant churches but with no clear division between the secondary and the more advanced levels. In 1735 the first important university, the University of Nagyszombat, was founded by the Jesuits. This institution is the predecessor of the Eotvos Lorand University in Budapest (Kosary, 1987).

From the second half of the 17th century, the Crown, increasingly pressured by its rivalry with Prussia, made education a state duty, removed it from the church's sphere of authority and placed it under state control. The educational policy adopted by Habsburg enlightened absolutism was drawn up after the Prussian model, claiming it the right and duty of the state to regulate public education in such a way that young people could be made into useful citizens. In practice, it meant the appointment of rectors faculty by the king, as well as the regulation of the curricula by royal decree.

The first important step in the emergence of a national educational system was Queen Maria Theresa of Austria's edict Ratio Educationis of 1777. The government, needing civil servants, set up four "royal academies" in 1777 offering curricula in philosophy and law. The queen took the Jesuit university under royal control, transferred it from Nagyszombat to Buda and, in 1784, to Pest. Its administration was restructured, following the model of the University of Vienna. A president, nominated by the royal government, and a "consistorium" ruled the university. The consistorium included the directors of the faculties. Below it was the "magistrate" to which members, rectors and deans were elected, but their power was limited. The university was given a diversified curriculum and a national role of supervising the royal academies and textbooks. Later, the consistorium was renamed the "senate," and the absolutistic centralized nature of the higher educational administration was maintained until the mid-19th century (Ladanyi, 1992).

The Hungarian liberal noble opposition strongly denounced the Austrian control over the universities, and the 1848 revolution brought about liberal legislation of higher education, guaranteeing the freedom of learning and the freedom of teaching as well. After the revolution, the governmental bureaucrats, lead by Leo Thun-Hohenstein, first focused on reconstructing the "order" in higher education, but later began their own reform, mainly following a Humboldtian concept of higher education. In this model the professoriate had a cultural mission as upholders of academic excellence. This regulation provided an autonomy for the faculty as a professionally connected body, rather than independence for the university as an autonomous institution.

The position of director of the faculty was eliminated, and instead, the faculty annually elected a dean. A university council was established, including the rector, prorector (the rector from the preceding year), deans, prodeans and electorates from each faculty. The council determined curriculum issues, administrative and disciplinary matters, etc. The nomination of a professor—the "habilitation"—was controlled by the faculty, although the government was also given the right to nominate private professors. Thun-Hohenstein's reforms included the guarantees of academic freedom and freedom of choice in learning.

In 1867 Hungary gained more independence within the newly established Austro-Hungarian monarchy. The monarchy retained control over military, foreign affairs and currency, but an autonomous Hungarian government was in charge of the rest of central administration, including education. From this dual structure of power, this period was called the "dualism."

The first Hungarian minister of education was Baron Jozsef Eotvos, who maintained the policy of guaranteeing professional autonomy and aimed to create a liberal system of higher education, although none of the governments could enact comprehensive legislation following 1867.

One of the most interesting sets of acts was issued by the next minister, Agoston Trefort, in 1873. It consisted of three laws, each regulating three universities. One—aimed at the restructuring of the University of Pest—included chapters determining the statuses of different professors, their protection and their autonomy. A second law sought to start the University of Kolozsvar in Transylvania, with similar regulations to that of Pest; and a third legislative effort aimed at reorganizing the "Jozsef" Technical

School, later to become the first University of Technology and Engineering in the country (Ladanyi, 1992).

Trefort's proposals supported the ideals of competition, secularization and liberty. These ideals were clearly present in his major legislative proposal for higher education, submitted in 1873. Although never enacted, it consisted of tuition for specific classes and protection of the status of professors, and removed the theological faculties from the universities. Freedom of learning and teaching was generally supported, but these freedoms appeared only in the internal regulation of specific institutions, instead of being enacted as general law.

In the meantime, universities had limited freedom in their finances and personnel. The main reason for the government to maintain its control over finances was to support its own expansive strategy by setting up new institutions. Expansion of the system was in conflict with the existing professional monopolies. The ministry maintained its right to appoint private professors; departmental chairs and deans were, however, decided by the faculty. This structure left the university caught between the ministry and the faculties, without much power.

Gradually, government influence over the creation of expertise was extended. The acquisition of certain qualifications as a prerequisite to becoming doctors or lawyers was controlled by the government, which thus regulated the procedures of studies and retained the Ministry's right of approval of the curriculum. The increasing conflicts between the government and academia were expressed by the battles around the nominations of professors, in which the government usually played the more liberal, sometimes lenient, role.

In 1919, after the First World War, two-thirds of Hungary's territory, including two of three newly established universities, was lost to neighboring countries. The general administrative framework of the higher educational system, however, was essentially the same as previously. The emergence of nationalism and fascism appeared mostly in the ideological content of educational practice and in some legislative changes.

The main legislative efforts during this period aimed at modifying the institutional structure and manipulating the admissions policy. To replace the lost universities, the government set up two new institutions, for which the personnel was re-cruited by the government from the universities of the lost terri-tories. Other reforms aimed to unify the system by concentrating the small institutions first in teacher training, then in technical, economic and agricultural training.

The most crucial governmental act was to manipulate ad-mission. Various pretexts and decrees were employed to main-tain a quota system, which aimed at providing positions for the children of the Christian middle class and limiting the admission of Jews to the university. The first "Numerus Clausus" in Hun-gary was enacted in 1920, 12 years before Germany enacted a similar act. Its vague language aimed at proportional participa-tion for different ethnic and religious groups in the enrollment. This act was modified in 1928 and softened the language of the regulation to please foreign governments; however, admissions practices remained in place. Finally, a 1940 act explicitly limited the admission of Jews to institutions of higher education.

In sum, by 1945, the system reflected a duality of (1) tradi-tionally high-level professional autonomy, possessed by the fac-ulty, and (2) increasing governmental influence, sometimes aimed at expansion, sometimes modernization and sometimes political manipulation. The first element was the power of pro-fessors, reflecting Humboldtian traditions, whereas the second was the dominance of the state, reflecting Prussian traditions. The struggle usually meant a confrontation between government intervention and protection of the academic monopoly by con-servative faculty. Furthermore, institutions were fragmented and, with the exception of four universities, specialized. The structure of the curriculum reflected legal and theological domi-nance over technical and economic disciplines, the admissions policy was politically manipulated, and growth in enrollment and graduation was delayed.

Politicized Higher Education after 1945

The short period of coalition did not bring about major reform of the higher education system. The parties that partici-pated in the coalition government basically agreed on some major strategies of reform but did not have enough time to implement them. Their programs included diversification of the vertical structure and separation of scientific training, research and professional training in order to counter the universities, which had conservative reputations.

The first reform, following the communist takeover in 1948, aimed at subordinating the system to the needs of the so-called populist democracy and of the planned economy. The dominance of the Soviet Union meant the introduction of Stalin-ist methods in every sector of social life. As education was part of the politically controlled socialist training system that aimed at the creation of the "communist man," higher education had to create the "communist intellectual."

The policy decisions of the central authorities changed according to the actual political and ideological processes, causing a cyclical motion in enrollments, graduations and standards. Hard-line communist political dominance in 1951, 1954 and 1957, for instance, meant strong ideological control, manipulation of admissions and graduations and low academic standards. Revisionist political turnarounds after the death of Stalin and during the period of consolidation in the 1960s brought about more pragmatic steps, higher academic standards and looser ideological ties. Policy decisions often reflected compromises because of the conflicting political objectives of the Party. These decisions focused on four issues: admissions, growth, centralization and polytechnicization.

Polytechnical Structure

The postwar period brought about radical changes in the structure of institutions and programs. The first signs appeared even before the communist takeover: decreasing enrollment in law and theology and increasing enrollment in technology, economics, science and medicine. Later, the Communist Party continued to divide the already fragmented institutional structure, so that it could strengthen central control over higher education. Medical training was detached from arts and sciences and the university and, as a separate institution, became subordinated to the Ministry of Health. The economics faculty of the University of Polytechnics was also closed, and a specialized University of Economics was created for training experts for the planned economy. Two new universities of technology were also founded in the early 1950s, one specializing in heavy industry in the town of Miskolc, and another in chemistry in the town of Veszprem. Legal academies, most of the legal faculties of universities and most theological institutions were closed, and the theological faculties of the Faculties of Arts were taken out and given to the churches with minimized roles and enrollments. Meanwhile, the Russian department of the Faculty of Arts in Budapest was reorganized as an independent faculty, called the Lenin Institute.

The polytechnical structure of the educational system was based on an ideology which effectively limited the increasing aspirations of people to participate in schooling. It appeared as a strategy to expand the system, but in reality it was a restriction of mass schooling. In practice, the polytechnical character of education was achieved by the vocationalization of secondary education, thus lowering the quality of academic learning; by the greater emphasis and proportion of apprenticeship programs at the secondary level, thus limiting the number of students eligible for higher education; and by the specialization of higher educational programs to meet industrial needs.

Political Manipulation of the Admissions

The role that the state played in manipulating admissions before the war remained during the Stalinist and post-Stalinist periods. During the first period the key political question was the participation of children of working-class parents in higher education. At first, this had a double rationale: to assure more politically reliable people for high administrative positions and to counterbalance injustices of the previous regime. Accordingly, the communist program in 1948 called for increasing admission for members of the lower classes and increasing attention to the "democratic education" of intellectuals. The program eliminated the maturity examination as a prerequisite for admission.

Later on, quotas based on class background were abolished, but preferences were still provided from time to time to families from working-class backgrounds. In fact this agenda was one indicator of the cyclical reassertion of hard-line political campaigns (Lukacs, 1989).

The proportion of manual workers' children attending higher education grew until 1951, when the Hungarian cultural revolution peaked (see table 1). The proportion grew again in 1955, when the Stalinist leaders returned following a period when their position was weakened as a result of Stalin's death. The next growth period for the children of manual workers was in 1959, during the ideological counterattack by the communist political elite after the revolution, and then in 1964 and in 1978—both times as periods of heavy-industry dominance, and the second time as a consequence of a campaign of economic and political recentralization.

TABLE 1. **The Proportion of Manual Workers' Children among Full-Time Freshmen in Higher Education**

Year	%	Year	%
1949–50	53.1	1969–70	37.2
1950–51	59.3	1970–71	36.9
1951–52	62.5	1971–72	37.5
1952–53	60.1	1972–73	36.4
1953–54	58.7	1973–74	36.8
1954–55	56.1	1974–75	40.0
1955–56	64.4	1975–76	40.1
1956–57	54.5	1976–77	42.5
1957–58	52.2	1977–78	42.4
1958–59	51.7	1978–79	43.6
1959–60	54.2	1979–80	42.0
1960–61	49.1	1980–81	41.7
1961–62	47.9	1981–82	41.5
1962–63	43.9	1982–83	41.0
1963–64	43.5	1983–84	39.5
1964–65	45.1	1984–85	39.7
1965–66	43.6	1985–86	38.2
1966–67	44.2	1986–87	37.7
1967–68	39.5	1987–88	37.0

Source: Lukacs, 1989.

The transition between secondary and higher education was regulated in such a way that high school performance strongly determined admissions. Consequently, the policies that governed the process of secondary education also dominated the admissions process from secondary to higher education at the expense of the universities, which could not effectively influence selection. The politicized process of selection for universities limited the influence of academic or other professional standards.

Despite the communist ideology, higher education in Hungary remained elitist. The percentage of the appropriate cohorts (20–24 years) participating in higher education remained relatively low (about 15% including evening and correspondence students, less than 10% without them), the lowest in Europe except for Romania. As a result, the level of education of individuals remained a relatively strong, almost exclusive indicator of social background. Thus education retained its role in recruiting the social elite, despite the cyclically reasserted blue-collar ideology of the Party. In fact, the percentage of children of manual workers among first-year full-time students decreased from 64.4% in 1955 to 37% in 1987 (Lukacs, 1989).

Inflation in the Enrollments

After the Second World War, admissions to higher education increased because of two factors: the admission of those who were earlier excluded because of the Numerus Clausus or the war, and the increasing participation of women in higher education. In 1945 the main political parties voted to give permission for universities to admit students who had not finished secondary school.

Between 1946 and 1976 the total number of students rose from 25,000 to 110,000. The increased admission was made possible by the creation of evening schools and extramural and correspondence courses for part-time students. In 1946 the proportion of students enrolled in these programs was only 5%, but since the 1950s the percentage has been about 40% (table 2).

TABLE 2. **Proportion of Full-Timers and Number
of Undergraduates per Teacher**

		Rate of Undergraduate Teachers per %		
Year	# of Undergraduate Teachers	Proportion of Full-Time Undergraduates	Proportion of Full-Time Students	Proportion of Part-Time Students
1950	32,501	81.6	—	—
1955	45,431	67.5	6.2	9.2
1960	44,585	65.8	5.2	7.9
1965	93,957	54.3	6.0	11.1
1970	80,536	66.8	5.5	8.2
1975	107,555	59.8	5.3	8.9
1980	101,166	63.3	4.6	7.3
1984	89,986	63.2	4.3	6.9

Source: Data collected by the Central Statistical Office.

Thus, growth and democratization of the system were achieved mainly by opening up lower-quality channels. Also, the growth was typically achieved in institutions with lower academic standards, reflected by the increasing proportion of non-university-level programs at the expense of university-level higher education.

The number of higher educational institutions in 1946 was 18. By 1965 this number grew to 92. The increase was achieved by transforming secondary technical and teacher training institutions into higher education institutions. Since then, as the result of combinations, the number of institutions has been decreasing (see table 3).

TABLE 3. Number of Higher Education
Institutions, Teachers, Students

Year	All Institutions	Universities	Faculties	# Teachers	# Students	# Students at Univ. Level
1950	19	–	43	–	32,501	–
1955	32	–	54	4,913	45,431	–
1960	43	14	60	5,635	44,585	32,637
1965	92	16	111	8,444	93,957	51,993
1970	74	18	102	9,791	80,536	44,722
1975	56	24	104	12,135	107,555	48,534
1980	57	24	95	13,890	101,166	45,357
1984	58	25	100	14,545	89,986	42,216

Source: Data collected by the Central Statistical Office.

Administration and Structure

The Party's most powerful measure, the first five-year plan
(1949–53), with the status of law, focused on quantitative development. A modification of the plan in 1951 even further increased the enrollment numbers of the period. Whereas the original plan called for an increase of 8,000 in the number of students
in higher education, the number was later raised to 30,000. The
five-year plan was later supplemented with 10- and 20-year
plans for the future labor needs of industry and the professions.
This planning system represented the most characteristic features of the socialist regime: both the centralized administration
and polytechnic structure subordinated higher education to industrial needs.

The growth of higher education was strongly connected to
the industrial expansion, which had generated a permanent
shortage of manpower, unskilled as well as skilled. The training
programs were oriented towards the fulfillment of these needs.
This meticulous planning system, however, could not guarantee

the appropriate employment of graduates, despite the efforts of the central bureaucracy, which tried to force graduates towards jobs where the shortage was most acute. Even by the final year of the long-term plan, 30% of students were employed in fields other than those for which they were trained.

Negotiations surrounding the content and size of programs took place between the National Bureau of Planning and the particular ministries responsible for the labor supply of specific industries and service sectors and subsectors. The institutions had to "produce" specialized labor for their industry. While the National Bureau of Planning provided the numbers, the ministries controlled the curriculum and the process of training and reported to the bureau on the manpower needs of their sector. Meanwhile employers, given the acute shortage of manpower, were more interested in hiring as many people as they could, but not at prestigious jobs or high salaries. The coordination of these bodies was in the hands of the Party apparatus.

Institutions of higher education were separated from scientific training and scientific research by the creation of the Hungarian Academy of Sciences. Research was given to the latter, and the granting of scientific degrees was controlled by an agency called the Scientific Qualification Committee under the auspices of the Academy. The right to appoint professors, control curriculum and reform the structure of programs was in the hands of the Communist Party. The right to appoint the deans and rectors was given to the Ministry of Education, also controlled by the Party, degrading the role of the faculty and university councils. Institutions and professors had to cope with direct political control over their curricula and the internal life of institutions.

Since the programs were specialized, and plan goals difficult to reach, the central authorities simply left out some elements of the curriculum which did not directly serve the short-term needs of employers. Soon, the courses of study were shortened, and campaigns were initiated against "unreliable" professors who wanted to "overburden" the students. Even at the Universities of Technology the course of study was shortened from five to four years.

In 1954, a year after the death of Stalin, the National Bureau of Planning decreased the number of enrolled students. The post-Stalin era brought about some changes in decision making. Most of the decrees came from the ministries, and the curricula of some programs were liberalized. In 1956 university students and the majority of the faculty were participating actively in the reform campaign prior to the revolution, and in fights during the revolution, too. As a consequence, after the fall of the revolutionary government, the new Soviet-backed political establishment returned to tight political control over higher education. After the repressive politics of the first few years, the Party (state) tried to install new governance procedures. This was called the period of consolidation. During this time, central control was relaxed somewhat and concessions were given to institutions. After 1962 appointments of heads of offices in higher education went from the ministries to the institutions, rectors and deans. After the introduction of the New Economic Mechanism and decentralization measures, university councils could include students and the councils had the right to elect department chairs. Professional curriculum control was given, with some limitations to the institutions as well. The ideologically relevant subjects (philosophy, history and social sciences) remained in central hands.

Although the political environment was somewhat relaxed, the basic elements of the centralized governance remained intact. The government strictly limited the autonomy of institutions, planned enrollment, subordinated quality to quantitatively determined goals, strictly specialized the character of programs and institutions and, generally, subordinated academic life to political and economic aims.

The changes did not affect the basic relationship with the National Bureau of Planning. The admission numbers remained subject to manipulation by the planning authorities, ignoring aspects such as demography, individual aspirations and academic standards. Higher education was still evaluated in terms of its congruence with the aims of central planning in service to the Communist Party's industrial strategy. Although centrally planned enrollment numbers gradually lost their mandatory character, lack of adequate support for higher education prevented institutional modification of programs. The financial difficulties were further exacerbated by the cutting-off of higher education institutions' ties to science, research and development. Except for some polytechnics, most of the schools relied exclusively on government finance.

Yet, within the framework of centralized governance some changes were taking place in the order of priorities. Beginning in the 1960s the government adopted a new campaign of economic and industrial development. It was the Hungarian version of Kruschev politics, aiming at peaceful competition with and victory over the West. Part of this strategy was to restructure the economic sphere by putting more emphasis on agricultural production, on the production of durable goods for households and on services.

The new politics required, among other things, the increase of relatively skilled manpower for these newly expanded sectors, and this need was accompanied by an expansion of higher education. The expansion in spending and enrollment coincided with the growth of higher education in Western Europe but had a different political and ideological background.

The new strategy was enabled by the Education Act of 1961, which made it possible for ministries to charter new higher education institutions. Although not intended as a step towards decentralization, the Act changed the way central control was practiced. It restructured the power relations within the governmental hierarchy, giving more authority to pragmatic, economic interests and less to ideology, at the expense of the ideologues in the Ministry of Education.

As a result, in the first half of the 1960s the proportion of higher education spending increased within the educational budget, although not within the overall budget of the central government. A typical example was the dramatic increase in the training of agricultural specialists. As a result, the management of agriculture, including managers of firms and central and regional bureaucrats, was gradually increased. The number of institutions designed to prepare personnel for specific service and industrial sectors was also increased. However, these institutions were created by upgrading former upper-secondary institutions.

As a result, from 1966 to 1980 higher education's position within the central budget was expanded, as shown in table 4.

TABLE 4. The Expenditures of Higher Education

Period	H.E. Percentage of Education Budget	H.E. Percentage of Total Budget	Education Percentage of Total Budget
1956–60	13.7	2.1	15.2
1961–65	15.5	2.0	15.7
1966–70	17.2	2.5	14.2
1971–75	17.1	2.4	14.2
1976–80	15.7	3.3	21.0
1981–85	13.7	2.8	20.2
1986–87	12.6	2.7	21.3

Source: Data collected at the Ministry of Finance.

The year 1968 represented an important milestone for the postwar period of Hungary. A new economic mechanism was introduced, which gave considerably more autonomy to economic enterprises than was given by other countries of the "peace camp." Yet, the new economic policy did not similarly affect the life of the higher education institutions, perhaps out of the government's fear that the 1968 student movements abroad would cause political upheavals in Hungary also.

During the 1970s higher education received additional resources as new groups of students gained entrance. Yet, by this time the political atmosphere and the power relations became more complex than those of the first two decades. There were conflicting interests within the central authorities of the Party and of the government and more competition for financial resources due to poor economic conditions. Within this environment higher education could not maintain its growth, and the expansive period of the higher education was over.

The most important reason of the slowdown was a reemergence of hard-liners in the political environment. The first half of the 1970s in Hungary represented a period of counterreform and centralization. It meant increasing preference given to the capital-consuming enterprises of the heavy industry sector. This expansion came at the time of the renaissance of the workers' power and of the weakening of the quasi-market reforms introduced at the end of the 1960s. The politics of the situation were translated into the language of educational policy as a need to strengthen workers' identity and their education, i.e., vocational training institutions. These institutions were basically apprentice schools in which trainees receive a basic level of preparation and socialization to work. In 1974 these schools were formally acknowledged as part of the secondary education system. But in practice, they were finishing schools, since they did not give a maturity exam, a basic prerequisite for higher education.

The increased focus on vocational secondary education brought about shortages of funding for both higher education and its source of students: the gymnasium. The last three time periods in table 4 illustrate these changes within education. The sector as a whole increased its share because of the demographic wave of large cohorts reaching school age. At the same time, the share of the higher education within the educational sector decreased.

Another reason for the weakening position of higher education was the poor economy. By the second half of the 1970s, it became clear that the Iron Curtain could not stop the oil crisis. Hungary faced an economic crisis because of the high debt service on loans made in the early 1970s and spent on expensive and unprofitable investments in the industrial and energy sectors. In 1979 the government designated a new strategy, the "New Path of Growth," but it was unsuccessful, given the absence of a free market, political legitimacy, or the capacity for innovation and entrepreneurship.

For higher education the crisis brought increasing restriction and deterioration. Resources were inadequate for maintenance, educational materials, technical equipment and facilities, and certainly not available for future development and modernization.

By the 1980s, the overspecialized nature of education created an awkward situation in which neither planners nor anyone else had effective control over the structure of higher education.

In addition, higher education institutions had few resources or possibilities for improving their programs or for integrating them into other academic or professional activities, such as research and development.

Participation and Policy-Making

During most of the communist period groups could influence educational policy-making only through direct connection with the state administration. Not only final decisions but also policy discussions were formulated exclusively in the Ministry of Education, government executive committees and Party councils. In other words, the only strategy that could be used in attempting to influence the system was political and oriented toward the highest levels of established power. The notions of independent interest groups and trade union strategies, for example, simply did not apply in a monolithic, centralized system. Furthermore, identifying the individual positions of the actors was hard, since conflicts among the policy-making elites, if they existed, were hidden or denied.

Nevertheless, educational policy-making in Hungary was far less homogenous than was perceived in the West. In the 1960s a movement toward decentralization began, and a pragmatic national government recognized differing interests. It was then that the control over educational decisions weakened and conflicting interests first became public. Initially, differences of opinion had emerged among administrators regarding educational structure, enrollment and finance on the basis of their geographical location and economic wealth (Halasz, 1986). This phenomenon of regionalism, both among the regions and between the regions and the center, was the consequence of increased administrative autonomy at the regional levels. These actors brought with them concerns about national manpower needs and about the linking of education with local economies, as well as the noneconomic preferences of educational agencies.

The recognition of regional differences was followed by a period of "pragmatic decision making" in educational policy. In the 1970s, despite the persistence of the centralized policy-making environment, local and national economic and social needs began to be taken into consideration. Ideological factors, which had previously been the overriding criteria for policy-making, weakened. Moreover, different kinds of "rationalities" appeared, which were related to politics, economics or professionalism.

During the 1980s, policy analyses in Hungary began to examine the structure of educational policy-making. An analysis of secondary schooling conducted by Gabor Halasz showed that in the centralized decision-making process, there were values and rationalities associated with interest groups (Halasz, 1986). The study used two dimensions (ideology and economy) to chart the position of interest groups. It distinguished between (1) ideologically committed educational groups, (2) ideologically less committed groups composed of economic planners, (3) ideologically committed vocational education groups and (4) ideologically less committed education groups. The analysis suggested that even a centralized decision-making system can produce distinctly different groups, though it does not have a participatory character; e.g., the higher education policy arena became segmented as more government agencies became involved, each with competing interests and agendas.

By the 1980s fiscal experts greatly increased their influence within the government. Their power was strengthened because of the diminishing influence of the five-year plans and by the increasing attention to financial balance. This was further strenghthened by the need to handle the rising deficit and the intense competition for public funds.

Although the planning authorities' influence greatly diminished by the 1980s, their role in the formal approval of the overall framework for the public sector, as well as their role as a forum in the preliminary negotiations between the competing interests, gave them a place in the policy-making process.

The ministries responsible for competing public spheres (industry, agriculture, health, environment, etc.) were partly consumers of and partly competitors in education. On the one hand, they asserted their labor needs in terms of numbers and qualifications for the educational sphere, and on the other hand, as subsidized sectors, they competed with the educational sector for the state resources. Even in the 1980s no democratic forum existed for negotiating the structure of public spending, so planning authorities and governmental agencies were the only places for these negotiations.

The Ministry of Culture, as the main agency of educational governance, was the agency at the central level which could defend the educational sphere's financial interests. Therefore, the Ministry was compelled, at least nominally, to pursue a policy of expansion to ensure the conditions necessary for its autonomous functioning. This task split the Ministry's energies: it was in charge of supervision and control, and also safeguarded and represented the interests of the sector (Darvas, 1989). This duality meant a top position in the hierarchy of educational governance and a bottom position in the hierarchy of political governance.

For higher education institutions the main issues concerned the institutions' professional, economic and physical conditions and their relative autonomy. These two issues gave an opportunity to simplify the negotiations between government and higher education institutions to two dimensions in the political arena: the possibility of expansion and the degree of institutional autonomy.

Although we have identified the main concerns of these governmental agencies and institutions, it is quite difficult to locate their influence in Hungary's centralized higher education administration. Negotiations and participation were hidden in the seemingly static relationship between the state and higher education. In different periods, however, we may observe different sets of priorities, according to which interest group has enough power to dominate the decision-making process at the central political level.

There are periods of centrally initiated reforms and periods of increasing but limited autonomy for the institutions. In the first period, the state subordinated higher education to its needs. It was either expansive in its decisions (complying, for instance, with the labor needs of industry) or restrictive (complying with the needs of some professions in training and research).

In the second period, the state did not introduce reform measures without offering concessions to higher education institutions, usually in the form of more autonomy in determining their own organization, mode of governance, and programs. Such concessions appear to stem from negotiations between the institutions and the state over the shortage of resources (Kornai, 1980). Accordingly, the state again introduced expansive measures or limited its higher education expenses.

This negotiation process was typical in the 1980s in Hungary, but the concessions that were offered to higher education institutions were limited by the continued strength of the centralized administration, by the weakness of professional representation and by the lack of interest on the part of the state in demanding more effective educational programs.

Using this analytical framework, one can recognize a sort of cyclical motion in the pattern of negotiations, compromises, agreements and policy decisions. This pattern gave emphasis intermittently to different interest groups and their respective policies (whether governmental or institutional) that had a distinct interest in expansion or autonomy.

Based on these main issues the analysis distinguishes between four types of higher education policy:

- *Group I*—the policy arguing that the lack of responsiveness of the higher education system can be explained by the lack of interest of the individual institutions and, therefore, the better system can be reached by further decentralization but without further growth.

- *Group II*—the policy requiring both greater autonomy and further additional state support for the higher education institutions.

- *Group III*—the policy arguing that a strong central administration could increase the effectiveness of the system and, therefore, further growth would not be needed.

- *Group IV*—finally the policy based on a centrally administered campaign of growth of higher education.

The position of those representing the different policies can be illustrated in a scheme similar to the one designed for secondary education by Halasz (1986) (see figure 1).

FIGURE 1.   Higher Education Policy Arena

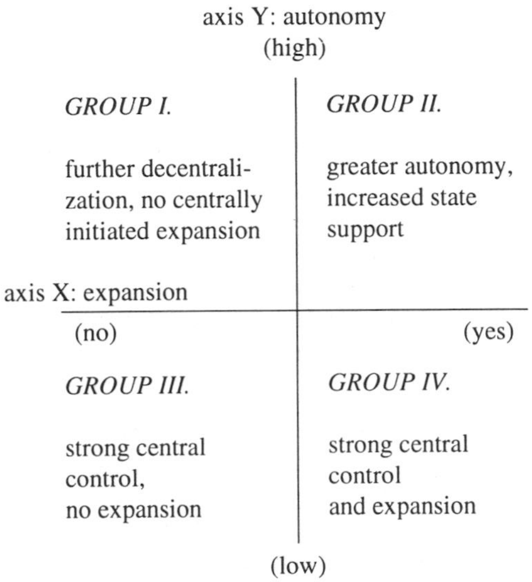

axis Y: autonomy
(high)

GROUP I.	GROUP II.
further decentrali- zation, no centrally initiated expansion	greater autonomy, increased state support

axis X: expansion

(no)	(yes)
GROUP III.	GROUP IV.
strong central control, no expansion	strong central control and expansion

(low)

In sum, the arena showed a limited scale of values which could be classified by two factors: expansion and autonomy. The interest sphere—namely, the professional, the administrative and the political—had distorted positions and limited space for their assertive strategies. Political representatives, instead of representing lay or outside interests within the system, channelled all the strategies into a centralized decision-making process. Neither the administrative-managerial sphere nor the professional-academic sphere could create its own effective representation. Instead, they were integrated to a monolithic system of covert negotiations, execution and loyalty. This system hid the existence of particularistic and competing interests and tensions and relegated the agreements and compromises to informal spheres.

Negotiations and Agreements in the First Half of the 1980s

In 1979 the Hungarian Socialist Workers Party for the first time explicitly admitted the existence of "deep problems" in the economy and, later, even the possibility of a crisis situation affecting other spheres such as education. For higher education this period brought about pressures from different directions. Initiatives to restructure the political arena eventually resulted in a changing role for the Party, the government, the higher education institutions and other participants.

By the end of the 1970s the Party had lost its resoluteness, which it still enjoyed in the early 1970s. The limits of its power were mainly noticeable in the implementation of decisions. In 1972 the Party was still able to initiate educational policy. At that time its policy was to limit efforts to implement minor changes in the curriculum for primary and secondary education. The usual track of decisions at that time was to bring about, or "enact," a new "Central Committee decision," which was voted by members of the Central Committee and had the highest prestige in the hierarchy of the decision-making process. The responsibility for implementation was then assigned to the Ministry of Education. Even the Parliament's legislative work was informally subordinated to this procedure.

In 1979 an influential member of the Politburo, Gyorgy Aczel, decided that a new developmental program should be designed for higher education and scientific research. Aczel was a key figure of the postrevolutionary political arena, and in the 1970s he was considered to be the second most powerful figure of the Kadar regime, often changing his position, moving among the top echelons of the Party and of the government. He was also known as a politician with broad informal contacts with the intellectuals, artists, scientists and members of the academic world. When he initiated the new higher education policy, he was the deputy prime minister and a member of the Politburo.

The preparation of the program was assigned to the deputy minister of culture, Andras Knopp, who, conforming to Aczel's style, developed the new program with the active collaboration of the academic world and higher education experts. We should note that for the first time the political establishment worked in strong cooperation with experts in preparing a "Central Committee decision." From then on, this pragmatic decision-making process was more and more typical of other Party decisions. Yet, in terms of implementing a new higher education reform, the political establishment, including Aczel and Knopp, did not cultivate the idea of either allowing the universities more autonomy or innovating on their own. Rather, they thought that reform should be implemented through a centrally administered operation.

The Central Committee decision on the Developmental Program for the Higher Educational System, introduced in 1981, aimed at a new pattern of development for the entire higher education system, a pattern to restructure the training programs and to expand both training programs and research activities. Understandably, the developmental program was a scientifically argued initiative to increase governmental support for higher education, since a reform of this scale would have required a considerable amount of money. However, the timing was the least optimal for this kind of proposal. The admitted crisis in the economy oriented the attention of the Politburo towards those who were working on the "New Path of Development" for the economy. Their main concern was to secure the employment of workers in endangered heavy industrial regions, mining towns and energy centers. These conflicts required short-term policy measures rather than long-term reforms investing in human capital. Since the centralized and politically determined decision-making system had but one top-level forum where all relevant interests and interest spheres competed for attention and intervention, the higher educational lobby could never get the required support, and their rather ambitious program was practically forgotten before implementation could begin.

In sum, the political program of 1981 to develop higher education is in the fourth sector of our scheme (see figure 1), and the members of the political establishment arguing for this policy belong to group IV. They tried to affect the system by cooperating with the academic world. Under Archer's terminology the politicians' strategy was to have their program appear as an "internal initiation" of growth.

The Party's central agencies served as a forum for the supporters of the program that called for expansion, rather than as a particular participant. The Central Committee and the Political Committee are institutions where efforts to expand the higher education sphere could be effectively represented and where financial support for these programs could be decided upon. This decision-making procedure also reinforced a belief that expansion could only be managed, controlled and protected from the top of the political hierarchy.

However, in spite of the cooperation and the complex elaboration of the asserted program, at this time the supporters of the expansion program could not win Party support. The Central Committee decided, in fact, to provide formal approval of the program but did not decide upon any additional financial means and directed the matter of execution to the governmental spheres.

The government, which was responsible for the administration of the higher education system through the recently reunified Ministry of Culture and by some other agencies, was caught in an even more contradictory situation. The minister of culture was Imre Pozsgay, who a decade later became one of the most prominent political supporters of political reforms within the Communist Party. Similarly to the Central Committee, he urged some financial resolution. But unlike the Party program, he did not call for a campaign of expansion and restructuring. Instead, his policy aimed at a more decentralized system where the Ministry could be a representative of the higher education sphere to the government rather than a bureaucratic executor of governmental decisions. Pozsgay's views, however, conflicted with the political reality of the 1970s, since the government was strongly controlled by the Party, its priorities reflecting the Party's priorities. As we have seen earlier, higher education did not enjoy a favorable status within the Party circles. The government was naturally obliged to accept the Party strategy. As a result, although the government verbally expressed its support for higher education, its support was only nominal and no resources were provided to back it up. As a result, the government alienated the leadership of higher education institutions, who were desperate, given the deterioration of the institutions, and who regarded the

Ministry as being unable to represent their interests in negotiations with the government.

Moreover, the plan to give the institutions more autonomy
could have caused anxiety. Decentralizing the administrative
system required radical intervention, which would have resulted
in the breakup of the existing power structure. The positions and
interests of influential personnel within the political leadership
could be endangered. Furthermore, the formal system of higher
education governance was built together with an informal system of negotiations and agreements, which itself represented a
sensitive balance of power. In practice, both the ministerial apparatus and the institutions depended on each other and counted
on the other side, when negotiating with external actors and
searching for resources. The danger that this balance might collapse could have alienated even the leadership of higher education institutions who otherwise would have welcomed more
power. From their perspective, the minister's initiatives were
trying to break down the bureaucratic structure and designated
more responsibilities without the necessary means.

In sum, the minister's initiatives aimed at a decentralized
system and at establishing a policy of increasing autonomy.
Ironically, the main support for this group (figure 1, group I) was
located in the Ministry of Culture, which itself was the principal
administrative body for higher education. Yet, we should
recognize that Pozsgay's program represented outsider,
politically determined interests, which used the sphere of higher
education to serve a more general call for reforming the whole
political system. This effort was clearly reflected later by his own
political strategy, which in different periods focused on different
issues and institutions and aimed at decentralizing, marketizing
or simply restructuring various spheres of the society. Thus, by
using Archer's conceptual system, we could call this type of
strategy "external transaction." In the meantime, he could have
been successful by using the same political hierarchy as the
competing interest groups. For him, the only way to succeed was
to get to a dominant position from inside the political system,
thus reaching decision-making status in a predominantly centralized structure and restricting other orientations. The irony of
Pozsgay's position was that he had to reach a top slot in the

centralized system to be able to decentralize it. Despite being inside the administration of higher education, he represented outsider values to the traditionally centralized administration.

It is therefore not a coincidence that two years later the minister had to leave his position. Typically, his resignation was caused by conflicts within the political circles around Aczel, the deputy prime minister. An additional irony is that Pozsgay's departure was crucial for later events. Being in a new position during the political transformation at the end of the 1980, he asserted himself with a new profile in a new political arena and represented a major force within the reformist establishment.

In the first half of the 1980s, given serious economic conditions, none of the expansive reform proposals could gain from the broader political system. In fact, not only the notion of expansion but even the notion of reform had low credit within the ruling political elite. Small and slow changes and restrictive strategies were dominant in governmental policies. For the higher education system, this meant the exclusion of radical proposals from both outside and inside. Both the size of the higher education sector and the absolute level of the governmental allocations to higher education decreased. Typically, the earlier mentioned expansive Central Committee Decision was not even made public before 1983, when it received some limited publicity.

Supporters of the restrictive policy, mainly from outside of the higher education sphere and under the support of the prime minister, Gyorgy Lazar, called for more efficient higher education training, which in their terminology meant stronger central control. From their perspective the two alternative strategies for change were first the radical way of reforms, which in fact meant more money to spend, and second to have a slow, "continuous" process of development with even some financial restrictions. This group believed in the second strategy, which is shown in the lower left section of our illustrative scheme (figure 1, group III).

The two alternating strategies confronted each other during the so-called Youth Parliament in 1983, organized by the Communist Youth Organization. Here the head of the Department of Education of the Party Apparatus, Mihaly Kornidesz, as the representative of the "slow-change strategy" stated that his conception was the "official" strategy. He criticized the "opposition" in the debate, represented by Mihaly Bihari, the head of the Department of Higher Education of the Ministry of Culture, who came from the academic world (he was a political scientist). He was also considered the right-hand man of the ex-minister, Pozsgay, and the representative of the "radical reforms." The confrontation of the two was a rare, if not unprecedented moment when tensions between different state institutions received publicity. The declaration of "officiality" by the Party bureaucrat signalled the prevalence of the policy avoiding, or at least postponing, radical changes. In sum, the third conception was initiated from outside the system: restriction and central control in higher education policy.

The last type of policy alternative (figure 1, group II) had a somewhat surprising, but understandable type of representation. Earlier we saw that the political, administrative and academic spheres had distorted interests and a distorted position in the political arena. One depended on the other, and formalized power relations were mixed with informal ties and connections. Furthermore, one sphere could effectively limit the initiatives of the other two. Therefore, a new political agenda could only be expected from new interest groups—ones which still had an important and established strength in higher education. An example was the newly activated student movement.

The student movement has been strongly controlled by the state since the revolutionary period of 1956. Even minor political initiatives were radically repressed during the 1960s and 1970s, out of the state authorities' fear of student unrest. The first student initiative to create an association was the Budapest Conference of Students in 1981. The participants of the conference expressed rather unusual ideas and political positions, which the authorities had not heard during the previous decades. Students called not only for an improved higher education, which caused anxiety among the political establishment, but also for self-governing institutions, which shocked the authorities. Furthermore, one can argue that the movement was initiated from below; despite strongly opposing official efforts, it gained a considerable influence in the political arena.

The most important challenges to the student movement came certainly from outside the higher education sphere. Critical attitudes toward the increasing crisis, the lack of further reforms and the inability of the political establishment to renew itself and the call for political democratization were traditionally stronger among the students than among the larger population. The feeling of dissatisfaction and hopelessness was exacerbated after the declaration of martial law in Poland in 1981. The radicalized political position was also fed by the deteriorating condition of both the physical facilities of universities and the quality of teaching.

Students in 1981 called for the establishment of an independent organization to protect their interests and for the reform of the teaching system in the direction of more flexibility. Although the timing of the desire for autonomy seemed to be provocative to the official political machinery, it was too strong to be simply repressed.

The student movement had a double result: on the one hand, it represented effective participation in the higher education policy arena, giving commendable support to those who urged major reforms in the system; on the other hand, the student generation of the 1980s began to emerge as an independent political force. Through the struggle for its own autonomous association, it helped the development of alternative representative institutions in the broader political arena, eventually resulting in the breakup of the monolithic political system.

Using Archer's concept, the student movement's strategy, in higher education policy-making, is an internal initiation of reform towards a democratic, better financed system. In our illustrative scheme the students represented such terms used above as autonomy and expansion.

In sum, the beginning of the 1980s showed strong signs of an eroding higher education policy arena. Four different policies could be distinguished. Among these, the ones that proved to be determinant were those with restrictive strategies. No efforts at expansion had a chance to be considered by the political establishment. On the other hand, this dominant higher education policy seemed to be even more conservative than its own political and social environment. While decentralization and autonomy became the main issues in the broader political arena, higher education seemed to be stuck in the trap of centralized finance. The forces which could shape the structure did not yet have enough political strength or economic resources to do it. Still, the system did not lack in tensions. But until the mid-1980s these tensions did not receive much publicity.

The Second Half of the 1980s: Possibilities and Doubts

In 1985 the slowing speed of the economy turned into stagnation and decrease of the GDP. The Hungarian model of "socialism with a human face," or Kadarism, began its agony. The political system—which was based on compromises between the varying but hidden partial interests of the state, the different institutions and individuals and which seemed to be successful during the last 25 years—collapsed. The rival approaches supporting and objecting radical reforms created a blockage within the political apparatus. This deadlock helped the postponement of radical changes. Within Party circles even the concept of "reform" had such a wicked name that no strategy could be sold under this title. The more pragmatic decision makers tried to bootleg some steps towards marketization and decentralization. The political system seemed to accept some of them as long as they did not reach the level of claims for political democracy.

In the educational system a growing skepticism was perceived concerning the former pattern of development based on centrally initiated reforms and tight central control. Politicians and educators not only realized that the economic resources were missing for such reforms, they also became aware of their unintended negative consequences. As a consequence, a new state educational policy was formulated for the primary and secondary system; this aimed at loosening central control, thus giving more autonomy to individual schools. The new policy of school autonomy was translated into the Educational Act of 1985.

Similar measures were not taken in the sphere of higher education. Not only were the institutions of higher education deteriorating, but their political proponents were also disenfranchised. The Party lost its credibility when its decisions resulted in the further decline of the institutional share of the state budget. The institutions were ambivalent about increasing their autonomy because of the danger of causing stronger student revolts. The central administration had the task of developing higher education, as given by the Party decision of 1981, but had no resources for execution.

The Ministry, with a replacement staff (those former reform-minded leaders had left the agency), began a regulatory campaign using a strategy that is usually chosen by the authorities in a centralized decision-making system. A new ministerial program was initiated, and its main promoter was the new head of the Department of Higher Education, Imre Torok. He, unlike his political scientist predecessor, was a professional bureaucrat, alternating his positions between those of the government and the Party apparatus. Torok believed that the society was in fact "educationally affluent" with an overabundance of intellectuals, and he blamed the institutions for the crisis. He claimed the main cause of the destruction of the system was their political efforts: lobbying activities by the institutions' representatives.

The Ministry began an intensive bureaucratic campaign, issuing about 140–160 decrees and 13,000–16,000 documents per year. At the height of these administrative efforts the Ministry initiated a new supervisory system to practice direct control over the activities of the university and over college faculty. Their proposal was called the "Uniform System of Requirements for Teachers" and aimed at connecting the salary system with evaluating teaching efficiency.

The Ministry's plan provoked strong resistance from the institutions. University professors and leaders regarded the program as an assault on their rights and on their relative autonomy and began openly to attack the administration which, in their opinion, instead of taking care of the deteriorating system, strengthened central control over it. The institutional protest succeeded in preventing the introduction of the program and in discrediting its designers in the political arena. The resolution of the conflict, however, did not lead to a new political balance.

In 1987, after eight years of political bargains the Party once more put higher education on the agenda of the Central

Committee. The Party's plan aimed at new efforts to develop the system. The political position of higher education was different from what it was before the 1980s. First, the Central Committee was not only totally discredited outside the central bureaucratic circles but also lost its legitimacy inside it as a negotiating political forum. Participants of the arena realized that the Party, even at the top level, did not have the means of designing or implementing any active strategy. On the contrary, it needed the contribution of the rest of the institutional system in order to realize its policy. The participatory framework of higher education and the structure of interests became so complex that without restructuring the decision-making process, no new developmental strategy could be successful.

The deadlock in the decision making can be illustrated by the way a new funding system was designed. The plans to restructure the decision-making system included the creation of a new institution for allocating resources, the Fund for the Development of Higher Education. Yet, compromises during the negotiations with other ministries and governmental agencies minimized the scope and the capacities of the fund to the level where neither restructuring nor considerable financial recovery could have been realized.

Parallel to the discredited centralized politics, new alternative movements emerged. The activization of the students continued in 1988, when students from universities in Budapest founded the first truly alternative political organization, the Association of Young Democrats (its Hungarian abbreviation is FIDESZ).

This organization was followed by others, and by the beginning of 1989 at least a dozen new organizations designed their own educational policy. This tendency was inseparable from the general process of democratization in Hungary. The earlier monopolistic position of the Hungarian Socialist Workers Party was replaced by a newly emerging process of pluralism, and it became clear that no further higher education development could be designed without the consideration of this tendency. Interestingly enough, many of the participants within and outside the reform movements had roles in the higher education policy negotiations in the first part of the decade. It shows that the crisis of higher education and the deadlock in its policy arena may have played an indirect role in the emergence of a new political structure. One should recognize that the political compromise between the system of party politics and the society was the result of the long-term economic and political crisis which led to, among other effects, deterioration in both the higher education system and its political arena.

Alternative Reform Strategies for the 1990s

Now that the economic structure of the country is rapidly changing, new demands are being placed on higher education to increase flexibility and improve quality and efficiency. In answer to these demands, the government faces an ongoing dilemma of choosing between two strategies. The first strategy means governmental withdrawal, deregulation and increased institutional and professional autonomy. In this, reform at the governmental level concentrates on creating permanent legal and institutional frameworks for negotiations and decision making. The government and the Ministry seek guidance from higher education institutions and professions, and allow universities, funding agencies, research institutions, professional associations and the like to negotiate as autonomous actors and to take some responsibility for change.

The second strategy means central intervention, in which the state becomes the modernizing force itself and the traditional model of centralized planning and control is somewhat sustained by the government, providing direct solutions to immediate problems in higher education practice.

In general, the political transition in Hungary did not have an abrupt, revolutionary character in which the rules of transition would be based more on political rather than legal legitimacy. In Hungary the transition went through legally constructed channels, without questioning the legality of the existing institutions. A new constitution was designed and enacted during the old parliament in 1989 before the first free elections. This constitution regulated the institutions of democracy in a similar way to that of most Western constitutions.

As a consequence of this direction in the transition, no action or movement broke with the previous domination of the state or centralized power of the government. One might argue that a new constitution might manifest the dissolution of this state dominance. Because this so-called constitutionalism was not a dominant legal process, the transition had to be driven by increased legislative and governmental activities. Indeed, the increase in the legislative activities of the parliament and of the government staff showed a clear tendency towards a prevailing state domination. In simple terms the reform process, as the essential element of the transition, was driven from above not through participatory actions of individuals or institutions of a civil society. One may argue that even the civil society was being re-created from above.

Higher education was not different in this aspect from the rest of the society. Both actions aimed at reforming the system, and the ones directed to encouraging participation were originated from above. Two issues on the agenda of higher education policy reflect the increased governmental and legislative activities. One is the preparation of a new act on higher education which will serve as a basis of both systematic and institutional reforms. A second issue is a general concept of higher education development in Hungary. Although in their content these issues are not independent from one another, one has to focus also on aspects that are beyond the substance of change: the initiation of reform and participation in reform. These may explain how actors emerge in the policy arena and what strategy they follow.

Among the new actors we find:

- New political parties arising from a more effective parliamentary system;
- Reorganized and new professional associations;
- Representatives from scientific circles and research groups;
- Rectors and other leaders of universities; and
- Representatives of various industries and commercial enterprises.

The most active members of the new higher educational policy arena are the Conference of Rectors (its Hungarian abbreviation is MRK), the Conference of College Directors (FFK) and the National Association for Higher Educational Interests (OFESZ), which is the association of students. Initially they were set up with the support of the government and, so far, they have been in close communication with it. However, in the future they may emerge as important and independent actors in the arena.

The major undertaking that they have participated in since December 1991 has been a "Concept for Higher Education Development Through 2000." It is a collaborative effort initiated by the above-mentioned organizations and sponsored by the government through its new Interportfolio Committee for Higher Educational Development. It calls for a reconstruction of higher education, restructuring of its system, transformation of its administration, integration of the institutions and, most of all, expansion of its teaching and research activities. The most important overall element of the program is the projected increase of 60% to 80% in the number of admissions. This increase in enrollment would put the Hungarian enrollment rate, which is presently the lowest in Europe, at a level similar to the less developed Western European nations, e.g., Portugal.

This expansion is also projected for a new higher education structure, to reflect the changing requirements of the economy and employment policy. Some specialized higher education programs (technical and agricultural) are overpopulated, and a surplus of graduates may be foreseen.

A second important proposal calls for the regional integration of institutions. According to this so-called Universitas program, nine "university alliances" and 12 "college alliances" would be created, each having its own structure and independent administration. These institutions would enjoy increased autonomy in negotiations with the government or with professional associations and business partners.

Governmental administration would be limited to financial means and accreditation. Both would be governed through councils, a Council on Higher Education and a National Council on Accreditation. In both the government, the institutions and representatives of the professions would be equally represented.

In the program we find chapters calling for the freedom to both teach and study. The latter would be facilitated through easier regulation of admissions, choice of specialization, cross-registration, retraining, etc.

Furthermore, the program focuses on stopping the decay of the system and on improving its facilities and infrastructure to fit the new plans. The program may be considered as a lobbying document for the individual institutions rather than as an integrated concept for development. Typically the matter of efficiency that is mentioned as a general goal for the system loses its significance and sense of emergency when the program discusses the development of individual institutions. Evaluations of effectiveness and financial efficiency remain vague and unfinished. Instead, the program becomes a lobbying document which urges the government to guarantee that it will sponsor the reconstruction of higher education. This way, the developmental program reinforces the status quo, in which the institutions themselves maintain their state dependency. This means that the developmental program reflects the contradictory relationship between state authorities and higher education institutions. The institutions' dependent economic position, contradicts their political position in which they call for more autonomy and jurisdiction.

A possible way to ensure a clear structure of authority is a new act on higher education, which the program urges. Hungary never had an act that exclusively focused on higher education. So far, acts on public education were supposed to regulate the higher education sphere, the latter being also predominantly public. This idea, however, raised the uncomfortable question of whether public schools and universities should have the same status.

As a consequence, one of the first steps following the adoption of the new constitution was the establishment of an advisory committee, the Committee for Preparing the Higher Educational Act, to design a text for debates. For two years, however, the proposals have been worked on by the same committee and debates have been held mostly behind closed doors. That the law has not been scheduled for parliamentary debate and legislation shows that its enactment has been subordinated to broader political interests and manipulation.

The debates over the act reflect the dilemma of whether a law should determine the direction and substance of reform or whether it should regulate the broad framework of rights within which institutions and actors would have extended autonomy and power to participate in the higher education decision-making process. The second type of legislation would fit a decentralizing governmental strategy, and the first would maintain an active state role in higher education government. The recent proposed text of the law suggests that higher education would preserve its traditional continental character, as it had before and after the Communist period. One noticeable sign of this is the detailed regulation of the internal organization and structure of universities in the act proposal. It is also striking that the accreditation function of the government is quite rigorous and that the government also regulates the terms for revoking institutional titles.

Overall, the patterns in the decisions about higher education suggest the prevalence of relatively strong governmental control and of the limited power of institutions. In the new period, however, strong governmental power will be practiced through normative finances and less through ideological control.

In the future this governmental control can possibly motivate higher education institutions to become more effective and financially efficient. This tendency may result in the appearance of market elements, tuition, strong business connections, etc., which, in turn, will allow a more decentralized decision-making system. Also, the newly established associations could serve as more democratic forums for political negotiations. However, these tendencies will only appear in the long term, since autonomous behavior cannot be introduced through governmental actions.

Appendix

The Structure of the Educational System in Hungary

A so-called general school gives, theoretically, the same type of elementary education for all 6- to 14-year-olds. It has a comprehensive, centrally regulated common curriculum all over the country. The secondary education system on the other hand is highly selective. Pupils after age 14 have three options (see table 5). One is the grammar school, which offers academic subject matter, with the promise of the traditional maturity exam and the promise of access to universities. It has high social prestige. The second possibility is apprenticeship, officially called "vocational training." It offers three years of professional training for occupations in industry, agriculture or simple services. These three years do not lead to the maturity exam, thereby blocking the road towards higher education. A third type of school is the vocational secondary school, which combines the character of the first two. All three types of secondary schools are controlled by the state and are free, but are obligatory only before age 16.

The second crucial point after the choice of career at age 14 is access to higher education at age 18. After 1956 admission was controlled through individual decisions on the distribution of free spaces for full-time students. Only 10% to 15% of an age cohort has a real chance to get in, which means a strict selectivity and a direct embodiment of the social hierarchy at the point of entrance to higher education.

TABLE 5. Distribution of Participants in Upper Secondary
Education (Who Were 16 Years Old between 1974 and 1983)
by Main Types of Institutions

	Attained Institution in %			
Social Group of the Father	Gym	Voc.	App.	Combined
Management & Brain-Work	60.6	26.7	12.7	100
Other Intelligent Professor	36.5	37.0	26.5	100
Skilled Worker	20.8	27.1	52.1	100
Small-Scale Production	16.8	33.1	50.1	100
Semi-Skilled Worker	14.1	22.6	63.3	100
Unskilled Worker	11.7	17.4	70.9	100
Agriculture Own-Account Farmer	13.8	15.5	70.7	100
Agriculture Manual Worker	15.3	19.6	65.1	100
Other and Unknown	9.6	26.7	63.7	100
Together	25.2	26.0	48.8	100

Source: Central Statistical Office, Budapest.

REFERENCES

Archer, M. S. (1979). *The social origins of educational systems.* Beverly
Hills, CA: Sage.

———. (1982). Theorizing about the expansion of educational systems.
In M. S. Archer (Ed.), *The sociology of educational expansion. Take-
off, growth and inflation in educational systems.* Beverly Hills, CA:
Sage.

Becher, T. & Kogan, M. (1980). *Process and structure in higher education.*
London: Heinemann.

Ben-David, J. (1977). *Centers of learning: Britain, France, Germany, United
States.* New York: McGraw-Hill.

Clark, B. (1983). *The higher education system: Academic organization in cross-national perspective.* Berkeley: University of California Press.

Daalder, H. & Shils, E. (Eds.) (1982). *Universities, politicians and bureaucrats: Europe and United States.* New York: Cambridge University Press.

Darvas, P. (1988). Reform policy and changes in the educational system. *Higher Educational Policy 1(3),* pp. 38–43.

———. (1989). *Felsooktatas es Politika* (Higher education and politics) Research Report. Budapest: Hungarian Institute for Educational Research.

Everman, R., Svensson, L. G. & Soderqvist, T. (Eds.) (1987). *Intellectuals, universities, and the state in Western modern societies.* Berkeley: University of California Press.

Green, F. T. (1980). *Predicting the behavior of the educational system.* Syracuse, NY: Syracuse University Press.

Halasz, G. (1986). The structure of educational policy-making in Hungary in the 1960s and 1970s. *Comparative Education 22(2),* pp. 123–32.

Jarausch, K. H. (Ed.) (1983). *The transformation of higher learning, 1860–1930: Expansion, diversification, social opening, and professionalization in England, Germany, Russia and the United States.* Chicago: University of Chicago Press.

Kornai, J. (1980). *A Hiany* (The Shortage). Budapest: Kozgazdasagi es Jogi Konyvkiado.

Kosary, D. (1987). *Culture and society in eighteenth-century Hungary.* Budapest: Corvina.

Ladanyi, A. (1992). A magyar felsooktatas fejlodesenek torteneti attekintese. (A historical overview of the development of Hungarian higher education.) Budapest: Hungarian Institute of Educational Research.

Lukacs, P. (1989). Changes in selection policy in Hungary: The case of the admissions system in higher education. *Comparative Education, 25(2),* 219–28.

Neave, G. & Rhoades, G. (1987). The academic estate in Western Europe. In B. Clark (Ed.), *The academic profession: National, disciplinary, and institutional settings.* Berkeley, CA: University of California Press.

Ringer, F. (1979). *Education and society in modern Europe.* Bloomington, IN: Indiana University Press.

Contributors

Peter Darvas, Hungarian Institute for Educational Research, holds a doctorate in economics from Budapest University of Economics. He is in the U.S. as a Spencer Fellow, National Academy of Education, working on a second doctorate at New York University, where he is an exchange scholar. His research focuses on policy changes regarding higher education in Central and Eastern Europe.

Helmut de Rudder, professor and chair of sociology at the University of Luneburg, Germany, is also director of the Institute for Higher Education Research. He received his doctorate in sociology from the University of Hamburg and joined the faculty at the University of Luneburg. He was elected and twice re-elected by his fellow faculty members to the post of rector (president) of the university, serving in that capacity 1971–73 and again 1985–89. A member of the State Higher Education Structural Reform Commission 1988–90, he returned to his own research interests, which include a recent comparative study of governing boards in the U.S. and the former West Germany. His interest in the transformation of the former East German higher education system arose from personal experience, for his government asked him to teach there once reunification took place.

Daniel S. Fogel received his bachelor's and master's degrees from the Pennsylvania State University and his Ph.D. from the University of Wisconsin. His international research and teaching have been conducted in several different countries including Brazil, Canada, Czechoslovakia, Hungary, Poland, Romania, Venezuela, Yugoslavia, the former Soviet Union, and throughout Western Europe. He was dean and project director for the

Czechoslovak Management Center in Prague, Czechoslovakia. He is currently director of the Center for International Enterprise Development, and professor of business administration at the University of Pittsburgh. His research and teaching areas are in organizational behavior and strategy including leadership, the design of human resource systems, organization development, and international management. He has published in behavioral studies, education, psychology, sociology, economics, and management journals, and has written several books, book chapters, cases, and popular press articles.

Kassie Freeman is assistant professor of education at Peabody College of Vanderbilt University. During the 1991–92 academic year, she was a visiting scholar at the Stanford International Development Education Committee (SIDEC), Stanford University. The summer of 1992, Freeman was a joint guest scholar of the Hungarian Institute for Educational Research and the Budapest University of Economics, Spencer Award. Prior to 1991, Dr. Freeman was director of planning and assistant secretary to the board of trustees at Spelman College. Dr. Freeman's research interests include equality and quality of higher education as they relate to economics of higher education. The focus of her research is the comparison of issues related to access to higher education between under-represented groups in the U.S. and Central Europe.

Yaacov Iram is chairman of the Department of Educational Foundations of the School of Education, Bar-Ilan University, Israel. He has been a post-doctoral scholar at the University of Pennsylvania, a Fulbright scholar-in-residence at Tufts University, and visiting scholar at Stanford University. He is an active member in international educational organizations and is the founder and current president of the Israel Comparative Education Society. He has published in a wide range of American, European, and Israeli journals on educational policy in historical and comparative perspective and on the social history of Jewish education. His research interests include educational policy in secondary education and universities and teacher training institutions from historical and comparative perspectives.

James E. Mauch, professor of administration and policy studies, is also associate faculty in the Center for Latin American Studies at the University of Pittsburgh. He has served as president of the senate at the University of Pittsburgh. He has been a Fulbright scholar in Peru, as well as a consultant to the OAS, AID, and USIA in Latin America. He also has been a consultant to the government of Papua, New Guinea, the Danforth Foundation, UNESCO, DHEW, as well as various state and local education agencies. He has served as former president, PA Educational Research Association, and chaired the review panel for senior Fulbright scholar awards. He received his doctorate from Harvard University, and previously taught at the University of Lima, Peru, and Monterrey Institute of Technology, Mexico. He has authored or co-authored books, monographs, and journal articles in the field of higher education.

Namgi Park, earned his Ph.D. from the University of Pittsburgh and his bachelor's and master's degrees in education at Seoul National University, Korea. He has been a researcher at the Institute of Higher Education in Seoul and assistant teacher at Seoul National University.

Paula L.W. Sabloff, lecturer, Department of Anthropology, Faculty of Arts and Sciences, and Administration and Policy Studies, School of Education, University of Pittsburgh, is a political anthropologist with experience in higher education administration. She is a member of the Institute of Politics and the Center for Latin American Studies at the University of Pittsburgh. Her bachelor's degree was received from Vassar College; her master's and doctorate are from Brandeis University. She served as executive director of the Governor's Commission on Higher Education, academic planner for the Commission on Higher Education in New Mexico, coordinator of strategic planning at University of New Mexico, and planning coordinator at the University of Pittsburgh before joining the faculty of Pittsburgh. Her research interests focus on state government-public university relations in the U.S.

Peter Scott is professor of education at the University of Leeds, England. He was editor of the *Times Higher Education Supplement* in London from 1976 until 1992. He was educated at Oxford where he received a first-class degree in modern history.

In 1973–74 he was a visiting scholar at the Graduate School of Public Policy, the University of California-Berkeley, while holding a Harkness Fellowship from the Commonwealth Fund of New York. He is the author of several books, including *The Crisis of the University* (1984) and *Knowledge and Nation* (1990). He holds honorary degrees from the University of Bath and the Council for National Academic Awards and has been elected a member of the Academia Europaea.

John Smyth, professor and chair of teacher education, Flinders University of South Australia, received his doctorate from the University of Alberta and has focused his research on teacher education and performance in Papua New Guinea, Australia, Malaysia, and the U.S. He has produced eight books, 15 book chapters, several dozen articles and monographs, and served on myriad boards both within his former university, Deakin University, and his discipline.

Index